PROGRESS

OF THE

WORKING CLASS

1832 - 1867

BY

J. M. LUDLOW & LLOYD JONES

[1867]

AUGUSTUS M. KELLEY • PUBLISHERS
CLIFTON 1973

First Edition 1867

(*London*: Alexander Strahan Publisher, *56 Ludgate Hill*, 1867)

Reprinted 1973 by

AUGUSTUS M. KELLEY PUBLISHERS

Reprints of Economic Classics

Clifton New Jersey 07012

Library of Congress Cataloging in Publication Data

Ludlow, John Malcolm Forbes, 1821-1911.
    Progress of the working class, 1832-1867.

    (Reprints of economic classics)
    Reprint of the 1867 ed.
    1. Labor and laboring classes--Great Britain.
2. Labor laws and legislation--Great Britain.
I. Jones, Lloyd, 1811-1886, joint author. II. Title.
HD8390.L93 1973   301.44'42'0942   72-77050
ISBN 0-678-00909-0

PRINTED IN THE UNITED STATES OF AMERICA
by SENTRY PRESS, NEW YORK, N. Y. 10013

Reprints of Economic Classics

PROGRESS OF THE WORKING CLASS

PREFACE.

A FEW months ago, one of the writers of this volume was solicited to write an essay on its subject for the then projected volume on 'Reform,' since published by Messrs. Macmillan. He reluctantly consented to do so, on having joined to him as coadjutor the friend whose name stands with his on the title-page, whose acquaintance with the subject was far more practical, and of earlier date than his own.

When the essay was written, it was found to form a volume. Too large to fulfil its original purpose, the best mode of dealing with it seemed to be to make extracts from it for insertion in Messrs. Macmillan's second volume of 'Questions for a Reformed Parliament,' whilst the whole work should appear as a separate publication. Hence the present volume, the text of which has, indeed, received large additions and not inconsiderable revision since the 'Questions for a Reformed Parliament' appeared.*

J. M. L.

* In the editorial note prefixed to the extracts in ' Questions for a Reformed Parliament,' the essay is by oversight represented as having been written for that volume. It was, however, as above shown, written for the previous one.

CONTENTS.

NOTE.

SINCE the following pages were printed off, all doubts have been cleared away as to the guilt of the managers of certain of the Sheffield Trades' Unions. By the confessions of Broadhead and others it is now known that what is called "rattening," that even assassination has been systematically resorted to, for the purpose of enforcing compliance with the rules of those unions.

The Commission decided to carry on the inquiry which led to these discoveries in Sheffield, because that town was, it may be said, almost exclusively the theatre of the outrages, the origin of which it was its duty to search out. It will be seen by reference to pp. 208 and 228 of the present volume, that the writers, when dealing with the character and progress of Trade Societies, treated the case of Sheffield as exeeptional, not only in regard to the secrecy with which the business of its unions was conducted, but also in regard to the practice of intimidation for trade purposes. Although one or two other places may be tainted in a less degree, the shocking revelations since made furnish no ground for altering the conclusion then arrived at.

It is well known to those who have given any attention to the subject that the artisans of Sheffield and its immediate neighbourhood are marked by special characteristics, produced by peculiarities in the trade of the district, and just such as might be expected to lead to the crimes which have been proved against them. The trades whose office-bearers have ordered or encouraged those outrages are (the brickmakers excepted) small bodies of men, with occupations purely local,—sickle and reaping-hook grinders, saw-grinders, edged-tool-grinders, fork-grinders, scythe-makers, and other trades of a like kind. For the most part they number from 150 to 400 persons each, and are deplorably destructive of life. The men engaged in them know that their time in this world is short, disregard all life-saving precautions, plot for high wages, which they too frequently spend in brutal indulgence, and meet the inevitable end with as much indifference as they seem to have manifested when plotting the destruction of others. These little corporations, or unions, are compact and manageable; jealous of encroachments, and passionate in their resentments against those whose conduct they deem injurious to the interest of their trade. There are varying degrees of strength and skill required in each, and the wages, as will be seen by the answers given to the examiners, also vary considerably; encroachments by the lower on the higher paid branches lead to strife; whilst any neglect of the unionist's received duties, such as failure in subscription, naturally begets personal hostility, frequently followed by rattenings, blowings-up, and shootings. The 160 forkgrinders of Sheffield, all told, whether in or out of union, always confined to the same locality, following a dangerous occupation from boyhood to the grave, in the same slough of local interest, prejudice, and passion, bear but a slight moral resemblance to the men of the engineering, building, and other trades who are associated in their tens of thousands, who pass continually from shop to shop and from town to town, acquiring information by experience, and rubbing off or lessening stupid prejudices and personal animosities by constant contact with fresh faces, new ideas, and altered conditions of life.

Nor must we forget that what we see is but the last flickering out, not the first outbreak of a baleful flame. The witnesses had to be stopped by the Commissioners from extending their revelations more than ten years back. There is no novelty in any of the outrages; the only novelty is the knowing all about them. At the time when the combination laws were repealed, they were common to many trades and towns, instead of being confined to a few trades in one or two towns; they have simply lingered in these since the time when every Trade Society was an illegal combination, and when personal violence was almost the only agency that could be employed to enforce the behests of committees.

Frightful, then, as these revelations are, they do not in the slightest degree modify the general opinions we have expressed as to the effect of Trade Societies. They are, indeed, a signal warning to the working class against what we may call the idolatry of trades-unionism. They show that the habit of exclusively considering the class interest of the worker may beget a temper as reckless, as deadly, as fiendish, as the religious fanaticism of a sect of Assassins. But the air-gun and the powder-can of the Sheffield unionist no more prove that all trade combinations should be suppressed, than the dagger of Ravaillac proves that all religious associations should be put down.

For ourselves, we are glad that the ugly truth is at last fully known. Its scorching light, better than any enforcement of the penal law against the offenders, will put a stop to the recurrence of such crimes. Worse perhaps even than the crimes themselves has been the toleration of them by at least a large number of the Sheffield working class. But the probe will now go to the bottom of the sore, and by judicious treatment it may be effectually cured. Whilst, on the one hand, the public opinion of the working men of England must be brought to bear upon the crimes themselves, with an earnestness which shall no longer allow another Broadhead to wrap his murder-buying in hypocrisy, and screen it behind sham offers of reward, on the other hand, the proved occasions and alleged excuses for those crimes must be taken away.

Rattening and other more objectionable modes of persecution, it will be seen, were chiefly resorted to for the purpose of keeping backsliding members of unions to their duty; whilst several witnesses stated that such methods of coercion would not have been resorted to, if there had existed any legal means of enforcing the claims of the committee. And it is moreover notorious that the most shocking frauds are being constantly committed against Trade Societies by their officers, without fear of legal punishment. It is not necessary to state here how the law ought to treat such associations; but if they must continue to exist (and we deem the man fit for Bedlam who would seek to put them down by law), it is absolutely necessary that something should be attempted by Parliament with the view of aiding them to secure such reasonable and legitimate objects as come fairly within the scope of their action. At present the relation between the trades' unions of the country and the law is in a very unsatisfactory state,* and it is to be hoped that no further time will be lost before organizations, which include such a large proportion of our best artisans, and which deal with such important interests, are treated in a spirit becoming the legislature of a country whose industry is one of the principal elements of its power and influence in the

---

* See Mr. Godfrey Lushington's admirable paper on this subject, in ' Questions for a Reformed Parliament.'

world. The true lesson of the Sheffield revelations is not to put Trade Societies *hors la loi*, but, on the contrary, to bring them resolutely within the pale of justice, compel them to publicity, and make of them, instead of intangible shadows, bodies legally recognized and legally responsible.

London, July 9, 1867.

INTRODUCTION.

A T no time within the history of our country have the
working classes been more talked of than at present.
The great work of the Session of 1866 is a Reform Bill, one
of the proclaimed original objects of which, according to the
Conservative leader of the House of Commons, by whom it
was introduced, was to restore those classes to the share of
political power from which he holds them to have been
excluded by the Reform Bill of 1832 ; whilst another of
its professed objects was to restrict their re-admission
thereto. Under these circumstances, it appears useful to
inquire into the late history and condition of a class whose
political influence forms thus the turning-point and the
problem at once of a great Constitutional change, and is
visibly both denied and dreaded by the same persons. Are
the working men advancing in the development of those
qualities which mark the man and the citizen, or are they

retrograding ? Is their advent to power to be deemed a blessing or a curse ?

The question is momentous ; the task of answering it conclusively, gigantic. If the writers of this volume had not been aware beforehand of the vastness of that task, the mere attempt to compass it would have sufficiently convinced them of their own inability to fulfil it. They believe, however, that they can contribute somewhat towards its fulfilment, and that the materials they have collected for the purpose may be of use to others. United by many years of friendship and fellow-work, they have, nevertheless, approached the question from quite different sides, and looked on it with quite different eyes. One of them, in the year 1832, was a working man in Manchester, having already wrought at his trade (then a highly paid one) in the South of Ireland and in Dublin. In the course of the few following years, he had occasion to travel throughout the whole of Lancashire and the surrounding counties, and subsequently to visit almost every large town in England and Scotland, residing for some years in Leeds and in Glasgow, as well as in London, and mixing everywhere with the most energetic and active-minded members of the working class. He believes himself, therefore, to have a practical experience of the condition and feelings of that class, more especially, perhaps, at the opening of the period which this volume proposes to embrace. His fellow-writer has, since the year 1848, taken part in several movements for the improvement of the condition of the working class. He has been led by his profession to consider especially the legal difficulties which stood in the way of that improvement, and the means of removing those difficulties ; and also, and in an increasing proportion of late years, the openings afforded by legislation for promoting the welfare of the worker. Without being able to boast of a very numerous acquaintance with working men, he has been fortunate enough to be placed in relation, from time to time, with a certain number of the most intelligent amongst them, and has enjoyed, and still enjoys, with a few, a friendship as sincere and hearty as that which binds him to members of any other class.

The terms "working class," "working men," will, in this volume, be taken in their every-day acceptation, as meaning those who work, chiefly with their muscles, for wages, and maintain themselves thereby. The phrase, "we are all working men," as used by the brain-worker, has a truth in it, but becomes a cant when carried too far. It is not, indeed, intended to deal with "the poor,"—*i.e.* those who may work, but cannot thereby habitually maintain themselves, otherwise than by an occasional glimpse at some of their efforts to raise themselves into the true working class.

Finally, it is not proposed to deal directly with the progress of any but the English working class, as being that with whose condition and feelings both writers are most familiar, although occasional illustrations of their subject may be derived from other quarters, especially from Scotland. Many of the measures, indeed, which will be hereafter referred to, embrace Scotland, or have been extended, in a modified shape, to that country, and to Ireland.

PART I.

CONDITION OF THE WORKING CLASS IN 1832.*

To understand the working classes of Great Britain, they must be looked at, and their proceedings studied, where they are active, thoughtful, outspoken, where they examine and decide for themselves, and, when the need arises, step out in advance of statesmen and legislators, and practically accomplish what Parliaments afterwards graciously approve of. Little therefore, we are afraid, can we say of those engaged in agricultural employment,—a class moreover, as the population returns show, amounting to less than half of the industrial class, and which diminishes as the latter increases.† Farm-labourers have few political thinkers

---

* Mr. Lloyd Jones is chiefly responsible for the contents of this part. He writes in the main from personal knowledge ; and although, for ease of reference to others, he may often quote printed evidence, it will only be where his own recollections enable him to vouch for the correctness of the statements he may have to borrow.

† According to the census returns of 1851 and 1861, the agricultural class had in the interval diminished from 2,084,153 to 2,010,454, whilst

among them. Ideas of social reform do not easily pene-
trate, or rapidly spread, among the solitary workers in the
fields. They are not given to association ;* are in no way
under the influence of " demagogues," of " designing
agitators," of trades-unionist " vampires,' who fatten on
their credulity; John Bright has never yet found an audience amongst them ; Canon Girdlestone seems for them to
be the nearest local approach to a George Potter.† Nevertheless, our legislators have not on this account treated
them with more consideration than the artisans of the
manufacturing districts. On the contrary, they have met
the persistently urged demands of the artisan classes by one
legislative enactment after another; whilst the labourer on
the land has generally had to make his virtue its own reward,—unless indeed in those very exceptional cases when
that reward has been supplemented by the thirty shillings,

the industrial class had increased from 4143 to 4,828,399, such increase
forming close upon one-third of the total increase of 2,088,615.

* At the soirée of Greening and Co., Limited, held at Manchester on
May 19, 1866, Mr. W. Lawson, of Carlisle, related, amidst shouts of
laughter from his audience of Lancashire operatives, how when he gave
his eleven farm-labourers the opportunity of voting by ballot on the subject of co-operation, labelling one bottle with that word, and the other
with ' every man for himself,'—" actually, ten of them voted for ' every
man for himself,' and only one put into the ' co-operation ' bottle !"

† It is a curious fact, however, that agricultural trades' unions were at
one time among the most conspicuous. The early years after the Reform Act are full of the case of the " Dorsetshire unionists." But the
severe punishment inflicted on these poor misguided fellows seems to
have quelled such unions so effectually that the late strike of the
Gawcott labourers for twelve shillings a week was treated by the ' Times '
as an agreeable novelty, and got a good word from almost the whole
press.

or the blue coat and brass buttons, of an agricultural society.*

But Newcastle, Birmingham, Leeds, Manchester, Glasgow, and yet other towns and cities, are centres of great districts, swarming with life, where men labour constantly and skilfully in the production of national wealth. For the purpose of the present inquiry, Manchester in particular may be taken as a typical centre. A circle drawn round it, with a radius of twenty-five miles or thereabouts, would hold within it a greater number of large busy towns than perhaps could be found within the same space on any other portion of the globe. Taking the Superintendent Registrar's boundaries, we find the population of the following towns to stand thus:—Bolton, 130,269; Bury, 101,135; Haslingden, 69,781; Blackburn, 119,942; Burnley, 75,595; Rochdale, 91,754; Oldham, 111,276; Ashton, 134,753; Wigan, 94,561; Stockport, 94,360.† These, and others besides, for commercial and social purposes, are all parts of one whole, and as it were the loose-lying limbs of an outstretched giant, of whom the great central city should be the heart. All are more or less en-

---

* The gang-system of the Eastern Counties seems at last about to receive its first check from legislation. But its evils are of old standing, and were exposed in print long ago; nor has the recent report of the Commissioners on the subject any substantial novelty to show to those who remember the letters on " Labour and the Poor " (the agricultural series) published in the ' Morning Chronicle' some seventeen or eighteen years back.

† These figures represent the populations of the various towns and their immediate neighbourhoods, as in the case of Oldham, which includes Oldham-below-Town, Oldham-above-Town, Chadderton, Middleton, Royton, and Crompton.

gaged in similar industries, all contain a vigorous, active, intelligent population, men who *will* busy themselves with public questions, will *not* confine themselves to the routine of their daily duties in workshop or factory; men who feel, and in many ways already have been able to prove, that they are not mere implements of production, but citizens of a great empire, connected by a thousand links with all other classes of that empire, and therefore concerned in the discussion and settlement of every question that can interest any. It is in such a district as this therefore (though the West Riding of Yorkshire, for instance, might furnish just such another) that the true character of the working men of Great Britain can be appreciated, their power estimated, their progress realized ; and it is upon what is seen in these people, of their powers of thought, decision of will, aptitude for organization, and practical business ability in dealing with the questions of the day, that all correct speculation as to their future political influence in the country must be based. What is true of them is true in a measure of the whole working class, for gradually, but surely, they are fashioning that whole class in their image. Without disparagement to the London working men, who have qualities of their own, it is certain that almost, if not quite, all great movements affecting the class have had their origin in the provinces. Time after time, the part of the Metropolis has been to crown a work which it had not begun.

It is no doubt the fact, that the germ of the progress of the working classes during the period which opens with the Reform Acts of 1832 is to be found, as respects legislation, on the one hand in Huskisson's great fiscal reforms of

1824–5, on the other in those measures of the same period which are chiefly to be associated with the name of Joseph Hume, the repeal of the Combination laws (5 Geo. IV. c. 95, 6 Geo. IV. c. 129), which made it no longer a crime for a working man to unite in self-defence with his fellows, and the Act "to Repeal the Laws relating to Artificers going to Foreign Parts" (5 Geo. IV. c. 97), which enabled him to thin the labour-market by emigration.* It is not less true, however, that up to 1832 changes, even of the most necessary kind, had been as a rule discouraged by those in power. The law, in every direction in which its operations were felt by working men, was adverse to, or jealously and suspiciously watchful of, all public movements that required the combination of large numbers of men. The Corresponding Societies' Act, passed in those dark early years of the Continental war (39 Geo. III. c. 79), by declaring unlawful (amongst others) "all societies composed of different divisions or branches," rendered all organization, except of the most rudimentary kind, impossible, or compelled it to secrecy. The Seditious Meetings Act, passed in the scarcely less dark early years of the peace (57 Geo. III. c. 19), laid meetings of fifty persons under severe restrictions. Either measure could be set in motion by any informer. But so many evils had arisen in connection with the political and industrial condition of the country; so much that was operating injuriously needed revision; and so much that was not operating at all

* Coupled with these in the statute book is an Act which will only bear fruit when Boards of Arbitration for trade disputes become a legal fact, the 5 Geo. IV. c. 96, " to Consolidate and Amend the Laws relative to the Arbitration of Disputes between Masters and Workmen."

required to be called into action, that voices previously stilled had to be listened to ; grievances hitherto overlooked to be examined, and in the end the most pressing and important demands of the sufferers to be granted.

Our cotton trade, which throughout the whole of the early part of the century had rapidly extended, grew up in an unregulated hap-hazard fashion. The old cottage system had given place to the rural factory, where the owner's necessities in regard to water-power secured for the workers the luxury of wholesome country air. This system again, through the application of Watt's invention, was superseded by the grouping of great establishments in the various large towns, so that a full supply of the labour of children might be obtained, without continuing the expensive practice which then prevailed of bringing pauper children from even the most distant parishes in the agricultural districts. Under these new conditions the cotton manufacture in Manchester and its neighbourhood had a rapid development. Large fortunes were made by numbers of men—enduring, sturdy, square-set—whose shrewdness in the management of business was much more conspicuous than their thoughtfulness or humanity in dealing with those whose labour was necessary to the success of their undertakings. Diligent and industrious themselves, they regarded the complaints of their "hands" about overwork as originating in a cowardly desire to shirk their duties as honest workers ; and if their bargains were well made, they believed implicitly that the world was the best possible world for all and sundry. It is true indeed that the evils of the new system were more severely felt in some districts than in others, and were frequently mitigated too by special conditions; in many cases by the kindly and generous intervention of humane factory owners. Gradually, however, the most dreadful results began to exhibit themselves. The absence of education stunted the mind, whilst increasing labour dwarfed and deformed the body, and the short hours of relaxation from toil allowed to the factory worker were commonly spent in the most sensual and degrading pursuits. The educational, moral, and physical condition of England's workers was beginning to be felt as altogether unbearable.

Commission after Commission was ordered by the Crown, with the view of prosecuting inquiries, all of which revealed abominations so shocking in their recital, that though the language in which they are described may be justified in the pages of a Parliamentary Blue-book, it is altogether unfit for reproduction here. A few passages, however, selected from evidence to which the least exception can be taken, must be given in justification of the general statement.

Speaking of Manchester in 1832, Sir J. P. Kay Shuttleworth—the value of whose testimony few will question—observes, " The population employed in the cotton factories rises at five o'clock in the morning, works in the mills from six till eight, and returns home for half an hour or forty minutes to breakfast. This meal generally consists of tea or coffee, with a little bread. The tea is almost always of a bad, and sometimes of a deleterious quality. The operatives return to the mills and workshops until twelve o'clock, when an hour is allowed for dinner.

Amongst those who obtain the lower rate of wages this meal generally consists of boiled potatoes. The mess of potatoes is put into one large dish, melted lard and butter are poured upon them, and a few pieces of fried fat bacon are sometimes mingled with them, and but seldom a little meat. Those who obtain better wages add a greater proportion of animal food to this meal, at least three times in the week; but the quantity consumed by the labouring population is not great. The family sits round the table, and each rapidly appropriates his portion on a plate, or they will plunge their spoons into the dish, and with an animal eagerness satisfy the cravings of their appetites."

After thus describing the half-savage domestic habits of the people, Sir James goes on to describe their general surroundings :—" The population nourished on this aliment is crowded into one dense mass in cottages separated by narrow, unpaved, and almost pestilential streets, in an atmosphere loaded with smoke, and the exhalations of a large manufacturing city. The operatives are congregated into mills and workshops during twelve hours in the day, in an enervating heated amosphere, which is frequently loaded with dust or the filaments of cotton, or impure from constant respiration, or from other causes. They are drudges, who watch the movements and assist the operations of a mighty material force, which toils with an energy ever unconscious of fatigue. The state of the streets powerfully affects the health of their inhabitants; sporadic cases of typhus chiefly appear in those which are narrow, ill-ventilated, unpaved, or which contain heaps of refuse or stagnant pools."

Let it be recollected that the evils of such a state of things pressed no less on the weak woman, the helpless child, than on the man. " From the whole of the evidence laid before us," say the Commissioners of 1832, " we find, first, that the children employed in all the principal branches of manufacture throughout the kingdom, work during the same number of hours as the adults." " In some rare instances," they say elsewhere, " children begin to work in factories at five years old. It is not uncommon to find them there at six. Many are under seven, still more under eight ; but the greatest number are under nine." For sheer fatigue, the poor creatures would go supperless to bed, be unable to take off their clothes at night, or to put them on in the morning. " Pains in the limbs, back, loins, and side," say the Commissioners, " are frequent. The frequency and severity of the pain uniformly bear a strict relation to the tender age of the child and the severity of the labour. Girls suffer from pain more commonly than boys, and up to a more advanced age." Again, " The effects of labour during such hours are in a great number of cases permanent deterioration of the physical constitution, the production of disease wholly irremoveable, and the partial or entire exclusion (by reason of excessive fatigue) from the means of obtaining adequate education and acquiring useful habits, or of profiting by those means when afforded."

"The deformities produced," says Mr. Robert Baker,[*]

* In a valuable paper ' On the Physical Effects of Diminished Labour,' to be found in the Transactions of the National Association for the Promotion of Social Science (which we shall take leave to call hence-

one of the Inspectors of Factories, who from 1828 to
1832 was, as a medical practitioner in Leeds, profession-
ally engaged in the daily and nightly visitation of several
factories, "consisted of in-knee, flat-foot, and curvature of
the spine. The first of these deformities was familiarly
known in the manufacturing districts as the 'factory leg.'
There was scarcely a thoroughfare in any of them where
they were not to be seen." Another gentleman whom he
quotes, Mr. S. Smith, Senior Surgeon of the Leeds Infirmary, says : " In 1832 I had frequent occasion to pass
through a district at noon, when the hands were leaving
work for dinner. A large majority of them were pale,
thin, emaciated, downhearted-looking creatures, showing
no disposition to mirth and cheerfulness. At the proper
age the hips were wide, but sharp and angular, the shoulders pointed, the head not held up, but a considerable
stoop." Such evidence is all the more valuable for our
purpose, as coming from a Yorkshire factory district, seeing that it exactly portrays the state of the workers in the
large towns of Lancashire.

That an education worthy of the name was impossible
for a population under such conditions, results avowedly
from the statements of the Commissioners of 1832. Factory workers were in those early days for the most part
grossly ignorant. Even the fine spinners, who were the
best paid, were only distinguished from the rest by their
extravagant riotousness. Topics of conversation were
limited ; power to converse rationally was possessed by

forth by its shorter familiar title of " Social Science Association ") for
1859, p. 553 and following.

few ; the noise of the factory was unfavourable to the exchange of ideas. Ignorant themselves, what wonder if they cared little to educate their children? saw in them too often only instruments for money-making, means of self-indulgence? Hideous instances might be quoted from the Blue-books of the driving of mere infants to the mill by their parents, simply that they might live in riotous idleness out of the fruit of their children's earnings. But the first great struggle of the Factory reformers was less for education than for its necessary condition—the relaxation of overtoil for the child; and hence the former subject appears only in a subordinate rank among the grievances detailed in the earlier reports. What, in fact, education must have been in 1832, appears thus best from such documents as the reports of the Inspectors of Factories from 1839 to 1843, when overwork was to some extent stopped, and the educational machinery of the Factories' Acts was already in operation. Thus in 1843 (30th January) Mr. Leonard Horner was able to report that in an area of 8 miles by 4, comprising the large borough of Oldham and that of Ashton, for a population of 105,000, there was not, at the date of his then last quarterly report, one public day-school for the children of the humbler ranks. And what was the education of those who were supposed to be receiving some? On July 7 of the same year, he felt himself entitled to say that out of 6872 children within his district (including Manchester), for whom certificates of school attendance were obtained, 4500 were receiving "no education whatever." Of these 2689, or 39½ per cent., were at private dame-schools, which he describes as " small assemblages of children brought together by indigent old men or old women, who nominally keep a school, they being incapable of earning a livelihood in any other way, but without any qualification for teaching." The factory schools themselves at the beginning, instead of constituting a real addition to the educational appliances of the day, were a mere mockery for the most part. " The engine-man, the slubber, the burler, the book-keeper, the overlooker, the wife of any one of these, the small shopkeeper, or the next-door neighbour with six or seven small children on the floor and in her lap, are by turns found teaching the young idea how to shoot, in and about their several places of occupation, for the two hours required by law,"—so reports Mr. Robert Baker to Mr. H. J. Saunders, one of the inspectors, in an extract appended to the latter's report of Jan. 1, 1839. And Mr. Baker did not think that among 500 mills under his superintendence in the West Riding he should be able to name a dozen where the education was really good.*

Such education as was given was, moreover, confined to the Sunday-school. We saw the case of Oldham and Ashton, with 105,000 population, and not a day-school. But in much more favoured localities, the disproportion of Sunday-scholars to day-scholars was overwhelming. At Macclesfield, Congleton, and Sandbach, Mr. T. J. Howell reported, on June 30, 1843, that for a population of 50,250,

* The following verbatim copy of a school-certificate, given in the report above quoted, speaks volumes :—" This is to sertfy that 1838 thomas Cordingley as atend martha insep school tow hours per day January 6."

the number attending Sunday-schools was 12,286, to only 2,028 who attended day-schools. And what was Sunday-school education? Even so late a document as the Report of the Commissioners appointed to inquire into the condition of the children of the poorer classes employed in mines and collieries, and the various branches of trade and manufacture in which numbers of children worked together, not being included in the provisions of the " Act for regulating the Employment of Children and Young Persons in Mines and Factories " (1861), will tell us. Mr. Fletcher, speaking of Oldham (within seven miles of Manchester), says of Sunday-school instruction : " The interval of six days between each day of instruction delays the attainment of any good result. . . . The number who say they can read an easy book is three-fourths, but this commonly includes all who can spell their way through words." Mr. Symons states that the masters in Yorkshire told him that they "do not usually question the children on what they have read;" and that the " uniform account of the clergymen and other witnesses is that the children forget what they learn one Sunday before they next return to school." Some of the scholars examined by the sub-commissioner for Derbyshire answered thus for themselves :—One " has been four or five years at a Baptist Sunday-school, cannot spell horse or cow;" another "has been to a Calvinistic Sunday-school four years, can spell neither church nor house;" whilst a third, who had attended a Methodist Sunday-school five years, " only reads a-b ab ; cannot tell what d-o-g spells."*

Whatever, therefore, the value of Sunday-schools might

* Education Commission Reports, 1861, vol. iii.

have been in giving habits of order and regularity to the young people attending them, or in causing early attendance on divine worship, it is quite clear that they had little effect in spreading education amongst the children of the working class.

What were the amusements of the masses, thus overworked, ill-fed, ill-housed,—left for the most part uneducated? Large numbers of working people attended fairs and wakes, at the latter of which jumping in sacks, climbing greased poles, grinning through horse-collars for tobacco, hunting pigs with soaped tails, were the choicest diversions. An almost general unchastity— the proofs of which are as abundant as they would be painful to adduce—prevailed amongst the women employed in factories, and generally throughout the lowest ranks of the working population. But drink was the mainspring of enjoyment. When Saturday evening came, indulgences began which continued till Sunday evening. Fiddles were to be heard on all sides, and limp-looking men and pale-faced women thronged the public-houses, and reeled and jigged till they were turned, drunk and riotous, into the streets, at most unseasonable hours. On the Sunday morning the public-houses were again thronged, that the thirst following the indulgence of the night might be quenched. When church hour approached, however, the churchwardens, with long staves tipped with silver, sallied forth, and, when possible, seized all the drunken and unkempt upon whom they could lay their hands, and these, being carefully lodged in a pew provided for them, were left there to enjoy the sermon, whilst their captors usually adjourned to some tavern near at hand, for the purpose of rewarding themselves with a glass or two for the important services they had rendered to morality and religion. In fact, sullen, silent work alternated with noisy, drunken riot; and Easter and Whitsuntide debauches, with an occasional outbreak during some favourite "wakes," rounded the whole life of the factory worker.

The ordinary artisan of the workshop was, indeed, a far different man. He was not tied down to the routine of a huge mechanical system, so expensive, whether at rest or in motion, that to be profitable it needed the regular aid of human labour. His freedom of intercourse with his fellow-workman was almost unrestricted. He had time for study, when inclined; and if he preferred the public-house to the workshop—which he too often did—it was a matter of choice, and he was open to correction when any sufficient influence could be brought to bear upon him. Besides, he was not put to work at so early an age, and, as a rule, had received more education, and experienced more fully the benefit of home influence. Still, the workshop of those days was by no means the most desirable school for a youth to commence the active duties of life in. In the highest-paid trades, work was not to be had on a Monday from the artisan; many men only began their week on the Thursday. The practice of "footings" was universal, the amount of which was invariably spent in drink.* Still, there were many good influences to be found in such work-

* In the trade to which the writer belonged, the new-comer was expected to pay 5s. down, to which the old hands added 1s. each, and the whole party adjourned at once to the public-house.

shops. There were grave men, who employed their leisure hours in reading or study—entomologists, florists, botanists, students in chemistry and astronomy. Men there were—politicians, dabblers in theology—who, when work was not actively on foot, kept the conversation amongst their fellows from sinking into inanity or vice, or who discouraged such practical joking as was mischievous or painful. But these men were exceptional, and sometimes, notwithstanding their studies, they were as fond of a glass as their most graceless neighbours.* Individual character was very strongly marked amongst these men. Some of them in their trades' meetings, when speaking on subjects familiar to them by experience, were eloquent, logical, and powerful orators; some quiet and business-like and clever in negotiation; others, again, were as ingeniously unprincipled as if they had been born to rule empires, full of quips and quillets — men "that would circumvent God"† for the gain or the glory of a triumph.

---

* Old Tom B— was an enthusiastic entomologist. Early in the morning, and at all other spare hours, his life was passed in the fields, or wherever else he could pursue to advantage his scientific inquiries. Every now and then, however, he would go "on the spree," but, whether drunk or sober, he was always bright and cheerful. One morning he came to his work after an absence of three or four days, and when questioned as to the cause of his absence, replied that he had been attending his own funeral, and making merry over his departure from the world. The truth was, he had gone to the officers of his burial club, and compounded his future claims for a certain amount of cash down, which he had spent in making himself jolly.

† J. B., or "Jemmy," as he was familiarly called, was an instance. He was a little man, with a huge black curly head, great blazing black eyes, and truly atlantean shoulders, but such very short legs that, when

It was with the soberest and most thoughtful of these men, as we shall show hereafter, that the agitation for the

seated, he looked a great brawny fellow, but little more than a dwarf when on his feet. There were two sets of victims Jemmy was always preying on—recruiting sergeants and landladies. He never finished a drinking bout without enlisting two or three times, to the great disgust of the men on the recruiting service, who at last came to know him and avoid him. Landladies, however, were a perennial source of profit and amusement to him. He shifted his quarters continually, never paying a shilling when he could avoid it, and thus, as he named it, ' opening the eyes ' of his landladies. Hence these forlorn females were constantly inquiring at the workshop for him. Jemmy worked on the first floor at a back window, and when the presence of one of these visitants was telegraphed to him, a looped rope always being in readiness, he slipped it over his shoulders, and his nearest shopmate dropped him out of the window on to the roof of a tiled shed, belonging to a dyer who oc-cupied the adjoining premises. One day, one of these importunate persons rushed into the workshop so suddenly, that Jemmy had to use the utmost speed to get out of the window. " I know he is in," cried the enraged woman, rushing upstairs ; but before any reply could be given, a horrible howl arose from outside the window. The men rushed at once and looked out, but Jemmy had disappeared through the roof of the shed. He was immediately pulled in,—and pulled out of a deep vat full of a strong indigo dye. As he fronted his adversary, bluer than Gainsborough's blue boy—face, hair, and hands being of the same colour as his clothes—for a moment he seemed confused ; but in another moment he had assumed a look of the most profound sorrow and humiliation. " I have sinned," he cried, "and I am punished ; my conduct has been abominably wicked. As sure as I am an altered man, Mrs. Smith, I'll pay you." Mrs. Smith, who was a pious woman, after a few more assurances disappeared ; and, as soon as the door had closed behind her, Jemmy gave his shopmates the most solemn assurances that he never would pay her a rap until he was an altered man, and until she had made good to him the value of the clothes she had caused him to spoil. " She is a credulous creature," he remarked solemnly, "and I take no credit to myself for opening her eye." Men like this were too often the heroes of the workshop.

Short Time Bill began. They saw and felt, much sooner than the factory workers themselves, what a curse the factory system as it then existed was. Certainly they saw the necessity of attacking it with a view to its correction before the factory operatives thought of moving in the matter. And it was not until the agitation had gone on for some time that those who were most directly interested in it could be brought to take much interest in the question. A friend of the writer's told him, at the time of the occurrence, of having gone to some village about three miles from Manchester to speak at a short-time meeting; he found himself, as he approached the spot where the meeting was to be held, in the midst of a crowd of factory operatives, moving eagerly in the direction in which he was going. Feeling gratified and elated, he spoke to one of those next to him, "We shall have a good meeting, I think."—"A what?"—"A good meeting, in favour of the Short Time Bill."—"Nay," shouted the man, "it's nobbut a dog-feet."

Moreover, as invention after invention brought new trades into the factory system, as the war of competition raged fiercer and fiercer, the members of these outlying trades were becoming always fewer and weaker in the midst of the swelling mass of factory workers; and if the strenuous efforts of many of them tended to pull that mass up, its weight was in turn always tending to drag them down. Means of common action there were but few, and as before stated, almost all outside of the law. There were. thus some Building societies, but few and bad; a number of Co-operative shops, but not successful except in a very few cases (one great success at Ripponden, in Yorkshire); the true principle of co-operative consumption, that of the division of profits on purchases, not having been yet discovered. The great Friendly societies, on account of their branches, secret passwords, etc., were positively illegal, and only connived at on account of their harmlessness. Political discontent was wide-spread, and discontent in those days was always very near to rebellion. The writer (who has since had the honour of serving, more or less irregularly, in her Majesty's Lanarkshire volunteers) must confess to having had his sharpened pike by him in 1832, ready for a march on London if the Reform Bill had not passed; and he was but one of thousands of Manchester working men who were alike prepared for the dread hazard of civil war.

Trade societies in particular, which some people nowadays seem really to look upon as new and unheard-of forms of evil, though generally ill-managed, were active, secret in their rules and deliberations, and too often tyrannical in their proceedings. In nearly all of them there was a tendency to violence.* Union men habitually refused to work with non-union men. "Knobsticks," as men who worked under price were called, were often maltreated; murder sometimes being the result. In those employments however which were not in union, proceedings

---

* The writer knew two men personally, who at different times and belonging to different trades, now perfectly free from outrages, were rendered totally blind by having vitriol thrown in their faces by men on strike. Similar outrages, but perhaps not often attended with such serious consequences, were of common occurrence.

almost as wicked, and much more prejudicial to the public welfare, took place. In the year 1829, for instance, a period of stagnation and distress, reduction of wages was proposed to certain classes of the factory operatives by some of their employers. The reply to such proposals was the assembling of riotous mobs. The factory belonging to the Messrs. Brocklehurst, of Macclesfield, was attacked and all the windows broken. In Manchester, several cotton mills were attacked and had their windows smashed and machinery demolished, one or two of them being burned. At Rochdale, now a model town, where co-operation and every other form of peaceful association flourish, the weavers broke into factories, destroyed looms and other machinery. Fifteen of the rioters were captured, and on an attempt at rescue being made, the military fired and killed six persons. The writer of these lines was present during the destruction by fire of one of the Manchester factories. The burning building was surrounded by thousands of excited people, whose faces, reddened by the ascending flames, expressed a fierce and savage joy. As the fire forced its way from floor to floor, darting through the long rows of windows, cries of exultation were shouted by the crowd; and when, finally bursting through the roof, it went roaring into the heavens, the maddened multitude danced with delight, shouting and clapping their hands as in uncontrollable thankfulness for a great triumph.

We have endeavoured to show, at least by means of a few typical instances, what was the condition of the working classes of this country about the time of the Reform Act of 1832. We would now wish to sketch out the history of their progress from that time to the present. Simply to attempt a complete history would require not pages, but volumes; it would be absolutely hopeless to carry the task out satisfactorily. For this divides itself under two heads, first, the story of the various forms of beneficent influence exerted upon the working classes from without; second, that of their own efforts for self-improvement. The former head would include, amongst other things, the record of thirty-five years' labours of almost every religious body, charitable society, educational institution, etc., throughout the kingdom, of the development of every industry and invention, the application of every scientific truth during that period,—enough to occupy the lifetime of a Methuselah. The latter head is in great measure that of the unrecorded, the unremembered, the undiscoverable. If it be true of all mankind that ' one soweth and another reapeth,' it is unfortunately true also of the working classes that with them the sower and reaper but seldom ' rejoice together.' The small ' mutual improvement ' society, without name or local habitation, which kept together but for a few years,—the healthy influence of one or two men in a shop,—the grip taken by one tenacious mind of a single fruitful thought,—may have been the real germ of some remarkable organization, successfully worked by men who are utterly ignorant of its origin. Physically and morally, it may be said that we all tread out our lives in the dust of past generations. But of none is this more true than of the working men. Owing to various causes,—frequent revolutions in mechanical processes, displacement of certain forms of industry, changes of domicile and of position, emigration, etc.,—oral tradition is with them at present singularly short-lived, and the leader of to-day will often be ignorant of the labours of his immediate predecessors, even when following in their very footprints.

There is one outward force, however, of which the action stands authentically recorded, and which is at once one of the most powerful regulators, and, in a free country at least, one of the best exponents of social progress, Legislation. Compelled to contract the proportions of our task, we shall attempt to present the reader with a sketch of so much of the legislation of the last thirty-four years (1832-66) as may be considered to have exercised a directly beneficent influence on the progress of the working classes; and then to show—1. How far the working classes have promoted or anticipated such legislation, or have influenced the policy of the country. 2. How far they have availed themselves of the means of improvement placed at their disposal by the law. 3. How far they have been able to do without it. We shall end by offering some considerations on the general moral progress of the working class during the period under review.

PART II.

PROGRESS OF LEGISLATION, 1832–66, AS RESPECTS THE WORKING CLASSES.*

ALTHOUGH, as we have stated already, the origin of whatever progress may have been made by the working classes since 1832 is to be sought in the earlier period, it may be stated without exaggeration that no equivalent period of our legislation hitherto can show a list of so many measures directly or indirectly contributing to the welfare of the working class, as the thirty-four years which closed with the Session of 1866. So numerous, indeed, are those measures, that in order to avoid losing oneself in a chaos, it seems necessary to marshal them in separate groups. We propose thus to consider successively—1. The Protective Acts, which are meant to avoid or restrain certain mischiefs arising out of the employment of labour. 2. The Enabling Acts, which emancipate, develop, or foster certain forms of activity amongst the working class. 3. Acts of general benefit, but which tend in a marked degree to the improvement of the class in question. We shall finally

* Mr. Ludlow is responsible for the contents of this chapter.

contrast briefly the progress of social with that of political legislation.

The distinction between the various classes of enactments to which we shall have to refer is indeed often so fine, that we must crave our reader's pardon beforehand for occasional misplacements of the measures recorded. Nor can we omit one caution. Our sketch will not pretend to be exhaustive. Every man of practical experience will no doubt be able to point out in it *lacunæ* with reference to his own particular field or fields of observation. Nor can it be otherwise. For in a body-politic like our own, where a strong current of national life circulates through all the members, it is impossible to separate definitely the laws which affect one class from those which affect any other. For good or for evil, all legislation ultimately affects the whole nation; the only difference between its effect on one or the other portion of the nation being that of time and of more or less directness of action. The "Act for the Abolition of Fines and Recoveries, and for the Substitution of more simple Modes of Assurance" (3 & 4 Wm. IV. c. 74) seems at first sight quite alien to the wants of the English working class. Yet many a working man's title to his house and bit of land, acquired through the medium of a Building or Land society, depends on it. The "Act to Provide for the Government of the Straits' Settlements" (29 & 30 Vict. c. 115), one might think, has nothing to do with the worker. Yet if it tends, as the colonists hope, to extend the trade of those settlements, it may set many a Manchester loom and Birmingham hammer at work.

§ 1. *The Protective Acts.*

The Factory Acts, so called, constitute the foremost section of the Protective group, which is indeed nearly coeval with the century; the first Act relating to cotton and woollen factories being dated 22nd June, 1802 (42 Geo. III. c. 73). The first Act of the period under consideration is the 3 & 4 Wm. IV. c. 103 (29th August, 1833; slightly varied by the 4 & 5 Wm. IV. c. 1). If we compare this with its immediate predecessor, the 1 & 2 Wm. IV. c. 39, we are struck in the first instance by an apparent retrogression, viz. that whereas the former Act forbade nightwork in cotton-mills and factories to all persons of either sex under twenty-one, the present only restricts it under eighteen. But the scope of the measure is now greatly enlarged. It now includes every "cotton, woollen, worsted, hemp, flax, tow, linen or silk-mill or factory wherein steam or water or any other mechanical power is used to propel or work the machinery." The labour of young persons under eighteen remains fixed at twelve hours a day, and sixty-nine a week, with one hour and a half for mealtimes, and the age of first admission for children at nine years. The employment of children under eleven, twelve, and thirteen years of age is to be gradually restricted from twelve to nine hours a day, or forty-eight a week. Regular holidays for children and young persons are secured; medical certificates are required before children can be employed; factory inspectors are to be appointed by the Crown; school attendance is made compulsory for all children whose labour is limited to forty-eight hours a week ; an abstract of the Act, and of the rules and regulations established by the inspectors, is to be hung up conspicuously in every factory.

This measure stood its ground for eleven years, when the " Act to Amend the Laws relating to Labour in Factories," 7 & 8 Vict. c. 15 (6th June, 1844), was passed. Besides elaborating the factory inspection system,—through the creation of sub-inspectors, the establishment of a recognized office, the requiring notice to be given to such office of the opening of a factory, the appointment by the inspectors of certifying surgeons, whose fees they may determine, etc.,—the Act contains provisions for protecting children or young persons employed in the wet-spinning of flax, hemp, jute, and tow, for the avoidance of accidents to children, the guarding of machinery, the inquiring into and securing compensation for accidents. The age of first employment for children is lowered to eight years ; the hours of their employment are reduced to six and a half or seven hours a day, or ten hours on alternate days. The employment of women is assimilated to that of young persons ; the cessation of labour on Saturdays for the protected classes is made absolute at 4.30 P.M. ; the hours for meal-time are to be taken between 7.30 A.M. and 7.30 P.M., with additional regulations as to meal-times and half-holidays (Christmas Day and Good Friday being made obligatory holidays in England, and days of sacramental fast in Scotland), and also for school attendance (with a singular exception as to children of eleven employed in winding and throwing raw silk).

The next year saw a new class of workers brought

under regulation by the "Act to regulate the Labour of Children, Young Persons, and Women, in Print Works," 8 & 9 Vict. c. 29 (30th June, 1845). These are placed under the control of the inspectors and sub-inspectors of factories; no works are to be opened without notice; no child is to be employed under eight; no child or young person without surgical certificate; no child or female during the night; the children are to attend school, and the Act and certain notices are to be hung up. The hours of school attendance in print works, it may be observed, were slightly modified by the Act of the 10 & 11 Vict. c. 70 (22nd July, 1847).

Next comes the 10 & 11 Vict. c. 29, the famous Ten Hours Act,—"an Act to limit the Hours of Labour of Young Persons and Females in Factories," 10 & 11 Vict. c. 29 (8th June, 1847),—restricting the hours of labour of young persons under eighteen and females, after 1st May, 1848, to ten hours a day and fifty-eight hours a week. It is well known that this Act has practically operated (until quite recently, when means seems to have been devised by some employers for employing adults only) as a general reduction of the hours of labour, in consequence of the interdependence of the labour of men and that of women and young persons. Three years later, the 13 & 14 Vict. c. 54, "to amend the Acts relating to Labour in Factories" (5th August, 1850), altered the forbidden hours of labour for young persons and females, which under the 3 & 4 Wm. IV. c. 103, had stood from 8.30 P.M. to 5.30 A.M., and under the 7 & 8 Vict. c. 15, had been made to commence on Saturdays at 4.30 P.M., to from 6 A.M. to 6 P.M.

on every day but Saturday, when they were henceforth to begin at 2, thus fully establishing the Saturday half holiday, but in fact allowing ten hours and a half work on other days. Meal-times must henceforth be between 7.30 A.M. and 6 P.M. The hours during which young persons and females could be employed beyond the regular limits for recovering lost time were restricted. On the other hand, children above eleven employed in winding and throwing raw silk were assimilated to young persons.

The Act last referred to not including children in its main provisions, it followed that these could be made both to begin work earlier and leave it off later than their elders. This anomaly was removed by the 16 & 17 Vict. c. 104, "further to regulate the Employment of Children in Factories" (20th August, 1853). Children, like young persons and women, were no longer to be worked except between 6 A.M. and 6 P.M., unless under certain conditions between 30th September and 1st April, when they might be employed between 7 and 7. In no case however, even to recover lost time, were they to be employed after 2 P.M. on Saturday, or after 7 P.M. on other days.

Seven years later (if we pass over an unimportant Act of the 19 & 20 Vict. c. 38, 30th June, 1856), an important extension was given to the system by the 23 & 24 Vict. c. 78, "to place the Employment of Women, Young Persons, and Children in Bleaching Works and Dyeing under the regulations of the Factories Acts" (6th August, 1860). the title of which sufficiently explains its scope. It contains a few variations of detail from the general system, the most noticeable of which is perhaps a permission of night work to recover lost time in certain special cases. The next year brought lace factories into the system, which had been specially excluded by the 3 & 4 Wm. IV. c. 103. The "Act to place the Employment of Women, Young Persons, Youths, and Children in Lace Factories under the regulation of the Factories Acts," 24 & 25 Vict. c. 117 (6th August, 1861), contains, like the last, some specialties, such as permission to employ youths between sixteen and eighteen for not more than nine hours between 4 A.M. and 10 P.M., and an exclusion of the provisions of the Factories Acts for the recovery of lost time and the fencing of machinery.   In like manner the Act of the 25 & 26 Vict. c. 8, "to prevent the employment of Women and Children during the night in certain operations connected with Bleaching by the Open-air process" (11th April, 1862), brought under the 23 & 24 Vict. c. 78, so far as respects night-work, a class of establishments which had been specially exempted from it.   The 26 & 27 Vict. c. 38 (29th June, 1863), extended the provisions of the Bleach and Dye-Works' Act to the employment within such works of females, young persons, and children in ca-lendering or finishing yarn or cloth of any material, where mechanical power is used.   And by the 27 & 28 Vict. c. 98 (20th July, 1864), those provisions were fur-ther extended to the processes of finishing, hooking, lap-ping, making up or packing of yarn or cloth, wherever carried on.

A still more important statute of the same session as the one last referred to is the 27 & 28 Vict. c. 48 (25th July, 1864), "for the Extension of the Factory Acts."

Subject to a few specialties, a whole group of fresh manufactures and employments—the manufacture of earthenware, except bricks and tiles, not being ornamental ones, of lucifer matches, percussion caps and cartridges, together with paper-staining and fustian-cutting—were brought into the system. In lucifer match-making, no child, young person, or woman was to take his or her meals in any part of the factory where any manufacturing process, except wood-cutting, is usually carried on. In fustian-cutting no child was to be employed before the age of eleven.

This Act completes, so far, the series of the Factory Acts, worked under the supervision and control of the Inspectors of Factories. We have now to turn to another series of Acts only less important than the former one, opening with the 5 & 6 Vict. c. 99, " to prohibit the Employment of Women and Girls in Mines and Collieries, to regulate the Employment of Boys, and to make other Provisions relating to Persons working therein" (10th August, 1842). By this Act, as indicated by its title, the unsexing labours of females in mines and collieries were absolutely forbidden ; boys were not to be employed under ten ; indentures of apprenticeship were limited to eight years ; no steam or other engine in certain cases was to be under the care of a person under fifteen ; and the payment of wages in public-houses was forbidden. Lastly, inspectors of mines and collieries were to be appointed, but armed with far narrower powers than factory inspectors,—in fact only those of entering, inspecting, and reporting to the Home Secretary.

The last-mentioned Act applies to mines generally ; the

two to be next noticed apply to coal-mines only. The first is the 13 & 14 Vict. c. 100 (14th August, 1850), "for Inspection of Coal-mines in Great Britain," providing for the appointment of inspectors of coal-mines, with somewhat more extended powers than under the former Act; for the giving notices of all accidents to the Secretary of State; and of all inquests upon deaths by such accidents. This Act (which was only to last five years) was repealed, and in substance re-enacted by the 18 & 19 Vict. c. 108, "to amend the Law for the Inspection of Coal-Mines in Great Britain" (14th August, 1855). The inspectors received increased powers; certain general rules for safety were enacted; special rules were to be established for each colliery, subject to the approval of the Secretary of State; both were to be conspicuously exhibited at the principal office of such colliery, and printed copies given to every person employed.

Five years later was passed the important Act of the 23 & 24 Vict. c. 151, "for the Regulation and Inspection of Mines" (28th August, 1860). The five first sections of this Act apply to all mines, and forbid the employment of boys under twelve, except such boys between ten and twelve who can either produce a schoolmaster's certificate that they are able to read or write, or who attend school for not less than three hours a day, two days in the week, during each lunar month. Eighteen is, moreover, fixed as the age at which youths may be placed in charge of steam-engines or machinery by which persons are hoisted up or down a vertical shaft or inclined plane. Still more important are the remaining provisions, relating to coal-mines

and " mines of ironstone of the coal measures, and worked
in connection with coal or any disused or exhausted coal-
mines." The general rules are extended; special rules,
before transmission to the Secretary of State, are to be
hung up for fourteen days at the principal office and place
of payment for workmen; provision is made, through the
agency of the inspector, for the removal of causes of
danger not provided for by the rules; wages are to be
paid in money, and in an office not " contiguous" to a spirit,
wine, or beershop; and where the payment of the employed is by weight, measure or gauge, they may, at their
own cost, station one of their own number at the place of
weighing, etc., to take an account of the weight, etc.
Connected with this series is the 25 & 26 Vict. c. 79
(7th August, 1862), which prohibits single shafts in coal and
ironstone mines within the last-mentioned Act, and gives
power to enforce compliance with its own provisions by
injunction.

It is impossible not to be struck with the difference between the series of the Factories' Acts and that of the
Mines' Acts. In both these are absolute restrictions
on the labour of children, of women; in both there is a
machinery of inspection. But the minute detail of the
Factories' Acts is absent in the Mines' Acts; their educational provisions are not to be found, except in a single
Act, as to boys between ten and twelve; the powers of
the inspectors are exceedingly limited. On the other
hand, the absolute exclusion of female labour, and of boy-
labour under twelve, or ten in certain cases, would of
itself show that the persons whom the Mines' Acts

have in view are mainly the strong, and not the weak. It is this which explains the unwonted rights given to the employed, of examining all special rules for their respective collieries before they are transmitted for approval, and of appointing persons to check the weighing and measuring of the fruits of their labour.

From coal to chimneys the transition is an easy one. We shall not, however, dwell here at length on a series of protective Acts affecting that pet trade of philanthropy, chimney-sweeping; a series older than the Union, and beginning as far back as 1788 (28 Geo. III. c. 48). Three belong to the period which is occupying us; the 4 & 5 Wm. IV. c. 35 (25th July, 1834), 3 & 4 Vict. c. 85 (7th August, 1840), and 27 & 28 Vict. c. 37 (30th June, 1864). The Acts are of always increasing stringency, and have an important social bearing, so far that by regulations as to the materials and construction of chimneys, and absolute forbiddance that any person under twenty-one be allowed to climb them, they have greatly promoted the good construction and safety of our dwellings. The extraordinary stringency of the enactments is in part explained by the difficulties, if not the impossibility of inspection, in a trade so exceptional as that of chimney-sweeping.

From black to white again, the transition seems a violent one. Yet the next protective Act which requires to be noticed is the " Act for the Regulation of Bakehouses," 26 & 27 Vict. c. 40 (31st July, 1863). This forbids the employment in bakehouses of persons under eighteen between the hours of nine at night and five in the morning, and imposes various regulations for the cleanliness of bakehouses, and as to the construction of sleeping-places on the same level with bakehouses in cities or large towns. The Act does not appear likely to be the last of its series.

From the Bakehouses' Act, we may pass to an enormous body of protective legislation, affecting a most important but peculiar class of our workers—sailors. Acts relating to this subject are of early date in our statute-book, going as far back as the reign of Richard II. The first of our period, however (3 & 4 Wm. IV. c. 88, 28th August, 1833), is a mere continuation Act, and has only in view the pecuniary interests of the sailor. The next (5 & 6 Wm. IV. c. 19, 30th July, 1835) has some sanitary provisions, and establishes a " General Register Office of Merchant Seamen." Sir James Graham's Act, the 7 & 8 Vict. c. 112 (5th September, 1844) has been called by a high authority, Dr. M'William (who, however, dates it erroneously in 1835), "the Magna Charta of British sailors."* The series culminates in two Acts of the 17 & 18 Vict. cc. 104, 120, the latter of which, the "Merchant Shipping Repeal Act, 1854," sweeps away all previous legislation ; whilst the former, the " Merchant Shipping Act, 1854," substitutes therefor a vast code of 548 clauses, with appended forms, which exhaust the alphabet down to W inclusively. The third part of this Act, relating " to masters and seamen," and the fourth, relating " to safety and protection of accidents," embody mainly the provisions protective of the seaman, who is not, however, represented in the " Local Marine Boards," bodies entrusted, in a great measure, with the carrying

* Transactions of the Social Science Association for 1861, p. 510.

out of the Act. The machinery of the Act comprises shipping offices (which may in London be Sailors' Homes) for registering seamen, superintending and facilitating their engagement and discharge, etc. ; the examination of masters and mates for certificates, without which no foreign-going ship or home-trade passenger ship is to go to sea; provisions for apprenticeships to sea-service, for the engagement of seamen, their discharge, the payment, allotment, remittance, recovery, etc., of their wages ; savings-banks for seamen ; clauses for their health and accommodation, through the survey of provisions and water, the providing or use of medicines, lime or lemon juice, sugar, and vinegar; the appointment of inspectors of medicines, medical attendance in sickness, burial in case of death, the carrying on certain ships of medical practitioners, the space to be allotted to each man, the protection of seamen from imposition, the removal of masters for incompetence or misconduct, naval courts, the " General Register and Record Office of Seamen," official logs, boats for sea-going ships, water-tight partitions in iron steamers, the equipment of steamships with safety-valves, fire-hose, signals, etc. ; the survey of passenger-steamers, etc. The Act was amended in certain respects by the " Merchant Shipping Amendment Act, 1855 " (18 & 19 Vict. c. 91), and the " Merchant Shipping Amendment Act, 1862 " (25 & 26 Vict. c. 63), the latter providing, amongst other things, that steamships required to have certificated masters should also have certificated engineers. Connected with it is the 27 & 28 Vict. c. 27 (23rd June, 1864), " for regulating the proving and sale of chain cables and anchors," which has an indirect but most important bearing on the personal safety of our sailors.

With the above Acts might be connected some relating to two classes of men closely connected with shipping, coal-whippers and ballast-heavers ; but as these, however interesting in themselves, are confined in their operation to the Metropolis, we shall not specify them here, though we may have to allude to them again hereafter.

None of the above Acts, it will be observed, are of a general character; all relate to certain specific trades or employments. Almost the only Act of the former description belonging to our period, which may be considered to be of a protective character, is that of the 7 Wm. IV. & 1 Vict. c. 67 (15th July, 1837), to amend the previous one of the 5 Geo. IV. c. 96, for the arbitration of disputes between masters and workmen; nor are its provisions worth dwelling on. Besides this we may, however, notice the 14 & 15 Vict. c. 11 (20th May, 1851), "for the better Protection of Persons under the care and control of others as Apprentices or Servants, and to enable the Guardians and Overseers of the Poor to institute and conduct Prosecutions in certain cases," repealed by the 24 & 25 Vict. c. 95, and substantially re-enacted by the 24 & 25 Vict. c. 100 (6th August, 1861); the purpose of which sufficiently appears from its title.

§ 2. *The Enabling Acts.*

We now come to what we have termed the Enabling Acts. These, again, may be loosely grouped under three heads—(1) those which facilitate or concern the banking operations of the working man; (2) those which concern the applications of his savings and of his energies; (3) those which relate to his physical and intellectual advancement.

(1.) Until the period which we are considering, the banking business of the working man was carried on exclusively by two classes of establishments : as respects the keeping of his moneys, by the Savings-Bank ; as respects the obtaining money on security, by the pawnbroker. The latter we may dismiss with a word, by simply observing that three Pawnbroking Acts belong to the period—the 19 & 20 Vict. c. 27; 22 & 23 Vict. c. 14; and 23 & 24 Vict. c. 21. The Savings-Bank system, which dates from 1817 (57 Geo. III. c. 105, 130), was equally completed at an earlier period (9 Geo. IV. c. 92), although several times modified during the one under consideration, between the 3 & 4 Wm. IV. c. 14 (10th June, 1833), and the 26 & 27 Vict. c. 87 (28th July, 1863), the latter restoring, under certain limits, the liability of trustees. In the 22 & 23 Vict. c. 53, "to enable Charitable and Provident Societies and *Penny Savings-Banks* to invest all their proceeds in Savings-Banks " (13th August, 1859), repealed but substantially re-enacted by the 26 & 27 Vict. c. 87, we obtain the first glimpse of the spread of provident habits amongst a class lower in the social scale than that for which the ordinary Savings-Bank was devised.

The Loan Societies Act, 5 & 6 Wm. IV. c. 23 (21st August, 1835), is the first new step in this direction. We wish by no means to give these institutions more than the straitest measure of approval. In many instances, they are, we fear, little more than usury shops of the most fraudulent description. Still, they are to the working man what the discount house is to the merchant, and, in the absence of anything better, it was perhaps wise of Parliament to make the legislation on this head, which had been hitherto only temporary, perpetual by the Act of the 26 & 27 Vict. c. 56 (21st July, 1863).

The most useful banking facilities have, however, been conferred on the working man through the medium of the Post Office. The Money-Order department of the latter (which received its first Parliamentary sanction in the Act of the 3 & 4 Vict. c. 96, 10th August, 1840), supplemented by its Registration system, has become the great channel for the transmission of his money from place to place. Still more important has been the institution of the Post Office Savings-Banks by the 24 & 25 Vict. c. 14, 17th May, 1861, (amended by the 26th & 27 Vict. c. 14, and extended by other Acts to be presently noticed), giving, in the words of the preamble, " the direct security of the State" for repayment of all moneys deposited. It is a remarkable evidence of the growth of those habits which the Savings-Bank was instituted to foster, that the premium to providence, which under the original English Savings-Bank Act of the 57 Geo. III. c. 130, was no less than 3*d.* a day, or £4. 2*s.* 11*d. per annum,*—no distinction being then made by law between the rate allowed by the State to the bank and that allowed by the bank to the depositor,—and which at the commencement of the period which occupies us was still (under the 9 Geo. IV. c. 92)

2½*d.* a day to the bank and 2¼*d.* to the depositor, or £3. 16*s.* 0½*d.* and £3. 8*s.* 4¼*d. per annum* respectively, has fallen in the Post Office Savings-Bank to £2. 10*s. per annum,*—the rate allowed to the private Savings-Banks, under the 26 & 27 Vict. c. 87, being £3. 5*s. per annum,* and to the depositor £3. 0*s.* 10*d.* Indirectly, further help has been given in this direction through the development of the Joint-Stock Bank system (chiefly through the " Act to regulate Joint-Stock Banks in England," 7 & 8 Vict. c. 113,—and the " Act to enable Joint Stock Banking Companies to be formed on the principle of Limited Liability," 21 & 22 Vict. c. 91), and the practice which has grown up in such establishments of receiving deposits of small sums at interest. And taking all these various influences into account, it will be found that an enormous extension has been given to the banking facilities of the working classes during the period in question.

(2.) Let us now consider those measures which refer to the application of the working man's savings and of his energies. One group of measures for such purpose seems at first sight conspicuous by its absence. Probably if the skilled working men of Great Britain were polled at the present day, in order to ascertain what form of organization they consider most important to themselves, and if they ventured to give a frank reply, from three- to four-fifths of them would answer that the Trade Society is that form now, whatever other may take its place hereafter. It is that however which the Legislature has till now most persistently refused directly to recognize. The contingency of want of work—although quite capable of calculation—

has never yet been reckoned as one to meet which a Friendly Society could be established. When, after long and vain efforts to put down Trade-Societies, the Legislature at last repealed the combination laws, it sullenly ignored the bodies which had successfully defied its power. The Trade-Society was no longer criminal *in se,* but remained, as it were, banished out of the realm of the law.

Still, by favour of measures of a more general character, Trade-Societies succeeded in improving their status. The 9 & 10 Vict. c. 33, " to amend the Laws relating to Corresponding Societies and the Licensing of Lecture-rooms " (27th July, 1846), enacted that proceedings under the 39 Geo. III. c. 79 and the 57 Geo. III. c. 19 should only be commenced in the name of a law officer of the Crown. Precarious as is the protection afforded by such a restriction, it has yet sufficed, thanks to the wisdom of the executive power and the control of public opinion, to allow the development of our great Amalgamated Societies, with branches all over the world.

One of the series of Friendly Societies' Acts, which will be presently noticed for other purposes, the 13 & 14 Vict. c. 115, " to Consolidate and Amend the Laws relating to Friendly Societies" (3rd July, 1846), timidly opened a door towards legal protection to Trade-Societies amongst others, in a clause affording certain of the securities of the Act to " benevolent and charitable institutions and societies, formed by voluntary subscriptions and benefactions for the purpose of relieving the physical wants and necessities of persons in distressed circumstances," which should register their rules. In the subsequent Friendly Societies' Act of the 18 & 19 Vict. c. 63 (23rd July, 1855), the last clause divides itself into two, the one giving many of the advantages of the Act, on the registrar's certificate, to " provident, benevolent and charitable institutions and societies . . . formed for the purpose of relieving the wants and necessities of persons in poor circumstances, or for improving the dwellings of the labouring classes, or for granting pensions, or for providing habitations for the members or other persons elected by them,"—the other giving the advantages only of the provisions relating to the settlement of disputes and the prevention of fraud or imposition, to societies formed " for any purpose which is not illegal," on a deposit of their rules, without certificate.   The latter clause has of late been largely made use of by Trade Societies, and the wisdom of the late Chancellor of the Exchequer had in consequence admitted them as Friendly Societies to the privileges of the Post-Office Savings-Bank.   Unfortunately a late decision of the Court of Queen's Bench (*Hornby* v. *Close*) has seriously damaged, if not destroyed, the securities afforded to Trade-Societies by the last quoted enactments.

One Act, however, directly affecting the proceedings of such societies, belongs to our period, the 22 Vict. c. 34, (19th April, 1859) "to amend and explain" the 6 Geo. c. 129, repealing the combination laws.   This enacts that the " peaceably endeavouring, and in a reasonable manner, etc., and without threat or intimidation, direct or indirect, to persuade others to cease or abstain from work," in order to obtain a certain rate of wages or altered hours of labour, is not to be deemed "a 'molestation' or 'obstruction' within the meaning of the said Act," nor to subject the workman to prosecution or indictment for conspiracy. The wording of the Act, it need hardly be pointed out, is not satisfactory. The " reasonable manner " of the endeavour to persuade is surely simply the measure of the judge's foot.

We enter now the first great field of exercise which for many years was allowed to the working man's energies, that of the Friendly Society, first recognized in 1793 (33 Geo. III. c. 54). Like the Savings-Bank, this institution belongs in its almost completed form to the period preceding that which we are now considering (10 Geo. IV. c. 56), but it received during the latter several important developments. The 5 Wm. IV. c. 40 (30th July, 1834) gave the important power of nomination to benefits, and authorized the formation of Friendly Societies for any purpose other than those enumerated in the Act, "which is not illegal." Omitting an unimportant Act of the 3 & 4 Vict. c. 73, the 9 & 10 Vict. c. 27 (5th July 1846) conferred several important boons on the working classes. Friendly Societies were for the first time expressly exempted, as such, from the provisions of the before-mentioned Acts relating to Corresponding Societies and the Licensing of Reading-rooms, 39 Geo. III. c. 79, and 57 Geo. III. c. 19 (the former of which, besides forbidding societies with "branches," declared unlawful all societies imposing any oath, test, or declaration not required or authorized by law). The removal of these restrictions for the first time enabled the great societies of Odd Fellows, Foresters, Druids, to obtain legal protection. Again, a clause was inserted which afforded the first legal protection to co-operative bodies, the so-called " frugal investment " clause, allowing friendly societies to be formed, under certain restrictions, " for the frugal investment of the savings of the members, for better enabling them to purchase food, firing, clothes or other necessaries, or the tools or implements of their trade or calling, or to provide for the education of their children or kindred." This clause was retained in the next Act on the subject, 13 & 14 Vict. c. 115 (15th Aug. 1850), which adds the " enabling any member, or the husband, wife, children, or nominee of such member to emigrate," to the purposes for which a society may be formed ; substituting, however, for the drag-net clause of " any other purpose which is not illegal," the far narrower one of " any purpose which shall be certified to be legal " by the Attorney General or Lord Advocate, " as a purpose to which the powers and facilities of this Act ought to be extended."

The purposes for which Friendly Societies can be established were a good deal contracted by the 18 & 19 Vict. c. 63, " to Consolidate and Amend the Law relating to Friendly Societies" (23rd July, 1865), the principal Act now subsisting on the subject. The Frugal Investment clause, with its educational facilities, the Emigration clause, and another which we have not thought it worth while to notice, for the insurance of live or dead stock, goods or stock-in-trade, implements and tools, have all dropped out. In the drag-net clause, the purpose is to be one " authorized" by a Secretary of State or the Lord Advocate, " as a purpose to which the powers, etc., of this Act ought to be extended." The Act was slightly modified by two others, the 21 & 22 Vict. c. 101, and 23 & 24 Vict. c. 58. The greater narrowness of the 18 & 19 Vict. c. 63, as compared with the 13 & 14 Vict. c. 115, is in great measure explained by the fact, that between the two was passed the Industrial and Provident Societies' Act, to be hereafter noticed, which carried out more adequately the purposes of the omitted "frugal investment" clause. It should be noticed, however, that the 29 & 30 Vict. c. 34, "to give further Facilities for the Establishment of Societies for the Assurance of Cattle and other Animals" (11th June, 1866), restored such societies to the privileges of the Friendly Societies' Act.

The Friendly Society must be considered as a sort of stock, on which many a graft has been successively made. The first of these, the Loan Society, has been considered already. The next, which has been for the working man a very fruitful one, has been the Building Society, recognized by the "Act for the Regulation of Benefit Building Societies," 6 & 7 Wm. IV. c. 32 (14th July, 1836), which was passed, as its preamble states, to afford "encouragement and protection" to "certain societies . . . established in different parts of the kingdom, principally amongst the industrious classes, for the purpose of raising by small periodical subscriptions a fund to assist the members thereof in obtaining a small freehold or leasehold property." These were established on the pattern of the Friendly Society, with trustees in whom the property should be vested, and certified rules.

The third graft is the Industrial and Provident Society, now quite detached from the stock. The first Industrial and Provident Societies' Act is the 15 & 16 Vict. c. 31 (30th June, 1852), probably the most important 'enabling Act' of the whole period, as the "Ten Hours Act" is the most important 'protective' one. Reciting the "frugal investment" clause of the 13 & 14 Vict. c. 115, and that "various associations of working men have been formed for the mutual relief, maintenance, education, and endowment of the members, their husbands, wives, children, or kindred, and for procuring to them food, lodging, clothing, and other necessaries, by exercising or carrying on in common their respective trades or handicrafts," it authorizes "any number of persons to establish a society under the provisions of this and the said recited Act, for the purpose of raising, by the voluntary subscriptions of its members, a fund for attaining any purpose or object for the time being authorized by the laws in force with respect to Friendly Societies, or by this Act, by carrying on or exercising in common any labour, trade, or handicraft, or several labours, trades, or handicrafts," except mining and quarrying abroad, and banking, subject to the provisions of the Act.

This Act,—which, if Sir James Graham's Merchant Shipping Act deserved to be termed the "Magna Charta of British sailors," might equally be termed the "Magna Charta" of co-operative trade and industry,—although amended by the 17 & 18 Vict. c. 25 and the 19 & 20 Vict. c. 40, left yet the working men associated under it—after the passing of the first "Act for Limiting the Liability of persons in certain Joint-stock Companies," 18 & 19 Vict. c. 133 (14th August, 1855)—in a position of disadvantage as towards their richer competitors, through the absence of such limited

liability. This anomaly was removed by the 25 & 26
Vict. c. 87, " to Consolidate and Amend the Laws relating
to Industrial and Provident Societies" (7th August, 1862)
—the Act now in force on the subject—which, departing
for the first time in such cases from the model of the
Friendly Society, made all societies registered under it
corporations with limited liability. Such societies might
be formed by not less than seven persons, " for the purpose of carrying on any labour, trade, or handicraft, whether wholesale or retail, except the working of mines and
quarries, and except the business of banking and of applying the profits for any purposes allowed by the Friendly
Societies' Acts, or, otherwise permitted by law." The
exclusion of all mines and quarries from the operation of
this last Act (the first one only excluded foreign ones) is
a serious drawback to its utility, since a large portion of
the mining population are deeply imbued with co-operative
ideas; and the Cornish miners, in particular, afford one of
the stock instances of successful co-operation, though only
in an elementary way. Nor is the exclusion of banking
justifiable in principle, especially whilst Loan Societies are
admitted to similar privileges.

We have treated the above Acts as special enabling Acts
for working men. The Industrial and Provident Societies'
Acts vindicate their own title to be so considered. Another common feature, however, pervades them all, which
hinders their ever being made largely available by the rich
—a limitation of the benefits to be derived under them.
Thus, the interest of a member or other person in a
Friendly Society is limited (under the latest legislation)

to £200, or, by way of annuity, £30 a year; in the Benefit Building Society, the share must not exceed £150, nor the monthly subscription 20s.; in the Industrial or Provident Society, the interest of members is limited to £200. They have also this in common—that they are all measures for associative self-help. There has now to be considered a late series of measures for facilitating the individual application of small savings for provident purposes, through the instrumentality of Government.

This series begins with the 16 & 17 Vict. c. 45 (4th August, 1853),—the title of which, "to Consolidate and Amend the Laws, and to grant• additional facilities in relation to the purchase of Government Annuities through the medium of Savings-Banks, and to make other provisions in respect thereof," by no means indicates its scope, as the first blow aimed at the private Savings-Bank system. Under former Acts (which we did not notice in reference to Savings-Banks on account of their provisions being superseded), the 3 & 4 Wm. IV. c. 14, and the 7 & 8 Vict. c. 83, small Government annuities might be purchased through the medium of Savings-Banks. The present Act enabled annuities, immediate or deferred, not being less than £4 nor more than £30, to be purchased directly from the Commissioners for the reduction of the National Debt by any depositor in a Savings-Bank, or person whom the Commissioners should "think entitled" to be or become such, and insurances, not exceeding £100, on their own death, to be effected by such persons with the Commissioners. Greater facilities were afforded for the like purposes by an Act rather more honest in title—the 27 & 28 Vict. c. 43—" to grant additional facilities for the purchase of small Government Annuities, and for assuring payments of money on death ' (14th July, 1864). The amount of annuity grantable by the Commissioners was now raised to £50 a year, and the machinery of the Post Office was made available for the receipt of moneys deposited for the purposes of the Act.

It is palpable that the above Acts not only tend to supplant by a Government machinery the private Savings-Bank, but also in a great measure the Friendly Society ; and the expediency of doing so was freely maintained during the discussions on the Bill. The former institution, which is merely a legalized charity, needs no great sympathy if a safer means of keeping the savings of the working classes can be devised. Without in the least wishing to blink the facts of the frequent mismanagement of Friendly Societies, and of the ruin which they have often entailed on their members, still, as institutions for associative self-help—for collective forethought—they occupy a far higher ground ; and it has yet to be seen whether the security of a Government machinery offers a sufficient equivalent for the discouragement of a form of co-operation which tends to educate men by its very failures, and, as respects the large body of the agricultural labourers, offers as yet almost the only field on which they may, to some extent, learn the art of self-government. Whilst anxious, therefore, to give the late Chancellor of the Exchequer credit for the most benevolent intentions towards the working classes, in offering them the security of the State for the investment of their small savings in the purchase of annuities or the effecting of life insurance, we venture to think that the suppression of the Friendly Society would be a most serious hindrance to the true progress of those classes, and that the careful reform of that institution is what should be aimed at.

But a last enactment remains, which, in social importance, probably far exceeds any machinery for Government cash-keeping or insurance as respects the working man,—we mean that clause of the " Act to Amend the Law of Partnership," 28 & 29 Vict. c. 86 (5th July, 1865), which provides that " no contract for the remuneration of a servant or agent of any person engaged in any trade or undertaking by a share of the profits of such trade or undertaking shall of itself render such servant or agent responsible as a partner therein, nor give him the rights of a partner." For the first time now it became possible for an employer, without legally risking his all, to do that which so many economists have recommended— associate his workers to profits. For the first time it became possible for the worker, without risking his little all in turn, to accept the benefits of such association.

(3.) Beyond the protective measures before considered, the most important class of Acts for the physical advancement of the working classes which requires to be noticed, is that for the improvement of their dwellings. The first is the Act of the 14 & 15 Vict. c. 28, " for the well-ordering of Common Lodging-Houses " (24th July, 1851), which provides for the registering, regulating, inspecting, and cleansing of such places. It is closely followed in the Statute Book by an Act of the same date, but meant seemingly to provide for a somewhat higher class, the " Labouring Classes Lodging-Houses' Act, 1851 " (14 & 15 Vict. c. 34), which empowers the Council of any Borough, any Local Board of Health, or Improvement Board, to adopt the Act, and carry it into execution out of rates or borrowed funds (which may be advanced by the Public Works Loan Commissioners), either by erecting "lodging-houses for the labouring classes," converting buildings into such, or purchasing existing lodging-houses. An attempt to promote the enterprise of private companies for the same purpose was made by the " Labourers' Dwellings' Act, 1855" (18 & 19 Vict. c. 132), which empowers companies of not less than six persons to be formed " for the purpose of providing dwellings for the labouring classes, with or without private gardens, and with or without common gardens or places of recreation for the use of the inmates of such dwellings, and for no other purpose whatsoever;" such dwellings to be let by the week or month, or demised for not exceeding twenty-one years, and the company not to hold at any one time more than ten acres of land without licence from the Board of Trade. The vice of this Act lies in its not allowing, under restrictions for the common benefit, alienation in fee of the dwellings to the inmates; otherwise it might have to a great extent most usefully superseded the Benefit Building Societies' Act. The parallel Act as to Scotland (18 & 19 Vict. c. 88) seems more liberal, but the peculiarities of Scotch law preclude us from going into its provisions. We cannot however forbear noticing the 23 & 24 Vict. c. 95, " to facilitate the Building of Cottages for Labourers, Farm Servants, and Artisans by the Proprietors of Entailed Estates in Scotland" (13th August, 1860),— a power which the owners of entailed estates in England do not seem to have been so anxious for, as it is only in the " Improvement of Land Act, 1864" (27 & 28 Vict. c. 114), that we find "the erection of labourers' cottages, farmhouses, and other buildings required for farm purposes, and the improvement of and addition to labourers' cottages, farm-houses, and other buildings for farm purposes already erected," enumerated among the objects for which landowners may borrow or advance money under the Act. The extension of State aid to such purposes is however carried out by the recent Act of the 29 & 30 Vict. c. 28, " to enable the Public Works Loan Commissioners to make Advances towards the erection of Dwellings for the Labouring Classes" (18th May, 1866), which enables such advances to be made, not only to any public authority entitled to carry into execution the " Labouring Classes' Lodging-Houses Act, 1851," but to " any local or other authority invested with powers of town or local government and rating" by Act of Parliament, " any local authority acting under the ' Nuisances Removal Act, 1855,'" or its amending Acts, any railway, dock, or harbour company, or any other company, society, or association " established for the purposes of the Acts, or for trading or manufacturing purposes," or any private person entitled to land in fee-simple, or to fifty unexpired years of a term.

One other group of enactments of the period may deserve notice in this connection, as likely to be of especial advantage to the working classes, although not specially devised for them, that which relates to the preservation of open spaces and the formation of recreation grounds. The General Enclosure Act of the 8 & 9 Vict. c. 118 (8th August, 1845), besides providing that no lands situate within 15 miles of the City of London, or within 2 miles of any city of 10,000 inhabitants, $2\frac{1}{2}$ of one of 20,000, 3 of one of 30,000, $3\frac{1}{2}$ of one of 70,000, or 4 of one of 100,000, should be enclosed without a special Act, and against the enclosure of village greens, contained a special clause (s. 30) for the appropriation or enclosure " of an allotment for the purposes of exercise and recreation for the inhabitants of the neighbourhood," of from four to ten acres, according to population. Mr. Slaney's " Recreation Grounds' Act, 1852" (22 Vict. c. 27), enabled grants of land to be made to trustees, "to be held by them as open public grounds for the resort and recreation of adults, and as playgrounds for children and youth, or either of such purposes," without being subject to the provisions of the Charitable Trusts' Act, and also empowered bequests not exceeding £1000 to be made "for the purpose of defraying the expenses of purchasing, preparing, maintaining, and preserving such grounds for the purposes aforesaid, and ornamenting the same." The 23 & 24 Vict. c. 30, "to enable a majority of two-thirds of the ratepayers of any parish or district, duly assembled, to rate their district in aid of public improvements for general benefit within their district" (3rd July, 1860)—which is unfortunately much narrower than its title—empowers the aforesaid majority of ratepayers, in parishes of more than 500 population, to purchase or lease lands, and accept gifts and grants thereof, " for the purpose of forming any public walk, exercise or playground," and to rate themselves at not exceeding 6*d.* in the pound (but only where half the estimated cost of the proposed improvement has been subscribed), for maintaining such improvement, for " improving any open walk or footpath, or placing convenient seats, or shelters from rain, and for other purposes of a similar nature." Lastly, the " Metropolitan Commons' Act, 1866," 29 & 30 Vict. c. 122—introducing a system which seems certain to be developed, and extended for the benefit of all large towns,—forbids the Enclosure Commissioners to entertain any application for the enclosure of any part of a Common situate wholly or in part within the Metropolitan Police District, and empowers them only to consider and approve of schemes for the " local management" of such Commons. And it would be unjust to pass over in complete silence the many Acts for the formation of local parks and other local improvements, including for the Metropolis the Victoria, Battersea, and Camberwell Parks,—the Halifax Park, etc.

We come now to those measures which have more especially in view the intellectual advancement of the working class. These are far more difficult to define. It is the working man, as such, who needs the protection of a Factories' Act, of a Mines and Collieries' Act; the benefits of the Friendly Societies' Act and of its congeners are expressly limited to the small capitalist, who must include the workman. But education, intellectual progress, has come to be viewed as a human, universal need, and from the moment we set aside the criminal and the pauper, we can hardly, in the province of legislation, distinguish between what is meant for the education of one class, and what is meant for the education of all.

One great fact, however, stands out in the period which is occupying us, the recognition by the State of education, as an object of national policy. Preceded, strange to say, for years by votes " for educating emancipated negroes," or " for education in Ireland," the first vote of £30,000 " for public education in Great Britain " occurs in the Appropriation Act of the 3 & 4 Vict. c. 112 (11th August, 1840), and was even reduced the next year to £15,000 (4 & 5 Vict. c. 53). Four years later, however, the 7 & 8 Vict. c. 37 was passed, " to secure the terms on which grants are made by her Majesty out of the Parliamentary grant for the Education of the Poor, and to explain the Act of the fifth year of the reign of her present Majesty, for the Conveyance of Sites for Schools" (19th July, 1844). This recognizes the authority of the Committee of Council on Education (first appointed by Order in Council in 1839), the principle of school grants, and that of Government inspection. The subsequent Act of the 18 & 19 Vict. c. 131 requires no special notice. By the date of the last Session, the grant for public education in Great Britain (though smaller than it had been) amounted to £694,530, supplemented by that for " Public Education in Ireland under the Commissioners of National Education in Ireland," of £336,130 (29 & 30 Vict. c. 91).

The latter half of the title of the 7 & 8 Vict. c. 37, indicates the connection with this part of our subject of a series of Acts which we need only most briefly notice, those for facilitating the conveyance of sites for schools and their endowment, beginning with the 6 & 7 Wm. IV. c. 70 (13th August, 1836), for the former purpose only, and the 4 & 5 Vict. c. 38 (21st June, 1841), which embraces both objects. The importance of the latter has, however, been impaired, and the facilities which the Government educational system had begun to afford for developing any signal intellectual gifts among the poorer classes contracted, through the mischievous, if not malignant influence of one whose object seems to be to keep at a dead level the classes which he has taunted with their inferiority.*

There are, however, other classes of educational institu-

---

* We would ask those to whom the above expressions respecting the tendency of Mr. Lowe's Revised Code may appear too strong, to read in the Transactions of the Social Science Association for 1866, the summary of the discussion on the subject at Sheffield in October, 1865, where they will find *every* speaker—teachers, inspectors of schools, clergymen, dissenting ministers, working men, etc.—declaring that the effect of the Revised Code has been to cause the higher branches of education to be neglected or abandoned,—in short, as Dr. Hodgson said, to produce the " deterioration and degradation " of our schools.

Since the above lines were written, the debates in Parliament of February 28 and April 5 have painfully confirmed the statements referred to, and in spite of Mr. Lowe's opposition, the Government, backed by a large majority in the House, has begun to retrace its steps. " When I found," said Mr. Corry, on April 5, " a great falling off in teaching power, and by the reduction in number of pupil teachers a great injury resulting to the education of the children, and when I found, further, a great diminution in the supply of candidates for certificates, threatening to break

tions which must not in this connection be left out of sight. We hold the distinction to be a profound one between the working man and the pauper. But there is one branch of the Poor-Law system which has for its especial object to raise the poor out of pauperism, to turn the pauper child into a self-supporting working man. And again, whilst we have avoided all mention of the penal law in dealing with the progress of the working classes, there is equally one branch of the system which belongs to our subject, that which seeks to raise the criminal child into an honest working man by education. To the former belongs the creation, under some of the provisions of the 7 & 8 Vict. c. 101, "for the Further Amendment of the Laws relating to the Poor in England" (9th August, 1844), of School Districts with their schools and District Boards, amended by the 11 & 12 Vict. c. 82, and the important Act of the 18 & 19 Vict. c. 34, "to Provide for the Education of Children in the Receipt of Outdoor Relief" (26th June, 1855). The transition between this class of enactments and the other is afforded by those relating to Industrial Schools, at first confounded with, but eventually distinguished from Reformatory Schools proper. The latter trace their origin to the

down the whole system of certificated masters,—it was my duty to take immediate action." So sweeping indeed was the destruction of teaching power effected by Mr. Lowe, that the pupil teachers had fallen in number between 1861 and 1866 from 13,393 to 8970 ; and those who remain, it is now complained, are very inferior in attainments, owing to the fact that, to use the words of Mr. Inspector Meyrick, as quoted by Mr. Corry, " geography, grammar, and history, all of them very efficient instruments for opening the mind, have disappeared as subjects of study, or, where they exist, are scarcely the ghosts of their old selves."

Act of the 17 & 18 Vict. c. 86, " for the Better Care and
Reformation of Youthful Offenders in Great Britain "
(10th August, 1854), which, reciting that " Reformatory
Schools for the better training of juvenile offenders have
been and may be established, allows the sending of youthful offenders, at the expense of the State, to any Reformatory School certified by an inspector of prisons to be useful
and efficient for its purpose." The 20 & 21 Vict. c. 48,
" to make Better Provision for the Care and Education of
Vagrant, Destitute, and Disorderly Children, and for the Extension of Industrial Schools" (17th August, 1857), reciting
that " industrial schools for the better training of vagrant
children have been and may be established," authorizes the
Committee of Council on Education to certify " any
school in which industrial training is provided, and in which
children are fed as well as taught," to which any children
may be sent who are " taken into custody on a charge of
vagrancy." The certifying power was by the 23 & 24
Vict. c. 108 transferred to the Home Secretary; by the
24 & 25 Vict. c. 113, the " Industrial Schools' Act, 1861,"
the whole system was revised, and brought into connection
with the Poor-Laws. " Certified Industrial Schools," which
were to be henceforth distinct from Reformatory Schools,
were to be those in which, besides industrial training and
feeding, children are also " clothed " and " lodged." Poor
Law Guardians, with the consent of the Poor Law Board,
were empowered to contract for the maintenance and education of pauper children in such schools, which might
also receive beggar and vagrant children, apparently under
fourteen, children apparently under twelve, having com-

mitted an offence, not being felony, punishable by imprisonment or some less punishment, and children under fourteen sent by their parents. The mingling of simply pauper
children with children presumably or actually guilty of
offences proving however, as it obviously is, objectionable, the 25 & 26 Vict. c. 43 (17th July, 1862) was
passed " to provide for the Education and Maintenance of
Pauper Children in certain Schools and Institutions " which
are to be certified by the Poor Law Board and inspected
by their Inspectors.   Lastly, the Industrial School system
was revised and extended by the " Industrial Schools'
Act, 1866 " (29 & 30 Vict. c. 118), which confined to
refractory children, or those of criminal parents, such as
Poor Law Guardians might send to a Certified Industrial
School.

If we pass from the education of children to that of
adults, we find no very distinctive measures for promoting
the latter among the working classes ; and on one point at
least, the omission in the later Friendly Societies' Acts of
"education" as a purpose for which such societies might
be constituted, a decided backward step was taken, which
for a time at least put the most admirable among the co-
operative stores to real incovenience.   The Act of the
6 & 7 Vict. c. 36 (28th July, 1843), "to exempt from
County, Borough, Parochial, and other Local Rates, Land
and Buildings occupied by Scientific or Literary Societies,"
seemed to have been almost studiously framed to exclude
the ' Mechanics' Institute,'—at the time the only available
means of adult education for the working man,—and
has been expressly decided not to apply to societies for

educational purposes (*Queen* v. *Pocock,* 8 Q. B. 729). In fact, the only piece of legislation which may be said to have directly promoted the education of the adult working man (and that only in common with all others), was the 17 & 18 Vict. c. 112, "to afford greater Facilities for the Establishment of Institutions for the Promotion of Literature, Science, and the Fine Arts, and to provide for their Better Regulation" (11th August, 1854). This expressly includes "every institution for the time being established for the promotion of science, literature, the fine arts; for adult instruction, the diffusion of useful knowledge, the foundation or maintenance of libraries or reading-rooms for general use among the members, or open to the public; of public museums and galleries of paintings and other works of art, collections of natural history, mechanical and philosophical inventions, instruments or designs." Grants of land not exceeding one acre may be made to such institutions ; means of suing and being sued are provided for them ; a power of making bye-laws is given, and provisions are enacted against the dishonesty of members.

But there is one other interesting measure, which may be considered in this connection, although perhaps it might also claim to rank among the Protective Acts, as its title implies,—the " Act for the Protection of Inventions and Designs exhibited at certain Industrial Exhibitions in the United Kingdom," 28 & 29 Vict. c. 3 (27th March, 1865), or " Industrial Exhibitions' Act." This recites that " exhibitions of objects of art and industry, manufactured or contributed wholly or in part by members of the industrious classes," have been lately held, or may be held, and empowers the Board of Trade to certify such exhibitions, after which the exhibition at the same, or the publication of descriptions during the same, or the use for the purposes thereof of any new invention, is not to prejudice the patent or registration rights of such inventor. The principle latent in this Act, as well as in those relating to larger exhibitions which suggested it, involves probably a wider alteration in our Patent Laws than was suspected by the framers. But at any rate, it is impossible to mistake the stimulus which it must afford to the inventive powers of the working man.

§ 3. *Measures of General Benefit.*

One other class of measures requires to be considered,—those measures of general benefit, which have however largely influenced the condition of the working class.

Foremost among these perhaps are the Fiscal Acts,—Acts for the repeal or alleviation of Excise and other cognate duties, diminishing the cost of articles of consumption,—Acts for the repeal or alleviation of Customs' duties, which in addition stimulate production by encouraging interchange with foreign countries,—of Stamp or cognate duties, facilitating transactions between man and man,—of Postage, helping every other reform, promoting all social, intellectual, and moral progress. The first series, which opens curiously with the repeal of the Excise on vinegar, 7 & 8 Vict. c. 25 (4th July, 1844), includes that of the duties on glass, 8 & 9 Vict. c. 6 (24th April, 1845), bricks, 13 & 14 Vict. c. 9 (17th May,

1850), soap, 16 & 17 Vict. c. 39 (8th July, 1853), paper, 24 & 25 Vict. c. 20 (12th June, 1861), and closes with that of the hop duties, 25 & 26 Vict. c. 22 (3rd June, 1862); the window duties being moreover replaced by the house tax, 14 & 15 Vict. c. 36 (24th July, 1851). The reforms of the second series, those of Customs' duties, are too many to be here enumerated ; suffice it to say that, beginning in 1842, the list closes with the reduction, by the 28 & 29 Vict. c. 30 (26th May, 1865) of the tea duties to sixpence a pound, which under the Act of the 3 & 4 Wm. IV. c. 101 (29th August, 1833) ranged from 1s. 6d. to 3s. ; that the temporary suspension of the corn duties, which led to their total repeal, belongs to the year 1847 (10 & 11 Vict. cc. 1, 2, 3, 64, 86); and that the final repeal of export duty on coals took place by the 11 & 12 Vict. c. 95 (14th August, 1850). In connection with both these series it would be unjust to overlook the property and income tax, 5 & 6 Vict. c. 35 (22nd June, 1842), which, whilst as a burden only grazing as it were the summit of the working class, yet by rendering possible the enfranchisement from taxation of all the chief articles of consumption, and of the elements of production, has indirectly been to that class a boon of priceless value. The third group, comprising the repeal of the auction duty, 8 & 9 Vict. c. 6 (8th May, 1845), various reductions of the stamp duties, and the reduction of the duties of fire-insurance by the 28 & 29 Vict. c. 30 (26th May, 1865), is generally of less direct importance to the working classes. We should except, however, the Acts relating to the Press, and beginning at an early period (6 & 7 Wm. IV. c. 76, reducing the newspaper duties; 13th August, 1836). The principal of these are (in 1853) the 16 & 17 Vict. cc. 63, 71, which both reduce the newspaper stamp and repeal the advertisement duties (besides in other respects relaxing the Press laws), and above all in 1855 (15th June), the 18 & 19 Vict. c. 27, which renders the newspaper stamp optional only. Among reforms in other stamp duties it would also be unjust to omit the reduction of the receipt stamp to one penny, and the introduction of the adhesive stamp, by the 17 & 18 Vict. c. 83 (10th August, 1854); the reduction of the agreement stamp to sixpence by the 23 & 24 Vict. c. 15 (3rd April, 1860), and the introduction of the adhesive agreement stamp by the 23 & 24 Vict. c. 111 (28th August, 1860); the abolition of probate duty on estates under £100, by the 27 & 28 Vict. c. 56 (25 July, 1864), and the introduction of the graduated scale of duties for conveyances under £25 consideration, which for the first time brought a vast number of the transactions of the poorer classes within the pale of the law. Among the group relating to the Post-Office we may notice the 6 & 7 Wm. IV. c. 54, allowing the free postage of stamped newspapers (13th August, 1836), the 3 & 4 Vict. c. 96, enacting the charging of postage by weight (10th August, 1840), and finally the 10 & 11 Vict. c. 29, which introduced the postage-stamp, and made the penny postage system possible, by the discretion which it left to the Post-Office (22nd July, 1847).

There is, indeed, a large body of legislation of a partly fiscal, partly social character, which, although its bearing on the physical and moral progress of the working classes is undoubtedly most important, we do not propose to treat of, on account of the many vexed questions which arise out of it,—that, namely, of the laws relating to the taxation and sale of spirituous and fermented liquors. Among these, we will simply mention the 23 Vict. c. 27 (14th June, 1860), as to refreshment-houses and wine-licences, as introducing a class of establishments deemed by many, at least, useful rivals to the public-house or the beer-shop.

Acts relating to the Public Health may next be considered, but form, again, a series too numerous to be set forth at length. The first group of them, perhaps, which deserves to be noticed is that of the Vaccination Acts, beginning with the 3 & 4 Vict. c. 29, " to extend the Practice of Vaccination " (23rd July, 1840), and of which the most important is the 16 & 17 Vict. c. 100, which made vaccination compulsory by law, though, unfortunately, it has not succeeded in rendering it universal in practice. Another valuable group opens with the Act "to encourage the Establishment of Public Baths and Washhouses " by boroughs and parishes, 9 & 10 Vict. c. 74 (26th August, 1846), amended by the 10 & 11 Vict. c. 61 (2nd July, 1847), but which eventually merges in the current of general sanitary or municipal legislation. The temporary " Nuisances Removal Act," of the 9 & 10 Vict. c. 96 (28th August, 1846), amended and made permanent by the 11 & 12 Vict. c. 123 (4th September, 1848) and the 12 & 13 Vict. c. 111 (1st August, 1849), and replaced, as respects England, by the 18 & 19 Vict. c. 121 (14th

August, 1855),—itself modified (together with the previous
" Diseases Prevention Act, 1855," 18 & 19 Vict. c. 116),
by the 23 & 24 Vict. c. 77 (6th August, 1860),—led the
way to the important " Public Health Act, 1848 " (11 &
12 Vict. c. 63), still substantially in force, although modified in various respects by the " Local Government Act,
1858," to be presently noticed, and (together with almost
all the other Acts on the subject) by the " Sanitary Act,
1866," 29 & 30 Vict. c. 90. Another Act of this category is the 23 & 24 Vict. c. 84, " for preventing the
Adulteration of Articles of Food or Drink " (6th August,
1860), which imposes penalties on every person " selling
any article of food or drink with which, to the knowledge
of such person, any ingredient or material injurious to the
health of persons eating or drinking such article has been
mixed," or selling " as pure or unadulterated, any article
of food or drink which is adulterated, or not pure."

The " Public Health Act, 1848," by the institution of
" Local Boards of Health," affords a transition to the
Municipal Acts, properly so termed, with which, from
henceforth, the Health Acts become, in great measure,
blended. The earliest in date of these, however, for the
period which occupies us, are the two great Acts of
1834-5—the New Poor Law, 4 & 5 Wm. IV. c. 76 ("an
Act for the Amendment and better Administration of the
Laws relating to the Poor in England and Wales, 14th
August, 1834), and the Municipal Reform Act, 5 & 6
Wm. IV. c. 76 (" an Act to provide for the Regulation
of Municipal Corporations in England and Wales," 9th
September, 1835). Of the first (with its various amend-

ment Acts, too many to notice), it will be sufficient to observe that, however imperfect is still the system which it established, yet by checking, as it did, the growth of pauperism, through the suppression of demoralizing modes of relief, and recognizing, at the same time, fully *the right to live*, it must have rendered especial service to the honest working man in town and country. And, although the tendency of the second was to curtail the class of freemen, comprising the bulk of the working men hitherto admitted to municipal privileges, yet the burgess's qualification, consisting simply of residence and three years' rating to the poor, was made low enough to admit all the more industrious of the working classes of the towns generally to the municipal franchise, except in the Metropolis. The enormous group of Acts amending or modifying the one last referred to, closing at present with the 24 & 25 Vict. c. 75 (6th August, 1861), can only be glanced at; although we may single out the 21 & 22 Vict. c. 43 (23rd July, 1858), which provides that, where the owner of a house is rated, the occupier nevertheless is to vote; and the 22 Vict. c. 35 (19th April, 1859), introducing nomination papers in municipal elections.

The "Local Government Act, 1858" (21 & 22 Vict. c. 98), although clumsily tagging itself on to the Public Health Act ("an Act to Amend the Public Health Act, 1848, and to make further Provision for the Local Government of Towns and Populous Districts;" 2nd August), is, in fact, a Municipal Corporations Act for the whole kingdom, since it may be adopted by any "place" with a settled boundary, and confers upon it government by means of a corporate " Local Board " (no longer " of Health "). It is, however, a far less democratic measure than the Municipal Reform Act. Instead of the simple rate-paying franchise of the latter, and of our old parochial system, the qualification of the electors,—which the Act seems ashamed of setting forth in express terms, and borrows from the Public Health Act, 1848—requires a minimum rateable value of £50 to confer a vote, increases the votes up to six for £250, or more, and gives votes to owners as well as to occupiers, and to owner-occupiers in both capacities. The Act, although recent, has, of course, a growing tail of amendment Acts—the last, 26 & 27 Vict. c. 17 (11th May, 1863). Parallel with it, for the Metropolis, is the " Metropolis Local Management Act, 1855 " (14th August), 18 & 19 Vict. c. 120, creating the machinery of District Boards, and of the Metropolitan Board of Works, which, however, maintains, in the first degree, the simple rate-paying franchise. This has also a large following of Acts, professedly or virtually amending it, down to the " Metropolitan Fire Brigade Act, 1865 " (28 & 29 Vict. c. 90), and a Superannuation Allowances Act of the 29 & 30 Vict. c. 31.

Through the operation of the above Acts, not only has a system been established which, however chaotic as yet, tends to secure to the population at large the primary elements of health, safety, and well-being, by means o sewerage and the application of sewage, water-supply, the prevention of fire and of smoke, the proper construction of buildings and streets, the removal of nuisances and obstructions, the prevention and combating of disease, the good ordering of public places, etc.; but in all localities to which one of the three municipal systems of the Municipal Reform Act, the Local Government Act, or the Metropolis Local Management Act extends, endeavours to meet these various purposes by means of local self-government, on a more or less extended scale. And, since the vast bulk of the working classes are dwellers in towns or in populous localities, it is obvious that they must have reaped the largest share of the benefits of the above system of legislation. As respects the purely agricultural population, some of the sanitary benefits sought to be secured by the Public Health and Municipal Acts proper have resulted from the long series of Acts for the drainage and improvement of land, authorizing public or private money to be advanced for such purposes, which begins with the 9 & 10 Vict. c. 101 (28th August, 1846), and of which the most important is the "Improvement of Land Act, 1864" (27 & 28 Vict. c. 114), already referred to for another purpose.

The Municipal Acts proper are, again, closely connected with a group of measures for general intellectual advancement.* Foremost among these is the "Act for Encouraging the Establishment of Museums in large Towns" 8 & 9 Vict. c. 43 (21st July, 1845), empowering the Town Councils of municipal boroughs of over 10,000 inhabitants to purchase lands, or accept gifts, grants, or devises, and to erect buildings for museums of art and

---

* To avoid controversial questions, we shall pretermit Acts of the period relating to religious and church matters, several of them, however, very important.

science, and to improve and maintain the same; to rate
themselves for the purpose at not exceeding one-halfpenny
in the pound of annual value, and to borrow money. The
13 & 14 Vict. c. 65, "for enabling Town Councils to
establish Public Libraries and Museums" (or "Public
Libraries Act, 1850"), whilst repealing the former Act and
taking away the powers of accepting grants, extended, as
its title implies, the principle to the formation of public
libraries. This was repealed in turn, and the system further extended, by the "Public Libraries' Act, 1855," 18 &
19 Vict. c. 70, which authorized the adoption of the Act
by all municipal boroughs of over 5000 population, and all
districts within the limits of any Improvement Act, and
parishes or groups of parishes of the like population, raised
the maximum rate to one penny in the pound, gave for
the purposes of the Act the powers of the Lands Clauses
Consolidation Act (*i.e.* of compulsory purchase, etc.),
added to those purposes the establishment of "schools for
science or art," and enacted that the admission to all
libraries and museums established under the Act should
be free. Lastly, the "Public Libraries Amendment Act
(England and Scotland), 1866" (29 & 30 Vict. c. 114),
rendered the last preceding one applicable to "any borough, district, parish, or burgh, of whatever population,"
besides reducing the majority of two-thirds, previously required for its adoption, to a simple majority. That the
last-mentioned group of Acts have been a decided benefit
to the working classes, we propose to show hereafter.

Indirectly, indeed, the working man is interested in
every measure for the spread of education; since he can-

not be taught himself except by those who have learnt something which they may teach. It will be sufficient, however, on this head, if we mention the 3 & 4 Vict. c. 77, "for Improving the Condition and extending the Benefits of Grammar Schools" (7th August, 1840), as initiating educational reform in those bodies which, after the National or British school, stand nearest to his reach. Let us finally notice in this connection an early Act of the period, the 5 & 6 Wm. IV. c. 2, "to Amend an Act of the 38th year of King George III. for Preventing the Mischiefs arising from the Printing and Publishing Newspapers, and Papers of a like nature, by persons not known; and for Regulating the Printing and Publishing of such Papers in other respects, and to discontinue certain Actions commenced under the provisions of the said Act" (20th March, 1835); which, by taking away (as in the case of the corresponding Societies' Acts, etc.) the right of the informer to sue for penalties, and confining its exercise to the law officers of the Crown, began that emancipation of the newspaper press which the fiscal measures before mentioned carried out.

Acts for the encouragement of invention form the midground between those for intellectual and for commercial advancement. The exorbitant charges of the patent system for a long time absolutely restricted the power of the ingenious or tasteful workman to secure a property in his own inventions within the field of the Acts for securing copyright in designs (beginning in 1787, with the 27 Geo. III. c. 38), which was confined until the present period to " linens, cottons, calicoes, and muslins," and was first extended—by two Acts of the 2 & 3 Vict. cc. 13, 17 (4th and 14th June, 1839)—to woollen, silk, hair, or mixed fabrics, and temporarily to other tissues and textile fabrics except lace; to the modelling, casting, embossment, chasing, engraving, or "any other kind of impression or ornament" on other articles of manufacture, or to their shape or configuration. The permanent Act of the 5 & 6 Vict. c. 100, "to Consolidate and Amend the Laws relating to the Copyright of Designs for Ornamenting articles of Manufacture" (10th August, 1842), was the first which gave a general copyright of ornamental design. The 6 & 7 Vict. c. 65, "to Amend the Laws relating to the Copyright of Designs" (22nd August, 1843), finally extended the principle to all articles of manufacture "having reference to some purpose of utility," so far as the design to be protected should be for "shape or configuration." Lastly, the 15 & 16 Vict. c. 83, the "Patent Law Amendment Act, 1852," chiefly by extending over a term of years the payments for letters patent, opened for the first time to the inventive workman a still arduous access to what seems often to him the charmed circle of patent-right.

Measures of pure commercial advancement come next. Foremost among them are the important though clumsy Acts of 1844, which first brought Joint Stock Companies and Joint Stock Banks openly within the pale of the law, the 7 & 8 Vict. cc. 110, 113, "for the Registration, Incorporation, and Regulation of Joint Stock Companies," and "to regulate Joint Stock Banks in England" (5th September), parents of a numerous progeny. Among these it will be sufficient to quote the 18 & 19 Vict. c. 133, "for

Limiting the Liability of Members of certain Joint Stock Companies" (14th August, 1855), followed by the already-mentioned 21 & 22 Vict. c. 91, "to enable Joint Stock Banking Companies to be formed on the principle of Limited Liability" (2nd August, 1858), and finally the now subsisting "Companies Act, 1862" (25 & 26 Vict. c. 89), which includes banking companies. Thanks to these Acts, and especially to the principle of limited liability, the working man has not only been able to contribute his small capital to large commercial undertakings, but to employ the machinery they supplied in co-operative undertakings of his own, which either exceeded the somewhat narrow limits of the "Industrial and Provident Societies' Acts," or which it simply appeared desirable to constitute otherwise than under these Acts. Finally, "the Act to Amend the Law of Partnership," 28 & 29 Vict. c. 86 (5th July, 1865), already noticed for another purpose, by enacting that the lending money "to a person engaged, or about to engage, in any trade or undertaking," in consideration of a rate of interest varying with the profits, or of a share of profits,' "shall not, of itself, constitute the lender a partner . . . or render him responsible as such," gave to the working classes, together with all others, further facilities for engaging in commercial undertakings.

The last referred-to Act brings us to the group of legal reforms proper. The most important of all these to the working man is the "Act for the more easy Recovery of small Debts and Demands in England,"—better known as the County Courts' Act, 9 & 10 Vict. c. 95 (28th August, 1846),—the first measure for centuries, it may be said, which brought the legal demands of the working man within the pale of civil justice. Among its Amendment Acts it will be sufficient to notice the 28 & 29 Vict. c. 99, "to confer on the County Courts a limited Jurisdiction in Equity" (5th July, 1865). Another Act, almost of the same date with the first County Courts' Act, the 9 & 10 Vict. c. 93, "for Compensating the Families of Persons killed by Accidents" (26th August, 1846), amended by the 27 & 28 Vict. c. 95 (29th July, 1864), has also proved of especial consequence to the working classes, whose lives are too often in daily peril through their daily toil. Whilst we wish to leave on one side the category of the penal laws properly so called, we cannot overlook the 6 & 7 Wm. IV. c. 114, "for enabling Persons indicted of Felony to make their Defence by Counsel or Attorney" (20th August, 1836),—to none more important than to the ignorant, the unpolished, and the comparatively poor,—nor the series of Acts (beginning at an earlier period) for the prevention of cruelty to animals (the principal of which is the 12 & 13 Vict. c. 92, 1st August, 1849), so important in their bearing on the brutal amusements formerly largely indulged in by the working class. The Charitable Trusts' Acts (of which the first is the 16 & 17 Vict. c. 137, 20th August, 1853,) tend to rescue from fraud and neglect many benefactions designed for the working class. The "Merchandise Marks' Act, 1862" (25 & 26 Vict. c. 88), besides its general tendency to purify trade, helps to secure to the working man quantity in his consumption, as the 23 & 24 Vict. c. 84, against the adulteration of articles of food or drink, helped to secure quality. (Compare also the Weights and Measures Acts, 5 & 6 Wm. IV. c. 63, 22 & 23 Vict. c. 59.)

§ 4. *Political Enactments.*

But now, as against all these measures of social legislation, what is to be said of political ? Let us see.

Putting out of sight the Boundary Act (2 & 3 Wm. IV. c. 64), as simply completing the Reform Act (2 & 3 Wm. IV. c. 45), the 5 & 6 Wm. IV. c. 36 (25th August, 1835), for limiting the poll in boroughs to one day, may be considered a real step towards purity of election in the boroughs. The 6 & 7 Wm. IV. c. 102, " for rendering more easy the taking the Poll at County Elections" (20th August, 1836), was a stir in the same direction for the counties. The Act of the 6 & 7 Vict. c. 18, "to amend the Law for the Registration of Persons entitled to vote, and to define certain Rights of Voting, and to regulate certain Proceedings in the Election of Members to serve in Parliament for England and Wales," is perhaps chiefly remarkable for its suppression of the claim-shilling, which seems to have proved such a powerful barrier to public spirit. Some slight extension of the borough franchise was effected by the 14 & 15 Vict. c. 14, " to amend the Law for the Registration of certain Persons commonly known as ' Compound Householders,' and to facilitate the Exercise by such Persons of their Right to vote in the Election of Borough Members to serve in Parliament" (3rd July, 1851). The year 1853 saw the example of the boroughs as to the duration of the poll followed, after eighteen years' interval, in the counties, by the 16 & 17 Vict. c. 15, "to limit the Time of taking the Poll in Counties, at Contested Elections for Knights of the Shire to serve in Parliament, in England and Wales, to One Day." The 21 & 22 Vict. c. 26, "to abolish the Property Qualification of Members of Parliament" (28th June, 1858), if it has not yet opened the door of the House of Commons to the working man, has at least unlocked it. The 24 & 25 Vict. c. 112, "for the Appropriation of Seats vacated by the Disfranchisement of the Boroughs of Sudbury and St. Alban's" (6th August, 1861), in creating the Parliamentary borough of Birkenhead, dividing the West Riding of York, and giving an additional member to South Lancashire, has to a trifling extent either given new votes to the working class, or extended the influence of districts where it is largely represented. The "County Voters' Registration Act, 1865" (28 & 29 Vict. c. 36) gave some further facilities to county voters. There is moreover a mass of Bribery Acts, Corrupt Practices' Prevention Acts, Election Petition Acts, which, considering late election disclosures, it seems best to pass under silence, since, however well meant, their influence seems to have been but small.

And this is all the progress of political legislation during thirty-four years. Compared with the stately march of social legislative progress, how slow and timid! Surely the record of the latter should have taught other lessons.

The Reform Acts of 1832 found the factory workers, under twenty-one, in the cotton trade, only protected from night work between 8.30 P.M. and 5.30 A.M.; those under eighteen restricted to twelve hours' labour, or nine on Saturdays; children under nine forbidden to be employed. 1867 sees the workers in all the leading branches of our textile industry—cotton, woollen, worsted, hemp, flax, tow, linen, silk, when worked under steam-power—enjoying the reduced hours of ten-and-a-half a day, with a Saturday half-holiday after 2 P.M. If children are allowed to work at eight years of age, provision is made for their education. Various other branches of industry, such as print-works, bleach and dye works, and lace factories, and processes connected with the protected manufactures, have been brought, with slight variations of detail, into the system; and finally, though by a measure which has not yet had time to produce any effects on a large scale, a number of other manufactures and employments; whilst an efficient system of inspection has been instituted to see the system carried out.

The Reform Acts of 1832 found our mines and collieries worked, in great measure, by women and children —those degraded, these crushed, by the labour. 1867 sees female underground labour absolutely prohibited, as well as boy labour unless educated, in coal or connected ironstone mines, under ten ; otherwise, both in these and in all other mines, under twelve ; whilst here also a system of inspection is at work, powerfully aided by the independent action of the workers themselves.

To say nothing of chimney-sweeps and bakers, the Reform Acts of 1832 found our sailors almost without protection in purse, health, or safety. 1867 finds a vast code in existence which endeavours to secure all three ; and although palpably insufficient in many respects (especially through the exclusion of the coasting trade from various of its provisions), shows at least a vast advance in public consideration for the merchant seaman.

The legislation in force in 1832 allowed the working classes no banking facilities except through the pawnbroker or the private Savings-Bank, no legalized field of associative self-help but the Friendly Society, to which all federative expansion was denied. 1867 finds the Savings-Bank system more efficient in itself, yet largely supplemented by the Post-Office Savings-Bank, which stakes the credit of the State on the safety of the poor man's deposit ; finds the Loan Society, the Benefit Building Society, the Industrial or Provident Society, recognized and regulated by law, the large Friendly Societies with branches or harmless oaths or tests brought within its pale, the Trade Society struggling for recognition, and last, not least, the association of the worker to profits allowed without the risks of partnership.

In 1832, Sanitary Science, as distinct from curative medicine, may be said to have been unknown, and the only protection to life against other than personally injurious action, to have lain in the common law of nuisance, and the Building Acts of the Metropolis, and of a few large towns. 1867 sees abroad a very flood of sanitary legislation. In every place large enough to maintain a Local Board, the right to pure air, pure water, safe and wholesome dwellings, sweet and well-ordered streets, and public spaces, is in fact recognized by law. Many special facilities and provisions have been enacted for the construction of dwellings for the poorer classes, and providing them with open spaces for recreation.

In 1832, the right of the English citizen, as such, to education was wholly ignored. By 1867, nearly £700,000 a year is spent by the State in furthering the education of the classes, able to contribute somewhat themselves for the purpose, who frequent our National, British, and other assisted schools; whilst district schools for the pauper child, certified industrial schools for the vagrant and disorderly, reformatory schools for the criminal, tend alike to convert the useless or the burdensome into useful members of society. The Mechanics' Institute of the earlier period has been able to develope itself and to obtain some legal protection. Legal facilities have been given for the establishment of free libraries, museums, and schools of art. The inventive powers of the working class have been stimulated by the Copyright of Designs' Acts, by an amended Patent Act, by the protection given to articles exhibited at industrial exhibitions.

1832 knew only a newspaper press shackled in a hundred ways,—operating under the constant terror of the common informer—weighed down by stamp duties, advertisement duties, paper duties. 1867 sees that press absolutely free from all impost,—the stamp only remaining as the price of an optional privilege.

Notwithstanding the initiation of commercial reform by Huskisson, the Reform Acts of 1832 left the whole trade of the country and the industry of the working man, doubly fettered by a mischievous fiscal system, which enhanced at once the cost of consumption and of production, taxed safety, cleanliness, providence, light; whilst leaving the income of the rich untouched. 1867 sees every necessary of life, every element of production, either free or subject to moderate duties; the window tax gone, with the soap, brick, and timber duties; the duty on fire insurance greatly reduced; property and incomes directly charged to the State. In 1832, the Post-Office was a burden on communication; it is now the most beneficent civil institution in the country.

In 1832, the association of capital, except by special privilege, did not, so to speak, exist. In 1867, almost every form of commercial association is practicable, under the Joint-Stock Companies' Acts. Limited liability has enabled the working class to contribute their small capital to the increase of the productive power of the country, and, by a late Act, has practically been extended from the company to private establishments.

In 1832, the stamp-duties threw the ordinary legal transactions of the working man, the expenses of justice, the enforcement of his legal claims, practically out of the pale of the law. The reduction of the former, on the one hand, the establishment (or rather, revival) of the County Court, on the other, have, by 1867, brought both within it. The Compensation for Accidents Act has created a new civil right, of especial importance to his class.

In 1832, the Poor Laws were pauperizing and degrading the whole country. In 1867, although the right to live is more fully than ever recognised, the growth of pauperism has at least been stopped, if the evil plant remains far still from being uprooted.

Municipal life in the corporate boroughs, was, in 1832, a chaos. It is, by 1867, a system, in which every rate-paying man, or even the occupier of a rate-paying house, can take part; whilst the small, but too often worn-out, machinery of our parochial government, is giving way on all sides before the busy meddling of Local Boards.

Was all this to go for nothing? Had all this accumulation of wholesome and beneficent, or, at least, stimulant legislation, been thrown away? Notwithstanding all these various efforts to render the great mass of the people, or to enable it to become a better fed, better clothed, better housed, more healthy, more orderly, more saving, more industrious, more self-reliant, better educated population, is it still where it was five-and-thirty years ago? Have only the summits of that mass been touched as yet? If it were possible to say so, we venture to declare that, in all the annals of legislation throughout the world, such a record of impotency could not be discovered.

But does not the history itself disprove such a possibility? With certain trifling exceptions in the case of factory labour, Friendly Societies, etc., and one lamentable one as respects education, that history is continuous—progressive. If the Factory Acts were injurious to the factory workers, we should not see so many trades successively brought under their operation, or under similar regulations. If there were not more small capitals being formed, more small capitalists seeking for advances, more provident habits being formed, more powers of associative self-help being developed, we should have seen no Post-Office Savings-Banks, no Loan Societies, no machinery for Government insurance or annuity-granting on a small scale, no Benefit Building Societies, no Industrial and Provident Societies. If working men's children did not care to be educated, there would be no need of a Government grant. If working men had never learnt to read, there need be no free libraries, and penny papers would be impossible. If working men had not learnt to write, the penny postage would have been a failure. If working men had not cared to work, the sweeping away of customs' and excise duties would have been ruin to the Exchequer.

In the general progress, therefore, of legislation itself, but especially as it affects the working classes, is contained implicitly the irrefragable evidence of the progress of these classes, comprising, as they do, the great bulk of the people. But if in one field alone the progress of legislation has been almost imperceptible, whilst enormous in most others, the inference seems irresistible that in that field legislation had, till now, lagged behind the facts. For we cannot reasonably suppose that political progress is inseparable from all other. We cannot suppose that men whose physical, intellectual, social condition has been raised, have remained on the same dead political level,— that better fed, clothed, housed, educated, thriftier, more capable of organization, they are yet no more fit to be trusted with political power than they were thirty-five years ago. The anomaly must have been in the law, and not in themselves.

Let no one, indeed, infer, from the long catalogue of beneficent social legislation which so far honours the dynasty of middle-class Parliaments inaugurated by the Acts of 1832, that we deem that work accomplished, or even near to being so. On the contrary, we know that in almost every department what has been done already is but the germ of what is to be. The extension of legislative protection over the woman and the youth throughout all processes and employments,—universal education, a reformed apprenticeship system, a reformed law of master and servant, the direct legalization of trade societies, the legislative establishment of boards of arbitration with, for some purposes, compulsory powers, a reform of our police,— such are some of the most prominent only among the social reforms which are already either in progress of becoming law, or at least looming large on the legal horizon; every one of them either representing the logical development or the legal embodiment of some principle already at work. *Noblesse oblige ;* and a country which has done so much already with such success for its workers, is bound to do more still. What we have to show now is that by their efficient co-operation in, and wise use of, the good already achieved, those workers have established their right to a far more powerful co-operation in that which remains to be done.

PART III.

INFLUENCE OF THE WORKING CLASSES ON LEGISLATION AND POLICY, 1832-66.

THOSE whose acquaintance with the manufacturing population of England reaches so far back as 1832, and who have personal experience, as well as the study of figures to aid them, will be aware that about that time many questions which since then have been settled, or partially settled, by the Legislature, were subjects of keen discussion amongst the thoughtful and intelligent portions of our working people in the manufacturing districts of Great Britain. It is satisfactory now, on looking back over the intervening time, and remembering the various beneficial measures which have become embodied in law, to observe that the working men, in all our great centres of industry, gave what strength and influence they possessed to that side which experience has since demonstrated to have been in the right. During the various agitations which have taken place, what they assisted to do does not require now to be undone, nor, luckily for the nation, have they or their friends to regret an opposition on their part to the practical legislation of the country which, if it had been successful, would have been seriously injurious to its best interests.

Notwithstanding the sad condition of the great bulk of the working class in 1832, there were to be found everywhere throughout Lancashire, Yorkshire, and the other thickly populated districts, large numbers of operatives who had received from their parents, in a moderate degree, the blessings of education. For the inquiring adult, the Mechanics' Institutes, founded within the last decade by Dr. Birkbeck, not yet overrun by the middle class, and still in the first fervour of their utilitarianism, had afforded the means of a somewhat arid self-education. In the absence of the newspaper, the only cheap literature (except that of the ' Penny Magazine,' just started, and its rivals) was book or treatise literature, either published by the " Useful Knowledge Society," or of a kindred character ; so that whatever intellectual training was to be had, was hard and bracing. There were thus numbers, too, of clever, strong-witted, self-taught men, who had by quiet thoughtfulness, patient inquiry, or keen discussion, found their way to at least a limited understanding of the duties men owe to each other in this world. There was also a not inconsiderable number of active sympathizers belonging to other classes of the community, who made common cause with the working men on questions specially connected with their interests as a class, whilst the operatives in return threw their weight on the reforming side on general questions, and thus by a wise co-operation helped forward all movements set on foot for the promotion of the public good.

Hence there was at this period what may be called a great awakening. National policies, industrial progress, social growths and social neglects of various kinds had been allowed to take their own course. There was no provision for education, no check to speak of on life-destroying labour, no true recognition of that in man which struggles upwards and lifts him out of the brute condition, giving him what God has willed he should have, a life beyond and above that of mere getting and spending. Men had opened their eyes and had seen, not their nakedness alone, but their corruption, their degradation. their rapidly approaching moral death.

Roman Catholic emancipation had been carried a few years before, and the Liberal operatives had helped powerfully in that movement. The Reform Bill had just passed into law, and on that question the working men had stood almost unanimously on the Liberal side, in the belief that the breaking down of an old political monopoly would certainly tend to the general advancement of all honest interests. They had little direct concern in that question themselves, but they were too sagacious not to understand something of the oppressions and corruptions that prevail, however cleverly they may be concealed, wherever power is concentrated in a class, and they knew too well, by an experience peculiarly their own,* to what cruel and unscrupulous means men will resort for the preservation of class privileges. Then again the education question

* The Peterloo massacre, never to be forgotten in Manchester, was perpetrated in 1819 on an unarmed meeting, called together to petition Parliament for reform.

was continually obtruding itself, and whenever it engaged public attention, it had no better or more sturdy friends than the active and intelligent amongst the working classes. At this time also the cholera paid England its first visit, and taught, as its great lesson, that foul air, filth, and over-fatigue are deadly enemies to human life; and sanitary reform became at once an important public question, which in all its successive stages was helped forward by the intelligent portion of the working people. It may be remarked that although some of these movements did not enlist very strongly the sympathies of the ignorant and apathetic amongst the labouring population, still none of them called forth their hostility, or brought them into any kind of active opposition to the men who were seeking to promote political and social changes in the interest of the community.*

The questions, however, which test most closely the intelligent forethought of the working people of Great Britain, and prove most clearly the value to the country of their power in influencing the course of legislation, are those which have originated amongst themselves, and which have been carried to a practical solution chiefly by their exertions. The question of Factory Labour is a strong case in point. Under the old system, children and women were worked in the factories sometimes twelve,

---

* The opposition of a portion of the Chartist body, some years afterwards, to the proceedings of the Anti-Corn-Law League, furnishes no contradiction to this statement. Such opposition was a policy on the part of unwise popular leaders, approved of and carried out by their most ignorant and intemperate followers,—a policy which in the end was one of the main causes of their destruction as a political organization.

sometimes fourteen. and sometimes even more than sixteen hours a day; and notwithstanding the dreadful effects
of this continued drudgery, visible in many ways, the employers, as a class, believed that any interference, come
from whence it might, to check or modify such a practice,
would inevitably end in the destruction of the cotton trade.
Those who remember the short-time agitation, and who
were so far mixed up with it as to understand the spirit in
which it was carried on, cannot have forgotten the determined hostility of the factory owners to that measure.*
The few men from outside the working class, who engaged
on the side of the latter in this struggle, were regarded by
the employers with a most intense dislike.   The present
Earl of Shaftesbury (then Lord Ashley), John Fielden,
Michael Thomas Sadler, Richard Oastler, and some others
fought nobly in this cause, and for their disinterested and
unflagging labours deserve to be gratefully remembered.
But as Inkerman has been called the soldiers' battle, so
the credit of this arduous conflict—ending as it did, trium-
phantly—belongs, in the sacrifices it called for, as well as
in the blessings it has brought to the community, to the
working men of England.

---

* It is impossible at the present day to read without a smile, in the
Parliamentary Debates of 1832–3, the speeches of the opponents of
factory legislation—including some whose names we will not be cruel
enough to quote,—so lugubrious are the prophecies they contain of certain ruin to the country if measures should be passed, which have since
been followed by a tide of unparalleled prosperity.   In short, were it
not for differences of name, one would fancy it was Messrs. Creed
and Williams descanting on the proximate ruin of the iron trade in
1866–7.

The question was taken up warmly by men engaged in every kind of labour. As before stated, the factory operatives themselves were for a long time far more apathetic—nor can this be wondered at, when the facts of their degraded condition are remembered—than those belonging to other branches of industry, who were drawn into the agitation more by their sympathies than by their interests. These men gave their money, their time, and their energies to the forwarding of this question, not because they themselves suffered directly from the evils of factory work, but because they saw around them the dreadful havoc it was making. But, as the agitation went on, it gradually took in large numbers of the factory people.

As early as February 1, 1832, Mr. Sadler presented a petition from 10,000 operatives of Leeds, chiefly employed in the factories, praying the House of Commons to adopt some means for limiting the duration of the labour of children so employed, and numerously-signed petitions were, in the course of the same session, presented from almost all the chief factory centres—from Bradford, a petition with 9,000 or 10,000;* from Huddersfield, one with 10,000; from the workers in the power-loom factories in Glasgow, one signed by between 6,000 and 7,000 in two days; besides the monster petitions of 130,000 and 138,000, presented by Mr. Sadler and Lord Morpeth; the

* The late Earl of Carlisle, in presenting this petition—which was signed by all the medical men of the town, the clergy, and some of the most extensive master-spinners—said that, " of all the towns in Yorkshire, Bradford had most distinguished itself by its opposition to the system of overworking children in factories."

latter, however, in particular, signed to a great extent by persons belonging to the agricultural population of York- shire. In the next session these numbers increased : Brad- ford sent 12,000 signatures in place of 9,000 or 10,000 ; Leeds, 16,000 instead of 10,000. After Lord Ashley had taken charge of the question, he declared (June 3, 1833) that "he had just as much right to say that he was em- powered to speak the sense of the operatives, as any honourable members had a right to say that they were empowered to speak by their constituents. Delegates had been sent to him from the manufacturing districts on the subject, and they had been as fairly elected as any member had been by any constituency. . . . Four delegates were in London who had been elected (the vote having been taken by universal suffrage) by the operatives of the West Riding of Yorkshire and Lancashire."

In vain were the workers assured by those who op- posed them that short hours would bring short wages, that their children would be compelled to run in idle- ness about the streets, and that women who then earned good wages would find themselves without the means of decent and comfortable sustenance ; and, above all, that foreign competition—that *bête noire* ever at hand to frighten those who sin against the canons of certain political economists — would, to a certainty, drive the cotton trade of the country into the hands of Continental rivals, whose operations were not interfered with by the unreasonable outcries of misled mobs. To these assertions the working men paid little regard. If need were, they declared that they would take the smaller wages ; but they were determined, whatever became of the Cotton Trade, to rescue their wives and children from the excessive toil that was killing them.* Upon one occasion, they exhibited the factory children in a great street procession just as they left their work,—stunted, distorted, and pale as spectres; a sight amongst the saddest ever seen on this earth since labour became a duty of life.†

The Protective legislation as to mines and collieries has followed pretty much in the same course as that relating to factories. It cannot be said that it originated in the efforts of the miners themselves as a class; otherwise the shocking state of things which was disclosed by Lord Ashley, in 1842, could never have subsisted unheeded. But from the moment that a way of improvement was opened by the first Mines' Inspection Act, the men made the question their own,—so that great as has been the influence exerted by the working class on factory legislation, it has from that time been perhaps even more so upon

* See, for instance, Mr. Sadler's speech of February 10, 1832, in which he said, "he had been before numerous meetings, some of them attended by 20,000 individuals, when the question had been broadly put to them—namely, Will you consent to a diminution of wages?"

† This procession of factory children took place one Saturday afternoon, on the occasion of a visit from Oastler and Sadler to Manchester. As it passed along, the people who lined the sides of the streets seemed awe-struck, and when, at Peterloo, where they were to be addressed by the two gentlemen named, they struck up a hymn, asking God to bless those who were labouring on their behalf, their plaintive voices sounded like an appeal to the Great Father to deliver them from the crushing oppression under which they suffered. On hearing this, men and women burst into tears, and, though delayed for years, from that hour the Short Time Bill was safe.

mining legislation; whilst owing to the wide divergence
of habits which generally separates the underground from
the surface worker, that influence has had to be almost
exclusively exercised by the class affected alone. The
Mines' Inspection Act of 1860, for instance, may be
considered to have been the work of the miners themselves. We have before us the ' Report of the Delegates
of the Amalgamated Association of Miners of Lancashire,
Cheshire, and Yorkshire, upon the means of obtaining the
Improved Mines Inspection Bill, 1860,' which shows that,
the former Act expiring in 1860, the men took time by
the forelock, met in conference at Leeds (9th to 12th
November, 1858), at Ashton-under-Lyne (2nd to 7th
May, 1859), drew up a form of petition for an improved
Act, appointed a council to obtain signatures and conduct
the general business, fixed upon a treasurer, and arranged
for an amalgamated fund to meet expenses ; that addresses
were issued, information obtained and circulated, meetings
held, delegates sent to London in July, 1859, and again
on the 19th February, 1860, who first obtained from the
Home Office the bringing forward of a new Bill, then
watched that Bill during its whole progress through both
Houses, until it finally obtained the Royal Assent, August
28th, when they left London. " In the afternoon and
evening," they say, " often into morning, the delegates
were in the House of Commons, explaining their case
and reasoning with the opposition, *so that in hot weather
and bad atmosphere, after miles of walking and hours of
standing, they were so weary as to long for the pit, the pick,
and home again.*" And although they could not get all

they asked, they obtained an Act, which, say they, " is a decided advance upon the old one, and if fairly worked, will prove of incalculable physical and social advantage to the operative miners in future"—the cost of the Act to the operatives, the delegates tell us, amounting to nearly £900. On the society to which the above report was presented, we shall have to say a few words hereafter.

Some further instances of the influence of the working class upon legislation will be given when we come to speak of those organizations which lie still outside the pale of law. But we may here observe that the Bakehouses' Act is also the result of many years' agitation of the subject by the class affected. We have before us a lecture delivered by Dr. Guy on " The Case of the Journeymen Bakers," delivered in Southampton Buildings, on July 6, 1848, referring to the " appeal of the Journeymen Bakers' Society," to " the question which you have raised, the right for which you are contending," etc.

In endeavouring to show how far the working classes have promoted or anticipated the beneficent legislation of the last thirty-four years, we must, moreover, observe that there is, among the enabling Acts above reviewed, a whole group which expressly state that they are passed but to regulate or encourage existing forms of activity.

Thus the Benefit Building Societies' Act is avowedly founded upon the fact (see its preamble above quoted) that societies exist " principally amongst the industrious classes, for the purpose of raising, by small periodical subscriptions, a fund to assist the members thereof in obtaining a small freehold or leasehold property." So is the first Industrial

and Provident Societies' Act, on the fact that " various associations of working men have been formed for the mutual relief, maintenance, education, and endowment of the members, their husbands, wives, children, or kindred, and for procuring to them food, lodging, clothing, and other necessaries, by exercising or carrying on in common their respective trades or handicrafts." Clearly the legislation embodied in both Acts, and in those which have grown out of the latter, has been anticipated by the spontaneous efforts of the working class. The Building Society, the Co-operative Society, is not the creature of Parliament, but the working man's own creation. Each has—as the Friendly Society, the Loan Society, the Savings-Bank, had before ; as the Trade Society, the Arbitration Council, is having now —a pre-parliamentary history, culminating or to culminate in some blue-book or blue-books of a Select Committee, which ends by recognizing the fact that the institution exists and has succeeded in maintaining itself outside of the law, and deserves or requires to be brought within it.*
And in every instance, we believe, in which these Acts have been amended, delegates have been empowered or sent up by the group of bodies affected by such amendment, who have conferred with the Government, or with

* As an instance of such an inquiry, we may refer to the blue-book of Mr. Slaney's Committee, " On Investments for the Savings of the Middle and Working Classes," 1850, on which the first Industrial and Provident Societies' Act was founded. In the ' Journal of Association,' 1852, a periodical connected with a society of which both the writers were members, will be found a list of upwards of 200 co-operative bodies in England and Scotland known to be existing at the time when the first Industrial and Provident Societies' Act was passed, and on

private members on the subject, and, when belonging to the working class, as they generally have done, have never failed to impress those with whom they came in contact with a high sense of their shrewdness and business capacity.

It is more difficult to measure the influence which the working classes have exercised over legislation of a more general character, or over general policy. That influence has often been exerted in ways of which few are cognizant. Take the following fact, which has never been mentioned in print, and is probably known to very few but those who, like the writer, were actors in it :—When the first grant of £30,000 was proposed by the Government for educational purposes, it was regarded as the narrow end of a very dangerous wedge by many ; especially by those who dreaded the strengthening of any influence not exercised by themselves. A certain section of the Church party in Manchester called a meeting in the Corn Exchange, to oppose the Government proposal. Canon Wray presided, and the Rev. Hugh Stowell was one of the leading speakers. A body of working men, favourable to national education, having taken the matter into consideration, decided that their views should be represented. To this end each of them agreed to go to one of the shops where the tickets for the meeting were to be had,

the practice of which the Act was in fact modelled. A much earlier co-operative movement, before the true principles on which profits should be apportioned was discovered, numbered in 1830, according to Mr. Alexander Campbell, (see summary of paper read before the Social Science Association at Edinburgh in 1863, ' Transactions,' p. 752,) " between 300 and 400 societies."

and get as many as they could. In this way they secured considerably above one-half the tickets, and quietly distributed them amongst safe men in certain large workshops, with instructions to attend in their " go-to-meeting " clothes. They did so ; and to the astonishment of the chairman and the speakers, decorously and quietly, without speech-making or amendment-moving, negatived all the resolutions except the vote of thanks to the chairman, and then dispersed and went to their homes as quietly as if nothing particular had happened. So far as the writer is aware, the conveners of the meeting never knew how their intended " pronouncement " against State-aid to education was defeated. But it was owing to the good sense of a number of working men that Manchester was saved the obloquy of declaring against a measure, of which all its then clerical opponents lived to avail themselves,—and lived also, we would fain trust, to feel heartily ashamed of having opposed it.

The war against the compulsory newspaper stamp, again, was one which, though it might be led by the publishers, could never have been carried to its eventual triumph without the rank and file of working men, always ready to support the unstamped newspapers. Much interesting matter might be supplied as to the heartiness with which many working men threw themselves into this crusade, hawking about the cheap papers at the peril of imprisonment, which was often no idle one.

To pass on to other questions, it is certain that, at a time when the working men of England had, God knows, grievances enough of their own to complain of, they never turned a deaf ear to pleadings for the rights of the African slave ; that anti-slavery meetings were always largely attended by the working class. In 1839–40, when an attempt was made by the British India Society to popularize the subject of Indian reform, a lively and intelligent interest in the subject was manifested by the working men in all large towns in which it was ventilated, and that interest has never wholly passed away ;* silently contributing, no doubt, to the fall of the Company's government, and to the inauguration of a *régime* which, however unsatisfactorily administered at present, may yet make India some day the pride and glory of England. In the agitation for the repeal of the Corn Laws again, notwithstanding the opposition of the Chartist body, and that of some of the most trusted leaders of the operatives (such as Richard Oastler), who were sincerely wedded to Protection, the working classes took a large part. Besides their "Working Men's Anti-Corn-Law Societies," numbers of them were enrolled members of the League, and filled its meetings in hall and theatre, whilst the pen of their own Ebenezer Elliott, the " Anti-corn Law Rhymer," gave the stamp of poetry to the cause.

But there is one crowning instance, fresh still in all our memories, in which the working classes may be said to

---

* At a seaside town, last autumn, one of the writers of this paper found the secretary and shopman of a co-operative store more alive to the horrors of the Orissa famine than nineteen-twentieths ot the persons he is in the habit of meeting. " India is a country that has always been full of interest to me, although only a working man," writes again (quite spontaneously) a London engineer (8th April, 1867).

have decided the policy of this country, when the voice of the people proved truly to be the voice of God.

At the time when every evil influence under heaven seemed combined to force England into abetting the slave-holders' secession, when the cotton-famine and blockade-runners' profits, the French despot and the 'Times,' the country party and the ship-owners, Mr. Carlyle and half the piety of England, were urging us on a course which all now feel would have been one of headlong and ruinous folly, the working men of Lancashire stood firm and fast to the holy principle of human freedom. Sublimely patient, far-seeing beyond speculators and statesmen, they could meet in the midst of their own deep distress, caused by the continuance of the war (31st December, 1862), to congratulate Abraham Lincoln on his proclamation of emancipation;* and, when any expression of sympathy with the cause of the Union was sure to meet with fierce scorn or self-complacent derision in the House of Commons, as well as on every "'Change" throughout the country, they never wavered in their firm faith of its ultimate triumph.

---

* "Under the circumstances," wrote Mr. Lincoln in reply (19th January, 1863), "I cannot but regard your decisive utterances upon the question as an instance of sublime Christian heroism, which has not been surpassed in any age or in any country."

PART IV.

USE MADE BY THE WORKING CLASSES OF IMPROVED LEGISLATION.

WE have now to prove by facts that the improved legislation of the last thirty-four years has not been a dead letter,—that the working classes have known how to avail themselves of it, for their own benefit and for that of all classes of the community.

To any thinking mind, the growth of general prosperity is sufficient to prove the fact. When Mr. Baines, in his speech on the Borough Franchise Bill, April 10, 1861 (Parliamentary Debates, vol. clxii. 3rd series), was able to say that the total amount of our exports and imports between 1831 and 1860 had risen from £97,623,332 to £373,491,000,* or 283 per cent., whilst the cost of the relief of the poor had diminished from 9s. 9d. per head to 5s. 6d.,† he surely quoted two facts which are utterly irreconcileable with the hypothesis of a retrogressive or

---

* The "Statistical Abstract for the United Kingdom, from 1851 to 1865," gives a somewhat higher figure, £375,052,224.

† " In the twenty-two years preceding the reform of the Poor Law in England, £143,000,000 was the sum spent for relief; but in the twenty-two subsequent years it was only £129,000,000, notwithstand-

stationary working class; which imply necessarily that the producers of this country have continued to work hard and work well, and have constantly advanced in all the wants of civilization. In the five following years the total amount of exports and imports rose to £489,993,285, thus showing an increase during that period of £116,502,285, or considerably more than the whole amount in 1831; the figure of pauperism however, although falling continuously since 1863, not having yet receded to a normal level from the exceptional height to which it had been carried by the cotton famine.*

But let us examine the question more in detail.

§ 1. *Results of Protective Legislation.*

(1) *The Factories Acts.*

It would be out of place here to attempt to trace how much of the working man's support of these measures, or the masters' opposition to them, proceeded from purely selfish motives. Amongst the operatives it is likely enough there were many who cared only for the relief from labour the Acts would bring them, whilst amongst the masters there must have been a large number

ing that the population averaged nearly 20 per cent. more in the latter than in the former period. This is equal to a total decrease of £33,000,000, or yearly more than 21 per cent. on the service of parish officers; but the reduction is really much greater, as formerly there was very large expenditure in labour-rates and otherwise which did not enter into the parochial accounts." (Mr. Edwin Chadwick, in paper on " Poor Law Administration," Transactions of Social Science Association for 1863, p. 721.)

* The exports of 1866 rose to £188,827,785, being an increase of 14 per cent. on the previous year.

who looked at the question as one of mere money profit or loss. But apart from these motives, it may not be amiss to glance at one or two facts which, to some extent, indicate the clearer views on the subject and better calculations of the working men.

The common prediction of the opponents of those Acts was that they would reduce wages, that they would diminish production, and that the workers would throw away the leisure afforded to them. The exact contrary has happened,—wages and production have increased, and a very large number of the workers, at least, have known how to make excellent use of their leisure.

The wages of factory hands, according to Mr. David Chadwick—quoted by Dr. John Watts, in his work on the cotton famine—rose, in the years between 1844 and 1860, from ten to twenty per cent. The number of spindles at work, in the fifteen years between 1850 and 1865, increased from 17,099,231, in the former period, to 30,387, 267 in the latter. The number of yards of cotton cloth produced in 1830, when factory owners worked all the hours they thought proper, without remonstrance or restriction, was 914,773,563 ; whilst in 1860, thirteen years after the ignorant operatives and " sentimentalists " had tied their hands, they produced 4,431,281,728,—an increase of 384 per cent. A few subsidiary facts may be referred to here, as curiously illustrative of the growth of prosperity in this branch of business, in spite of the evil prophecies uttered during the short-time agitation. In 1850, the moving power in our cotton factories was equal to 50,286 horses. In 1860 it was 205,827 horses, being an increase of 300 per cent. It appears that, from 1851 to 1861, the increase in the population of Lancashire, the great seat of the cotton manufacture, was 20 per cent. ; but the increase in those trades whose activity gives special evidence of prosperity, was very much higher than this. Bricklayers and joiners increased 29 per cent.; paper-makers, 50 per cent ; letter-press printers, 37 per cent. ; engine and tool-makers, 50 per cent.; coachmen in private families, 180 per cent. ; and gardeners in private families, 532 per cent.*

Mr. Alexander Redgrave, one of H. M.'s Inspectors of Factories, addressing the Congrès International de Bienfaisance, held in London in 1862, under the presidency of the Earl of Shaftesbury, quotes additional figures to the same effect. In 1838, the imports of raw cotton amounted to 5,000,000 cwt. ; and the exports of cotton yarns and manufactures were valued at £24,550,000. In 1860 the imports of raw cotton were 12,419,000 cwt. ;† the value

---

* The disturbance caused by the American War neither employers nor employed could foresee ; but as this disturbance affected all nations, according to the extent of their reliance on America for cotton, the falling off in our trade consequent upon it has little to do with our present inquiry. Recent statistics, however, show that our exports of cotton manufactures and cotton yarns have again risen, from £54,856,289 in 1864, to £57,254,845 in 1865, the value of the imports of raw cotton being respectively £78,203,729 and £66,032,193, figures showing, as is observed by the ' Statesman's Year-Book,' the vast consumption of these articles within the United Kingdom. In 1866, the exports of cotton yarns and manufactures rose to £74,565,426 value,—the highest figure they have ever reached.

† The figures of Mr. Redgrave do not quite tally with those given by Mr. Edmund Potter, M.P. for Carlisle, in his paper " On the Position of the Cotton Districts, read at the Edinburgh meeting of the

of cotton yarn and manufactures exported, £53,000,000. In 1838 there were 4,217 factories, giving employment to 356,684 persons. In 1860 there were 6,378 factories, giving employment to 775,534 persons. We do not for a moment wish to give the Factories' Acts credit for the whole value of these results, which are undoubtedly due, in great measure, to many of the other reforms of the period above enumerated, and, in particular, to the repeal of the Corn Laws, and the general improvement of our fiscal system. But it is undeniable that the rise in wages, the increase in production, and the development of protective legislation, have proceeded simultaneously—that the one has not hindered the other.

A result, however, which is more directly traceable to protective legislation, has been the improvement in the health of the workers. The most cheering evidence to this effect is contained in a before-quoted paper, by Mr. Robert Baker, one of H. M.'s Inspectors of Factories, "on the Physical Effects of Diminished Labour," read before

National Association for the Promotion of Social Science " in 1863, and given at p. 649 of its ' Transactions ' for that year. The following data may be extracted from his paper :—

Exports of Cotton Goods and Yarns,			1830	.	£19,400,000
„	„	„	1848	.	22,681,000
„	„	„	1858	.	43,000,000
„	„	„	1860	.	51,959,000
Population in Lancashire		.	1831	.	1,336,854
„	„	.	1841	.	1,667,054
„	„	.	1851	.	2,031,236
„	„	.	1861	.	2,429,440

Mr. E. Potter gives also at about 450,000 the number of persons employed in cotton-spinning and weaving.

the Bradford meeting of the Social Science Association, in 1859. "There were," he writes, "in 1856, and there are at the present moment, employed within the factories of the United Kingdom, 682,517 persons, compared with 354,684 in 1835. Of these, 387,826 are females, compared with 167,696 in 1835; and 46,071 are children between eight and thirteen years of age, as compared with 56,455. There is," he says, " a gross increase of workers of 92 per cent.,—the increase of females being 131 per cent., and nearly as many children as there were formerly; *and yet all the diseases which were specific to factory labour in 1822 have as nearly as possible disappeared.* We seldom or never now see a case of in-knee or of flat-foot ; occasionally one of slight curvature of the spine, arising more from labour with poor food than from labour specifically. The 'factory leg' is no more amongst us, except an old man or woman limps by, to remind one of the fearful past. . . . The faces of the people are ruddy, their forms are rounded —their very appearance is a joyous one." So, Mr. Smith, senior surgeon to the Leeds Infirmary, as quoted by Mr. Baker:—"What has struck me most is the wonderful change in the condition of the female part of the population since the passing of the Act. . . . They are now fair and florid, strong and muscular,—not only cheerful, but full of fun. Instead of the sharp angles formerly seen in their figures, all the outlines are well rounded off, particularly at the hips and shoulders. So striking a difference in twenty-five years I could not have believed, had I not marked and seen it with my own eyes." In short, Mr. Baker quotes the testimony of medical men, "who weekly visit mills which employ, in the aggregate, upwards of 70,000 persons, of whom upwards of 40,000 are females, and 4500 are children, and who all testify to the same fact, viz. the almost entire disappearance of deformity, and the non-appearance of any other disease specific to factory labour."*

Let us now turn to the effects of the educational machinery of the Factory Acts. And here let us at once dispose of an objection which has been made to that machinery, viz. that it has driven children into those employments which are not subject to inspection. That this has been the case to some extent may be inferred from the fact that the number of children employed in factories has diminished instead of increasing. In 1835, there were 56,455 children at work in factories ; in 1838, only 29,283 ; in 1858, 46,071, population meanwhile having largely increased. It is moreover remarkable, that of the figure last mentioned no less than 44,769 were employed in England, 1188 in Scotland, and 114 in Ireland.†

The contrast between these numbers will serve to explain the different views which have been taken of the results of the Act North and South of the Tweed. Thus Mr. J. D. Campbell, Sub-inspector of Factories, in a discus-

---

* It is not, however, to be denied that factory labour still tends to engender or promote various diseases. It seems also to stunt the stature. See in the same volume of 'Transactions,' p. 725, the summary of Mr. John James's paper, " On the Condition of the Factory Operatives of Bradford."

† See a paper by Mr. George Anderson on "The Factory Half-time System, and the Educational Test," in the Transactions of the Social Science Association, 1860, p. 379.

sion on " Educational Tests for Employment,"* "gave it
as the result of his observation, that the educational clauses
of the Factory Act had " almost totally failed " in the
Glasgow district; " and he believed he might state that this
was the experience of the other inspectors also. Parents
preferred sending their children to those trades where they
would get full wages. Even when children were sent to
factories under the half-time system, they went, as soon
as they got the opportunity, to other places where they got
full wages, and the consequence was that owners of factories would have nothing to do with half-time youths."

This testimony is irrefragable, as far as it goes, though
little creditable to either Scotch employers or operatives.
But from England the testimony is far other. Mr. Redgrave, in his before-quoted paper, read before the ' Congrès International de Bienfaisance ' in 1862, says:—
" Before the Factory Act passed the Legislature, but few
of the children had any opportunity of attending school.
. . . For the last thirty years every child under thirteen
works in a factory for only half the day, and attends
school for three hours on the same day. At this time
upwards of 24,000 children are so attending school,
making good progress and attending to the earnings of
the family. . . . They now attend the best class of schools,
whereas in the early days of factory inspection the schools
were merely nominal. A comparison of the alteration in
twenty years in my own district shows the following results:—In 1843 only nineteen per cent. of the factory
children attended National, British, and Denominational

* Social Science Transactions, 1860, p. 419.

schools, that is, public schools under the management of committees or other public bodies, whilst forty-five per cent. attended 'dame' and other private schools. Now nearly seventy per cent. attend public schools, and only fourteen per cent. frequent private schools, not one of which is a 'dame' school; and further, the public school of to-day, the mode of teaching, the apparatus for teaching, and the qualifications of the teachers ensure to the factory children still greater advantages than could have been obtained in 1843."

So Mr. E. D. J. Wilks, Secretary to the British and Foreign School Society, in a paper read before the Social Science Association, at Bradford, in 1859,* says of the Educational Clauses of the Factory Acts: "I have no hesitation in avowing my conviction, based . . . upon actual, long-continued, and widely-extended observation, that, generally speaking, their operation has been most healthful, not only in an educational, but also in a social point of view. . . . The results have proved the principle sound in theory, wise in legislation, and practical in working. Evils that were dreaded have not been realized, and advantages of a kind that could hardly be anticipated have accrued." Among the last may be reckoned the fact, more pregnant in social consequence, perhaps, than any other ascertained in this age, of the superiority of the half-time over the whole-time system, as a means of education, or, in other words, of learning *plus* work over 'learning alone. Wherever good factory schools have been provided, it has been proved, to use the words of Mr. E. Chadwick, at

* Transactions, p. 363.

Glasgow, so far back as 1860, "that in three hours the half-timers eventually obtained as much book instruction as the children detained in the same schools for five or six hours daily ; the fairly taught half-timers were . . . intellectually more apt than the long-time scholars, taught by the same teachers, and under the same system."

To quote one testimony more :—Mr. Akroyd, at the Congress of the Social Science Association in 1864, said that " he and his father had been opposed " to the half-time system, but he now " advocated the extension of the principle embodied in the Act to all classes of workers, and argued from experience that the measure which had been so beneficial to the children in the factory towns, would be equally advantageous for those in the agricultural districts."*

Experience has thus shown that the educational results of factory legislation, wherever its provisions have been efficiently carried into effect, have been as cheering at least as the physical ones ; and if it has failed on this head in some districts, it is simply because the principle remains too restricted in its application. With education, morality has greatly improved among the factory hands, the females especially. In one Bradford mill, " where 500 girls were employed, the average yearly number of illegitimate children did not amount to more than three, and those were mostly to suitors, who afterwards married the mothers," says Mr. John James in his before-quoted paper, read before the Social Science Association, in 1859.

And now let us look at the more general results. " The

---

* Social Science Transactions, 1864, p. 479.

Factory Acts," says Mr. Edmund Potter, "were resisted by many of us as economically unsound, and as an unjust interference with the rights of labour and capital. *They have been socially beneficial.* . . . The cotton district population has rapidly and soundly improved during the last thirty years.* . . . No working population has existed in the kingdom of so high and healthy a moral and physical standard. It has been a material strength to the cotton trade ; if to be kept up, it can only be by the process which has brought it thus far. High-class machinery requires regularly employed and well-trained hands and good physical condition."

"The masses," says again Mr. Redgrave, "have proved themselves worthy of the boon conferred upon them ; they have not abused the gift ; their intelligence has increased ; their habits have improved ; their social happiness has advanced ; they have gained all, and more than all, they expected from factory legislation ; and they have not been intoxicated with success. Much might be said of what the operatives have done with their leisure hours ; how evening schools have been frequented ; various mutual improvement societies have been appreciated ; how the Easter and Whitsuntide holidays have been spent in more rational enjoyments than formerly ; how the intelligence, subordination to authority, and the general tone and bearing of the operative have kept pace with the advancement of the age."

* "No greater contrast of misery and ignorance, comfort and education could exist," says the same gentleman elsewhere in his paper, "than that shown, for instance, in the districts of Blackburn and Colne in 1820 and 1860."

So again Mr. Baker: " The living and flourishing institutes for intellectual improvement, the lectures, the musical meetings, the allotment gardens, and all the other
sources of pleasure and profit which are to be found, not
only in the towns, but in almost every hamlet of their
factory districts . . . only take their date from the possession
of the privileges which restricted labour conferred upon the
people, I mean the Saturday afternoon,—of itself one of
the greatest blessings ever conferred upon them,—and the
certainty of knowing when the master's time ends and
their own time begins."

We have seen that in 1832, sinking as they were daily
under the burthen of over-toil, both premature and excessive, the factory population was below, not above the
general level of the working class. This condition of
things is now, by competent observers, alleged to be re-
versed. " It is, I think, no libel on the working classes in
the mass to say that, in respect of natural acuteness, the
cotton workers are their superiors," says Mr. R. A. Arnold
in a paper " On the Cotton Famine," read before the York
meeting of the Social Science Association.*

Two years previously, at the height of the Cotton
Famine, the Rev. J. P. Norris, in a paper " On the Half-
Time System," read before the London meeting of the same
association,* had said :—

" It was only last week that one of the largest employers of labour in Manchester, speaking of the patience
and fortitude with which a population of many thousands

* Transactions, 1864, p. 612 and following.
† Transactions, 1862, p. 278 and following.

of operatives are now enduring an unprecedented amount of privation, said to me, ' I know nothing in the range of my experience more remarkable than the development of the Lancashire character in the last fifteen years ; ' and he ascribed it chiefly to the beneficent operation of the Factory Laws, adopted as they have been by the master manufacturers as their truest interest."

But perhaps the most remarkable result of the Factory Acts has been their effect upon the employers. As some of our quotations have already shown, from being the virulent opponents of legislative interference, the manufacturers now, for the most part, cordially accept it, and as Mr. Redgrave truly says, " are now generally the foremost advocates of improvement,—promoting the erection of factories and schools, the establishment of educational institutions, donors of parks, baths, washhouses, for the express use of the factory operatives." Hence those magnificent establishments, such as Saltaire and Akroydon, which have come to rank among our national glories; hence the princely public benefactions of the Crossleys, and of so many others. It would scarcely be too much to say, that the humble factory worker, through his perseverance in enforcing righteous legislation, has been the great civilizer and moralizer of his employer.

We may seem to have been devoting too much time to the subject of factory legislation, especially in the cotton districts. But this is, in fact, a typical instance in many ways. In the first place, it must be recollected that our cotton exports alone amounted in 1860 (in round numbers) to £52,000,000 out of £135,000,000, or nearly 39 per cent. of the whole.* Again, it is in the cotton districts that the system of protective legislation to the worker has had its longest trial (extending now over a generation), and has had its results, through the exceptional calamity of the cotton famine, most severely tested. Now we know that the very results of the famine itself, on a population trained by our factory legislation, were positively good; that crime, and generally drunkenness, decreased ; that education extended. " Great progress," says Mr. R. A. Arnold, in a before-quoted paper, " has been made in education during the period of the cotton famine. Generally the number of children in attendance at the schools increased, and the concurrent testimony from all sides is that they were more regular in their attendance, and made better progress than in previous years." A system which has stood the double ordeal of time and of an unprecedented temporary strain, cannot be a bad one.

We have, therefore, every ground for concluding, from the thorough success of protective legislation in the cotton districts, that slowly but surely, in proportion to the time during which, and the extent to which it has been applied, it is working similar effects in all other employments to which it has as yet been extended. Even as respects those which have been only brought into the system by the Factory Acts' Extension Act in 1864,† there is

---

* After falling in the intermediate years, the proportion was somewhat more in 1865, £74,500,000 out of £188,800,000, or over 39 per cent.

† Under this Act, about 50,000 workers were added to the 775,534 who, in 1862, were employed in the various trades comprised in the system.

evidence that beneficial results are being obtained, whilst the employers, taught by the experience of their fellows, readily co-operate in carrying out the Act. " There can be no longer any doubt," says Mr. Baker, June 5, 1865, " that the wisdom of Parliament in assimilating the hours of employment one to another in various trades will be productive of the happiest results."*

(2) *Results of the Mining Acts and Merchant Shipping Acts.*

It would be alike tedious and superfluous to attempt to follow up in detail the results of protective legislation in other employments. The history of our mining industry, for instance, would show a quite similar development of production side by side with that legislation; and most active in precisely that branch which enjoys the largest share in that legislation, viz. coal-mining. When the first of the Mining Acts was passed in 1842, the condition of the mining population was in many respects even worse than that of the factory population ten years before. At the date of the census of 1841, the total number of persons employed in mines in Great Britain and the British Isles was 193,825, of whom 118,233 in coal-mines. In 1861, the number of the last alone had increased to 235,590. The number of collieries at work increased from 2397 in 1853 to 3088 in 1862, producing in the latter year 83,635,214 tons of coal, with nearly £21,000,000. At the present time the number of mining operatives has reached 400,000, of whom no less than 307,000 are em-

---

* Quoted in Mr. H. S. Tremenheere's Paper on 'The Extension of the Factory Acts,' Social Science Transactions for 1866, p. 291.

ployed in coal mines. The quantity of coal raised and disposed of during 1865 was 98,150,583 tons, being an increase on the previous year of 5,362,714 tons, and of nearly ten millions on 1863, and the total value of minerals obtained was £41,745,404. It has been recently stated that the increase in the annual value of mines in Great Britain, from 1853 to 1864, was nearly £69 per cent., being at the rate of over £6 per cent. per annum.

The development of our shipping shows in precisely like manner that the protective enactments of our Merchant Shipping Acts have in nowise hindered commercial activity; that that activity is greatest precisely in the class of ships which are most carefully regulated by the law. From 1852 to 1865, the number of sailing vessels employed in the foreign trade had diminished from 7431 to 7384, though the tonnage had increased from 2,365,995 to 3,629,023, and the number of men from 103,618 to 110,501; but the number of steamers so employed had increased from 149 to 756; the tonnage of these, from 83,367 to 523,698; the men on board, from 7151 to 28,860. And the last published Trade and Navigation returns show that the shipping of the United Kingdom at the end of 1866, as compared with 1865, had increased by 131 vessels of 123,995 tons, manned by 4375 men, such increase being all in steam-vessels, the number of sailing-vessels having decreased.*

---

* The total shipping of the United Kingdom amounted to 25,160 sailing vessels, of 4,845,142 tons, and 2708 steamers, of 821,731 tons, making together 27,868 vessels, of 5,666,873 tons.

But let us test in one or two other ways the progress of these two great groups of protected workers,—miners and seamen.

Our colliers form still, we fear, beyond question, one of the most ignorant classes of our population. But they are anxious for education. In a petition to the House of Commons of the "workers in the coal and iron-stone mines of Great Britain," signed by many thousands of working miners, and presented in 1860, the petitioners, who express themselves as "deeply sensible of the benefits which have resulted from the statutes . . . . for the inspection of coal-mines, and for the prohibition of females and young persons under the age of ten years from working in coal-mines," and "anxious that the same may be extended to iron-stone mines," ask, amongst other things, that "training-schools be established for the purpose of educating miners, so that they may become skilled and competent to undertake the management of mines." They "submit that the practice of employing boys in mines from the age of ten to fourteen years for more than eight hours per day, does not afford sufficient opportunity for obtaining an adequate amount of education, and is also the main cause of the low social condition of the miners in general;" and they pray, therefore, "that some provisions may be introduced into the next bill for the education of the young employed in mines from the age of ten to fourteen years." With the above petition was circulated a statement or representation, signed, by order of the miners' deputation, by its chairman and secretary, part of which runs as follows:—"9. As all experience has proved that no permanent improvement can be achieved without a corresponding advance in knowledge, intelligence, and habits, the operative miners above all desire that a good, sound system of intellectual, social, and moral education may be provided for their children and youth of both sexes, to be carried out upon the *principles* of the Factories' Act education clauses, or in such way as may secure to the rising generation the knowledge felt by them to be so essential to all future social progression."* This petition, it must be observed, was not the first embodying similar requests. In the 'Report of the Commissioner (Mr. H. S. Tremenheere) appointed under the provisions of the Act 5 & 6 Vict. c. 99, to inquire into the operation of that Act, and into the state of the population in the mining districts, 1859,' will be found (p. 49) a notice of another, expressly asking "that the half-time system should be introduced, and children between ten and fourteen obliged to go to school for four hours daily," whilst a standard of education is suggested which would suffice to make every collier a mining engineer. But, as in the case of the Factory Acts, the educational provisions urged by the men were resisted by the masters. Although embodied in Mr. Clive's Bill of 1860, they were sought to be wholly struck out, and were actually struck out in the Lords, to be restored only in their present negative form, which, it has been stated, "has excluded the ignorant," but "has not furnished education, or promoted its extension." The miners, however,

---

* See this petition and statement in the 'Report of the Committee on Trades' Societies,' published in 1860 by the Social Science Association, pp. 47–51.

do not lose sight of the subject, and in the 'Transactions and Results of the National Association of Coal, Lime, and Iron-stone Miners of Great Britain, held at Leeds, November 9, 10, 11, 12, 13, and 14, 1863,' from which the above statement (p. xv) is quoted, will be found the draft of an Education Bill, requiring that no boy under twelve shall be employed in any mine, nor " without the certificate of a competent schoolmaster that he can read and write, and is versed in the first four rules of common arithmetic." " The council," it is said a little before, " have great faith in the power of education, and therefore earnestly press upon the Government the necessity of immediate attention to this momentous question, with a view to further legislation on the subject, believing that, in proportion to the miners becoming educated and informed will their foolhardiness and demoralization diminish, while substantial happiness and the comforts of home will thereby be increased and secured." (Ibid. p. 142.)*

We have thus shown that, under the influence of protective legislation, the ignorant miner has shown himself anxious for the education of his children. If we show that, under similar influence, the spendthrift sailor is beginning to become provident, we shall have afforded

---

* Of the progress of the mining population in a district not considered one of the best, take the following account, from the pen of the assistant secretary to the (late) Wolverhampton Working Men's College :—" Few classes have improved so much as the colliers. . . . The collier of former days was foremost in bull-baiting, dog-fighting, cock-fighting, man-fighting, and all low amusements. It was his greatest honour to have the best bulldog and game-cock. But these amusements have, I think, entirely disappeared. What is considered lowest in the collier's

strong evidence of the power of the working class to avail itself of legislative benefits.

The ordinary Savings-Bank we do not consider an institution of which the development affords a very satisfactory test of the condition of the working class. We believe the working man, so-called, invests far more rarely in it than the poor clerk, the small tradesman, especially than the domestic servant. But there is one kind of Savings-Bank which does afford a very satisfactory index to the provident habits of the class for which it is devised,—we mean the Seamen's Savings-Banks. Scattered as they are on all the seas, our sailors had, by the 20th November, 1864, a fund of £40,625. 5s. 11d. deposited with the Board of Trade, and in November, 1865, this balance had increased to £44,714. 16s. 10d. We cannot, however, forbear noticing here that the Merchant Shipping Acts not having been originally the result of the direct pressure of the class of workers affected by them, have not yet proved themselves sufficiently adapted to the wants of that class to command popularity. Although amended in many respects,—chiefly, it would seem, through the exertions of the seamen's trade societies,—they contain yet several

amusement now is pigeon-flying. Scores of them have cottages and huts of their own ; and the older ones, who were ignorant, have mastered the elementary part of education, and are giving their children some education too. Many Methodist chapels contain a large proportion of them in their congregations ; and I am told that scores of them are preachers. The collier attends to his home, and most of them take a newspaper on the Saturday. Of course there are disreputable men amongst them, but . . . their progress is something wonderful." We shall revert to this subject.

provisions much disliked by the men. Hence the "black flag" of the seamen in the Reform demonstration of February 11th, 1867. Still, we may trust that Captain Fishbourne did not go beyond the truth when, in a paper read on the 'Means employed to raise the Condition of British Seamen,' before the Congrès International de Bienfaisance in 1862 (vol. ii. p. 65 and foll.), he said that the varied machinery of the Acts, of Sailors' Homes, etc., " has been gradually impressing sailors with. the idea that they are cared for, that they are not considered, as they supposed they were, an Arab class, designedly excluded from the common benefits of society, but valued members of the community."

§ 2. *Results of Enabling Legislation.*

(1) *Savings-Banks and Friendly Societies.*

From the results of protective legislation we must now pass to those of enabling.

Agitations like that for the Short-Time Bill, originating in the perception of wrong done, and sympathy with those who suffer, if justified in their origin and wisely conducted, having once passed a certain point, carry everything before them. A certain amount of conviction, operated on by the press and from the platform, at last blazes up into an enthusiasm which puts opposition out of the question. Argument having done its work, a determined self-will takes its place, which claims and insists, until sovereigns and parliaments and classes submit to the demands of the public voice. It may be said of the working men of England, however, that much of what they have accomplished since 1832 has been done without the excitement of public agitation, or the stimulus of that vague hope, which is always more or less active, when legislative changes of importance are sought.

For reasons above given, we shall not dwell on Savings-Bank deposits as a test of the progress of the working class, believing that such test is to a great extent a fallacious one.* The circumstances of different localities, however, vary much in this respect. Thus, in Bradford, it was stated by Mr. John James before the Social Science Association in 1859 (Transactions, p. 726), " there were 430 factory girls, who had £8139 deposited, and 133 married factory women, having £3897 deposited," whilst there were " not more than 506 domestic servants, with deposits to the value of £12,756,"—figures which, however, are sufficient to show that the servant invests more largely than the worker for wages. A more genuine index to the spread of provident habits among even the poorest classes is afforded by the Penny Savings-Bank,—an institution now widely spread throughout almost every rural parish, but which seems to have received its highest development in Yorkshire. From a paper by Mr. E. Akroyd, read before the Social Science Association in 1860 ('Transactions,' p. 864), it appears that the Yorkshire Penny Savings-Bank (a registered institution), which began business on the 11th May, 1859, had on the 30th September, 1860, 105

* On the 20th November, 1866, the Trustee Savings-Banks held £33,840,096 of deposits (about £5,000,000 less than in 1861), belonging to 1,376,890 depositors. The Post-Office Savings-Banks held about £8,000,000 of deposits, belonging to between 700,000 and 800,000 depositors.

branches in active operation, £18,000 of invested funds, and had received from 25,000 depositors above £24,000, the withdrawals having been about £6000. The connection of these institutions with others of a higher class is sufficiently shown by the fact that 39 Penny Savings-Banks had been opened in connection with the Yorkshire Union of Mechanics' Institutes, to be presently noticed.

Friendly and Benefit Societies have long been known to our working people, but the true principles upon which to base them, and the best mode of managing them, were, till a comparatively recent period, far from being well under-stood. The old sick and burial clubs were defective in many ways. Societies like the Odd Fellows, Foresters, Druids, and others were for a long time outside of the pale of legality. Even so recently as 1842 the Odd Fellows had to take counsel's opinion on the question of their legality. From 1832, or thereabouts, a very rapid growth had, however, taken place in all these bodies. In 1835, Mr. Ansell's work, followed by Mr. Neison's in 1845, enabled them to put themselves right in calculating the rates of payment by members, and the benefits to be received in consequence. The exception of Friendly Societies from the provisions of the corresponding Societies Acts in 1846 enabled several of the larger bodies to obtain legal protection.* The present magnitude of the interest which these societies represent may perhaps be inferred from the figures put forth this year by the Manchester Unity of Odd Fellows. After making deductions for deaths, this society

* Some very considerable bodies, however, have no local branches. Thus the 'Royal Standard,' instituted March 6, 1828, and which in

now possesses 387,990 members in 3671 lodges, with a reserve fund of over £2,000,000. During the year, 4831 members and 2967 members' wives had died, and the money paid to their relatives amounted to the magnificent sum of £64,433. 8*s*. The "Ancient Order of Foresters" in 1863 numbered 224,000 members, and its annual sick contributions were about £220,000. Space will not admit of detailed reference to the proceedings of the many thousands of benefit societies existing in England. Mr. J. T. Pratt, Registrar of Friendly Societies, furnishes in his last report some very interesting information; but his returns, elaborate as they are, give only a portion of the case.* Of course it would be difficult to guess with any degree of correctness the number of members, or the amount of funds possessed by the 15,128 societies which, according to the statement of the Registrar, have made no returns, or by the many associations which have not put themselves into connection with the Registrar General's office. The Rev. Nash Stephenson, in a paper "On Benefit Societies,"

1863 had 4910 members and £58,981 capital, and had paid £138,128 of claims, and by the end of 1865 had increased to 5438 members, and £67,381. 9*s*. 9*d*. of capital, having paid £161,426. 2*s*. 2*d*. of claims, is organized in 'Divisions,' numbering 500 members each, meeting monthly on separate days. A more recent society organized in divisions is the 'Hearts of Oak,' which, according to its 24th Annual Statement, commenced the year 1866 with 9988 members and £37,753. 3*s*, 1*d*. assets, and concluded it with 10,771 members and £40,466. 14*s*. 6*d*. assets.

* Under date 16th July, 1866, he says, "In December, 1865, the Registrar sent out 22,834 forms of annual returns of the general statement of the funds and effects of Friendly Societies, and the same number of forms of return of sickness and mortality required from Friendly

read before the Social Science Association in 1859 (Transactions, p. 672), reckons the total number of members of
all the societies at not less than 3,052,000, the amount
of their annual contributions at £4,980,000, and their
accumulated capital at £11,360,000. This is probably
an under-statement, and Mr. Charles Hardwick, in his
paper on the Odd Fellows Friendly Society, read in 1862
at the Congrès International de Bienfaisance, was perhaps
under rather than over the mark, when he said that "the
entire Friendly Societies of Great Britain possessed reserved
capital amounting to twenty millions sterling."*

Many of these societies, when they first began to appeal openly by public procession and otherwise to the people for support, adorned themselves in strange costumes,
scarfs, aprons, and badges,—ludicrous enough to all, save
those who felt themselves dignified by such grotesqueness,
foolish enough and harmless enough, no doubt. But of
late years these things have been kept in great measure (except by the Foresters) in the background, whilst the real
objects of such associations have been brought prominently

Societies, pursuant to 18 & 19 Vict. c. 63, s. 45. Of the Annual Returns only 7706 have been received back previous to the 1st of July,
1866, 170 of which omitted to give the name of the society and place
where held. In the Appendix will be found the names and addresses
of the Friendly Societies from which returns have been received, and
the amount of the funds of each, and also the number of members, and amount of funds in each county. The 10,345 Returns show
the number of members to be 1,374,425, and the amount of funds
£5,362,028."

* Some further details may be found in Mr. T. Y. Strachan's paper on
Provident Institutions, Social Science Transactions, 1863, p. 663.

forward. Nor can we omit noticing the change that has taken place in many of these large societies as regards their places of meeting. At one time there was no escape from the public-house; now, in every town, and in many a village even, halls and independent lodges, apart from the tavern, are fast springing up, and show at least a growing desire to escape from the working man's worst temptation. In short, making every allowance for the mismanagement and dishonesty of many of the smaller societies, it seems impossible to deny that the accumulation by bodies composed largely, and in many cases exclusively of working men,* and the administration by them, for their own benefit, of the large sum mentioned by Mr. Hardwick, shows a very remarkable growth of thrift and forethought amongst our working masses.

Nor must it indeed be supposed that the exercise of the working man's forethought in the way of insurance is confined within the Friendly Society, or only tends to the use of the later facilities for Government Insurance. Several of the ordinary insurance offices are largely used by the working class. We are here quite out of the range of statistics, but we may quote as an instance the " British Prudential Insurance Society," which, we are informed by a correspondent, has issued in Durham and Northumberland 32,500 policies, most of them to working men.

(2) *Building and Land Societies.*

But,—to proceed to a form of providence yet more dis-

---

* It is difficult in any way to estimate the proportion of the different classes comprising these Societies. From the 42nd Annual Report of

tinctive of the working class,—Building Societies, again, are now firmly established in all great centres of industry, Liverpool, Manchester, Leeds, Birmingham, London, etc. ; and in these places the men may be counted by tens of thousands who, in addition to having a sick and burial fund to rely on, have also homes provided in which they are their own landlords, or in a fair way of becoming so. Messrs. Chambers, in their tract on " Building Societies," describe with considerable fulness the gratifying results attending their operations in Birmingham. The statute within the provisions of which they act, was passed in 1836, but their existence dates only from 1847, when the Freehold Land Societies started with the intention of manufacturing forty-shilling freeholders, by purchasing estates in bulk, and subdividing them amongst their shareholders. That object is now quite a matter of secondary consideration. The shareholders may not care less for the freehold, or the political power it confers ; but their leading desire is to add a house to the land, and thus secure free homes. At the time when the writer visited Birmingham, from 8000 to 9000 of these working men's homes were erected. The aggregate number of enrolled members was 10,000, the annual receipts £150,000, and fully

the " London Friendly Institution," an old and quiet society, founded in 1824, and which, on the 30th September, 1866, had 2372 members, £24,538. 12s. 8½d. capital, and had paid £84,330 for benefits,—it appears that out of eight candidates for the direction, one was a clothier's foreman, one a cooper, one a warehouseman, one a mason, one a carpenter and builder, one a pianoforte maker, one an ironmonger, one an engraver's block maker ; another warehouseman being a candidate for the auditorship.

90 per cent. of the persons enrolled were working men, whose wages varied from 12*s.* to 40*s.* per week. One group of these Societies, doing business in the same office, during sixteen years had received £520,000 in millions of small sums, and not a penny had been lost by error or default. It may be added that upon the committees managing this group of societies, " there are not more than two or three middle-class men, and not one of the upper classes;" and " the same proportion is said to exist in all the other Birmingham Societies."*

Mr. Hole, in his admirable work on ' The Homes of the Working Classes' (London, 1866), gives later details. " About 9000 working men in and around the town have supplied themselves with superior dwellings of their own. . . . In six societies, comprising 14,973 members, the amount of money actually received up to June 1, 1865, was £865,000, and the amount advanced on mortgage was £561,000 ; of which the sum of £302,500 has been absolutely redeemed, leaving £259,000 now due on mortgage. These Societies are only those connected with the Freehold Land Society ; but there are several other Societies in Birmingham whose operations may be safely estimated at about half as much more."

The progress of these Societies in the West Riding of Yorkshire is still more remarkable. Mr. Dibb, the Deputy

---

* The moral effect of these societies was testified to by Mr. J. A. Stephens, before a Committee of the House of Commons. " Freehold Land Societies encourage provident habits, diminish drunkenness, induce the working classes to invest their earnings, and behave better ; so much so, that twelve years ago, when the population was 50,000 less than now, 420 police were necessary, but with this increase of population

Registrar of Deeds for the Riding, stated in 1858 that the number of deeds annually registered on behalf of such Societies since 1843 had risen from 31, to 637 in 1857, the numbers in quinquennial periods having been:

From 1843 to 1847 192
„ 1848 „ 1852 1372
„ 1853 „ 1857 3044

Total 4608

Mr. J. Arthur Binns wrote in 1859 of the then four principal Societies of the West Riding,* that they had received during the previous year £222,522, and had advanced on mortgage £632,457. The "Leeds Permanent Building Society"† alone had, between 1848 and 1858, received in subscriptions, £519,568; in loans, £103,226; and had advanced on mortgage £340,692; the cost of management being £8102, or £1. 5s. 6d. per cent. on receipts,—a higher figure than in two of the others. By 1864, as Mr. Hole shows in his above-quoted work, the receipts in subscriptions had risen to a total of £1,200,598. 6s.; in loans, to £251,461. 4s. 6d.; the advances, to £749,864. 6s. 11d.; the subscriptions received in 1864 alone amounting to £150,567. 3s. 7d.

there has been a decrease of police, and 327 are now sufficient to preserve the peace."

* Social Science Transactions for 1860, p. 680, and following.

† Building Societies are either "terminating," *i. e.* established for a certain period, or "permanent." They are, again, either "mutual," where every member looks to becoming a house-owner, or "investing," where members are admitted who merely seek a profit for their money. Minor distinctions, as of "Starr-Bowkett Societies," etc., we need not enter into.

In Sunderland the progress of these societies has been no less signal. From a letter by Mr. John Robinson, dated July 11, 1866, and published in the 'Sunderland Times,' it appears that the number of societies in operation in the borough in 1859, was 40, in 1866, 60, being an increase of 50 per cent. in seven years; the members numbering 13,401, against 3823 in 1859; the capital, £1,768,025. 10s., against £582,001.

It would be difficult to procure an accurate return of the number of Building Societies in England, and the number of persons in the aggregate belonging to them; but as there are few forms of association so general, and as nearly all the great popular societies of the kingdom have Building Societies attached to them, they must be very numerous. Mr. Baines, in 1861, estimated the number of members at 100,000, their annual subscriptions at £1,750,000, the amount advanced by them to their members at £6,000,000. Latterly, says Mr. Chambers, "these institutions have been introduced into Wales, between which and the borders of Scotland there are now few towns without them. Throughout England and Wales there are said to be 2000 Land and Building Societies, comprehending more than 200,000 members. The money paid into these societies now amounts to eleven millions, of which upwards of eight millions has been invested in property." Not the least interesting feature of the Benefit Building Society consists in the facilities which it affords to benevolent employers and others for providing houses for the working classes.*

* How it has thus been made available by Messrs. Akroyd and

And although all classes now freely enter into such societies, they are still especially favoured by the working man. Mr. John Holmes, in Leeds reckons that " one-half at least " of the money received by them in Leeds " is the frugal saving of the wage-class." In Sunderland, six societies are expressly named " First," " Second," etc., "Working Man's" Society. How low in the class their influence may reach is shown by the extraordinary fact mentioned in Mr. J. Robinson's letter, that one of the Sunderland Societies, the " Durham County," having within the last three years established a Penny Bank, has through it received upwards of £7000. Of the character of the dwellings erected by these Societies it is needless to say much. " Wherever," says Mr. E. Potter in his before quoted paper, " On the Position of the Cotton Districts," " by the aid of Clubs, or by the hands themselves, cottages have been built for the use of the working classes, they have been of a high class, comfortable, cleanly, and good ; except that they almost invariably want drainage." " The working man building a single dwelling for himself," says Mr. Hole, " will have it substantial. It may be ugly, but there will be no ' scamping ' if he knows it." On the other hand, it is made a reproach to Building Societies that they are " too regardless of the sanitary conditions of the

Crossley, and by the Leeds " Society for the Erection of Improved Dwellings," may be seen in the pages of Mr. Hole's book, in Mr. Akroyd's paper " On Improved Dwellings for Workpeople, with a plan for building them in connection with Benefit Building Societies," read before the London meeting of the Social Science Association in 1862 (see Summary, ' Transactions,' p. 805), and in Mr. John Holmes's paper on " Houses for the People, and how to provide them," read before the York meeting of the same Association, in 1864 (see Summary, ' Transactions,' p. 680).

property on which they make advances," and that they will "lend money on public-houses and beer-shops." In other words, they are apt to become mischievous in proportion as they depart from their title, and become mere channels for investment.

(3) *Co-operative Societies and Partnerships of Industry.*

No form of association, however, proves so much in favour of the moral and intellectual progress of the working people as Co-operation. No other system is so intricate in its organization, so complicated in its workings, so exacting in the demands it makes on the forethought and reasonableness of those who enter into it, and at the same time so completely the result of the working man's own thoughtfulness. Working men matured the plans, experimented on them, and carried them out to a successful issue, without advice or aid from any outsider.

Savings-banks ask simply for the prudence to deposit. Friendly Societies demand little beyond this, except the management, which the members supply ; but as the objects are limited and definite, simple unchanging routine makes the labour easy. Building Societies require more skilful handling, but the duties are not greatly varied, or numerous, and the principle upon which the business is to be done once settled, slight experience makes the work easy. The Trades' Union, again, is more complicated than the Building Society. The levying of contributions, distributing donations, providing and arranging for strikes and lock-outs, with many other equally important functions, call for much good sense, discretion, and honesty. But the Co-operative Store, even in its simplest form, goes far beyond any of these. It is an arrangement to promote economy of expenditure amongst its members. It has to provide for buying all sorts of merchandise of the best quality at the lowest price; for selling at a sufficient profit; for recording sales, so that the profits realized may be distributed again amongst the purchasers, in proportion to the extent of their purchases; with much more that can only be carried out successfully by a wise supervision, a steady application to business, and an exercise of intelligence and honesty of a very high order.

Curiously enough, the first attempt at co-operation was made somewhere about the time when the various other forms of association which have been noticed were either coming into existence, or striking those roots which have since nourished their vigorous growth. Co-operative Stores were meant chiefly as a defence against the inroads of the distributing classes on the working man's pocket; and also as a means of promoting ready-money dealings, and the prudence in expenditure which usually accompanies such dealings. It would be difficult now to conceive the state of things that then existed. The back streets of the manufacturing towns swarmed with small shops, in which the worst of everything was sold, with unchecked measures, and unproved weights. The customers at these shops were the persons who drank and danced as long as they had money, and who, when they had none, had no other resource than the " stuff shop." The business to the shopkeeper was profitable, when he got regularly paid on the Saturday night; but regularity in payment was not the rule, and great losses were sometimes suffered. The business upon the whole was a bad one. Hence, when Co-operative Stores first began their much needed operations, the general indebtedness amongst the working people made success almost impossible. At this early period, nothing was known of the admirable plan on which they are now worked. A certain number of persons supplied the capital in small shares, and divided, in proportion to the capital invested, whatever profit was made. Such concerns had no special attraction for artisans or for the public, nor could they furnish any guarantee against fraudulent dealing. The enthusiastic young men who stood behind the counter in the evening, when the stores opened, used to preach self-denial and prudence to their few stray customers. Such preachings in a pecuniary sense, however, were found to be unprofitable ; and as rent and taxes were to be paid, and goods sold with sufficient dispatch to be kept from spoiling, the co-operative shops had to be shut up, except in a few cases where, as joint-stock concerns, they became very successful. There is yet one at Ripponden, in Yorkshire, which has for many years done a very large and flourishing business, profitable to the shareholders, but having no other relationship to the general public than if it belonged to a private individual.

Beyond all question, however, the first true beginning of the co-operative store movement was the Rochdale Equitable Pioneers' Store, and the chief ground of its success was the admirable plan upon which it started,—a plan which cannot be too often stated or too closely studied. The great difficulty with the first stores was to bring custom, and failing in this, they broke down. In Rochdale, however, they said to the public, " Invest in the trading capital here, and you shall have five per cent. on your money, inasmuch as we bind ourselves not to put it to risk by speculative trading, no credit being given. In the next place, whatever remains as profit, after paying interest on capital, will be divided as bonus on the amount of money spent in the store by each member." The advantages of this proposal soon began to make themselves apparent. Presuming a hundred men invested twenty shillings each, one shilling each would be due to them at the expiration of the year, as five per cent. interest on their separate investments. They had each done precisely the same as investors, and each was justly entitled to the same reward. But custom is as necessary as capital for the production of profit ; and in contributing this all-important element, they almost necessarily differed from each other. The family income made a difference ; the number in the family made an important difference. In fact, a poor workman with a large family was a far more profitable customer than a well-paid artisan with a small one. These poorer men, therefore—the most difficult to move, because usually the most encumbered by debt—were the most directly appealed to by the new plan. There was no interest in buying inferior articles and selling them at high prices, no temptation to adulterate anything sold, no inducement to give short weight or measure, inasmuch as anything taken from the consumer by fraud would go back to him again as increased bonus. And as everything purchased had to be paid for in ready money, the whole frightful system of indebtedness, which, up to that time, crushed the people, must disappear.

Faithfully carried out by the shrewd and strong-backed working-men of Lancashire, these methods of business led to marvellous results. No words could paint these so eloquently as the following figures, showing the progress of the society, which are tabulated in their almanack for the present year :

Year.	Members.	Funds.	Business.	Profits.
		£.	£.	£.
1844	28	28		
1845	74	181	710	22
1846	80	252	1,146	80
1847	110	286	1,924	72
1848	140	397	2,276	117
1849	390	1,193	6,611	561
1850	600	2,299	13,179	880
1851	630	2,785	17,638	990
1852	680	3,471	16,352	1,206
1853	720	5,848	22,760	1,674
1854	900	7,172	33,364	1,763
1855	1,400	11,032	44,902	3,106
1856	1,600	12,920	63,197	3,921
1857	1,850	15,142	79,788	5,470
1858	1,950	18,160	71,630	6,284
1859	2,703	27,060	104,012	10,739
1860	3,450	37,710	152,063	15,906
1861	3,900	42,925	176,206	19,020
1862	3,501	38,465	141,074	17,564
1863	4,013	49,361	158,632	19,671
1864	4,747	62,105	174,937	22,717
1865	5,326	78,778	196,234	25,156
1866	6,246	99,989	249,122	31,931*

* To test these figures a little more, it may be added that, in the June quarter of 1866, when the dividend was the smallest for the then last five years—in great measure " on account of the butchering de-

These figures show a business of nearly a quarter of a million a year, done at a profit of £31,931, of which sum almost all goes back again to the members as bonus on purchases, the economy of management being so great that including interest on capital, the working expenses amount only to 2 per cent. on the returns. But this is not all. There is also in Rochdale a Corn-mill Society, selling to the stores of the neighbourhood, which during the June quarter did a business of £50,212. 18s. 0d., or at the rate of £200,000 per annum. There is a large Cotton-mill as well, a Sick Burial Society, and a Building Society, besides some Turkish Baths, all of which have sprung out of the original Store. Now if it be considered that Rochdale is returned in the last census as having a population of 38,000 inhabitants, and 7700 inhabited houses, it may be seen at a glance what proportion of its people are engaged in this co-operative business, especially if it be borne in mind that the members of these stores are nearly all heads of families,—and in this store alone there are about 5326 members. In Halifax, the Co-operative Store, in the number of its members, is ahead of Rochdale; at the end of 1865, according to the Registrar of Friendly Societies' returns there were 5775 persons belonging to it. The cash received for goods, however, only amounted to

partment yielding so small a gain, . . . caused by the great restrictions arising from the cattle plague,"—the total cash received for goods sold was £60,904. 9s. 6½d., being an increase of £3,587. 0s. 2½d. compared with the last quarter ; and the profit was £6,917. 0s. 2½d., which, after allowing £275. 18s. 6d. for depreciation of fixed stock, and £137. 7s. 4d. for the educational fund, allowed a dividend of two shillings in the pound to members.

£147,963, and the profits to £12,541. There is also here a large flour-mill, and as the inhabitants and the number of inhabited houses are much the same as in Rochdale, the proportion of persons engaged in co-operation compared with the number of inhabitants may be taken as about the same in both towns.*

Mr. Tidd Pratt's return for 1865 shows that the number of societies certified to December, 1864, was 651, of which, however, only 417 had sent returns, whilst 52 had been dissolved. The 417 returning societies held together £761,313 of share capital, owed £112,733 on loan; they had done business for the year to the amount of £3,063,088 for goods purchased, £3,373,837 for goods sold; had a balance of £136,923, possessed assets to the amount of £1,105,685, and were accountable for £273,480 of trade liabilities. Thus their balance in hand exceeded their loan capital, and their trade liabilities were less than a quarter of their assets. Sounder conditions of trade can

---

* The following papers on co-operation, in the later volumes of the 'Transactions of the Social Science Association,' may perhaps be usefully referred to:—1860, Paper by M. D. Hill, Recorder of Birmingham, p. 748; and see Summaries (Mr. H. Fawcett and Dr. Watts) and Discussion, pp. 870-5. 1862, Summaries (Mr. J. Wilson, Rev. H. Solly, Mr. Holyoake) and Discussion, pp. 801-5. 1863, Paper by Mr. H. Pitman, p. 624; and see Summaries (Mr. Alex. Campbell, Mr. J. Plummer) and Discussion, pp. 752-6. 1864, Paper by Mr. Holyoake, p. 618, and see Summary (Mr. John Gurdon), p. 693. 1865, Paper by Mr. Holyoake, p. 480, and see Discussion, pp. 529-35.

See also the article on "Co-operative Societies," in the 'Quarterly Review,' vol. cxiv. p. 418.

The 'Co-operator' journal has howevei for years now supplied the chief record of co-operative progress.

hardly be imagined. The 148,586 members who composed them were scattered nearly all over the country (though Rutland and a few Welsh counties do not figure at all), but far more thickly through the manufacturing and mining districts,—71,332 being numbered for Lancashire, 34,909 for Yorkshire, 6855 for Durham, 4000 for Northumberland, over 3000 for Northamptonshire and Cheshire, etc.*

These figures cannot, indeed, be considered as strictly accurate. Wherever different co-operative bodies exist for separate purposes in one town, the same men are generally members of both. Thus the 849 members of the Rochdale Corn-mill are probably all included in the 5326 of the " Equitable Pioneers;" whilst again, the 24,005 members of the " North of England Co-operative Wholesale Industrial and Provident Society" are almost all of them members of retail stores within the area which is supplied by the society. But, on the other hand, if we take into account the fact that 182 societies had sent in no returns; that 216, certified since December, 1864, were not included in the return, which is made up to 31st December, 1865; that another twelvemonth has elapsed since then; and that a vast number of societies never register at all, we shall see that the figure of 148,586 members must be below the reality, rather than above it.† Let us take it at about 200,000, and let us

---

* See, in the 'Co-operator' for October 1, 1866, "The Co-operative Directory."

† If we allow 35,000 as the number to be deducted for persons members of more than one society, there will remain 110,586. But

suppose that three-fourths of these are engaged in retail shopkeeping, the last third in wholesale trade, or in some process of manufacture, whether that of flour, as in the corn-mills, so flourishing especially in Yorkshire, or some other. What does this show? That nearly 150,000 of the working class have raised themselves collectively, if not individually, by this means alone, into the position hitherto occupied by the shopkeeping class, forming the vast bulk of the £10 occupiers in boroughs; whilst about 50,000—whose business requires premises, if not of free-hold tenure, at least held for some fixed interest or term of years—have raised themselves collectively in like manner to a position equivalent to that of the independent classes of county voters, freeholders, copyholders, or

182 societies have made no returns, 216 were registered in 1865, and it may be presumed that at least an equivalent number were registered in 1866, making 614 in all. Now if from the 417 returning societies we exclude all with more than 1000 members (18 in all, having together 65,771 members), there will remain 399 societies, with 82,815 members, or over 207 each, as the average number of members in those societies. Let us take the average number of members in the 614 societies above mentioned at 150 only, this will make 92,100 to be added to the 110,586, or 202,686 in all. Reckon the unregistered societies at only 200 more, and these at only 20 members each, this will make 4000 additional, or 206,086. But again, the great bulk of the existing stores are always increasing in number. Thus, to take an instance elsewhere than in Lancashire or Yorkshire, the " Sunderland Equitable Industrial Society" is set down in Mr. Tidd Pratt's return for December 31st, 1865, at 1174 members; its Report for December 15th, 1866, shows a net increase during the year of 102, or nearly 9 per cent. Reckon the increase at only 6 per cent. on the whole number of 148,586, this for two years will make 17,830, swelling the previous total to 223,916; or throwing out the odd thousands, the figure of 200,000 above mentioned.

leaseholders. Let it be observed, moreover, that this co-operative movement has lately successfully traversed the crucial experiment of a cotton famine, that it is growing officially, as Mr. Tidd Pratt's return shows us, at the rate of over 200 societies a year, or say, at 150 members each, 30,000 men, to whom must be added over 8000 a year for the increase of numbers in existing bodies; in all nearly 40,000,* of whom at least three-fourths must be taken to belong to the working class, commonly so-called.

But the co-operative movement cannot be sufficiently appreciated unless it be followed into its higher branches, —wholesale trade, or production. What an instance of developed capacity in the working class is shown by that " North of England Wholesale Co-operative Society, Li-mited," of Manchester, which, as its advertisements in the ' Co-operator' tell us, after two years of life, is now doing business at the rate of a quarter of a million sterling per annum ! Take again the " Wolverhampton and Brewood Industrial and Provident Plate Lock Manufacturing So-ciety," founded during a strike by the Plate Locksmiths of that town in 1864, with seven men and £13 capital, and which, after enduring the fiercest competition on the part of the masters,—who forced down prices to crush it to that extent, that the society was actually losing £15 per week on its sales,—has nevertheless succeeded in maintaining itself, conquered a footing second to none in the trade, had

* The ' Co-operative Directory' above quoted shows, between 1864 and 1865, an actual increase of 18,825 members among the returning societies only, which may be safely doubled for the non-returning, newly registered (for two years), and non-registered societies at the present day.

in August last* sixty men at work, producing £100 worth of goods weekly; sent to the Dudley Exhibition last year a case of plate locks which were put on a par with those of Messrs. Chubb and Cotterall; and have now, according to a friend who visited them 24th April, 1867, " as much business as ever they can do."† It is to be regretted that this Society has not sent in its returns to Mr. Tidd Pratt.

In London, again, the " Working Gilders' Co-operative Association," which began with £8 capital, never received more than £18, never registered at all as an Industrial Society, yet did last year over £2500 of business,‡ and

* See a paper by Mr. Foxwell, in the ' Co-operator' for 15th August, 1866; also ' Co-operator' for 1st September, 1866.

† " I went this morning," writes the friend in question, " to visit the Co-operative Lock Manufacturers' premises, and deeply interested I was in the result. The workmen generally seemed somewhat elderly men, except at the forge, where only younger men can do the work. They do all their business on ready-money principles. Although working but at a small profit, the men subscribe 2s. 6d. out of every sovereign towards paying off liabilities incurred in the time when they were selling at a loss."—" We are as unflagging in our zeal as ever," writes the secretary to the society, " to better our condition, and the condition of the trade generally, both by improving the general articles of trade, and by bringing out such new samples and designs as may prove beneficial to the workman and to the public."

‡ See, as to the history of this very interesting group of Co-operators, a paper by one of the writers of the present volume, in the ' Industrial Partnerships' Record' for May, 1867. The following figures exhibit the steady growth of the business of the Working Gilders' Association during the last four years of its independent existence ·—

1863	£2062. 12s. 2½d.
1864	2353 4 9½
1865	2460 18 5½
1866	2529 11 2

the last year having been notoriously one of great stagnation in trade.

has lately transformed itself into a " Frame-makers' and Gilders' Association, Limited," by amalgamation with the business of a former employer and landlord, the whole management of both branches of business being transferred, by the express desire of the employer who coalesces with the co-operative workmen, to the foreman of the co-operative shop, as one of the managing directors. The joint establishment stands very high in the trade, employs about forty men, and is doing business at the rate of £6000 a year.

It is true indeed that, with a few exceptions, associations for co-operative production, formed on the principle of dividing profits among the workers, are but of limited extent; the large flour-mills of the North, the various bakeries, etc., being only established for purposes of consumption, and dividing profits upon purchases. Of the movement for co-operative production in 1850–2, but few remains subsist; the best known being perhaps the "Working Tailors" and "Working Hatters" Associations of Manchester. Within the last few years, however, a similar movement has recommenced in the Metropolis, of which the successful "Working Gilders' Association" may be considered to have been the pioneer. Among the results of this are to be reckoned the "London Co-operative Cabinet Manufacturing Industrial Society," 1865 (established, though by working men, like the last-named company, on the "industrial partnership" principle of allowing a large share of profits to capital), followed more recently by the "Metropolitan Co-operative Deal Cabinet Manufacturing Industrial Society, Limited," by Co-operative Societies of Working Dyers, Packing Case Makers, and Working Tailors.

Co-operative production, however, has a moral value which is not indicated by the number of men whom it sets at work, or the figure of its business. If a co-operative workshop has sufficient elements of vitality to outlast the inevitable struggles and storms of its first few years, it begins to develope a most remarkable series of results. Co-operation first expels from the shop drunkenness and all open disorder, which are found to be perfectly incompatible with its success; introducing in their place a number of small adjustments and contrivances of a nature to facilitate work or promote the comfort of the worker.* By degrees it exterminates in turn the small tricks and dishonesties of work which the opposition of interests between employer and employed too often excuses in the worker's eyes; it is felt to be the interest of each and all that all work should be good, that no time should be lost. Fixity of employment meanwhile, coupled with a common interest, creates new ties between man and man, suggests new forms of fellowship, till there grows up a sort of family feeling, the only danger of which is that of its becoming jealous and exclusive towards the outsider. Let this state of things last awhile, and there is literally evolved a new type of working man, endued not only with that

---

* The effects of co-operation on the health of the worker are most marked. The gilding trade is a decidedly unhealthy one; yet, with one or two exceptions, it would be difficult to find a healthier-looking body of London artisans than the Working Gilders could show at their yearly excursions.

honesty and frankness, that kindliness and true courtesy, which distinguish the best specimens of his order wherever they may be placed, but with a dignity, a self-respect, a sense of conscious freedom which are peculiar to the co-operator. The writer of these lines met with this type first in the "Associations Ouvrières" of Paris; he has since had the happiness of seeing it reproduced, with variations as slight as the difference of nationality might render unavoidable, in English co-operative workshops, and he therefore believes that its development may be confidently looked forward to as a normal result of co-operative production.* The great problem of such production lies indeed in the choice of a manager. It is sadly true that in the majority of cases hitherto these men prove unequal to their task; that the exercise of power too often tempts them to dishonesty, to reckless speculation, to arbitrary conduct. Where, however, the right man can be found, the most admirable results arise from the habit of an authority which rests not upon the possession of capital, but

---

* The above statements are made as the result of the personal experience of the writer. In corroboration of them may be quoted a passage from a letter by Mr. Thomas Jones, Secretary to the "Wolverhampton and Brewood Industrial and Provident Plate-Lock Manufacturing Society":—

"The co-operative movement has proved a great blessing to many of our men, both socially and morally, for it has stimulated almost every workman to use his utmost skill to bring out a superior article, that would command both an influence and a sale in the market. Some who formerly were given to habits of indolence and intemperance are now become sober, industrious, and respectable. On the whole, the Co-operative Plate-Locksmiths are far in advance of those of the same trade who work for employers, both intellectually, socially, and morally."

upon that combination of intellectual and moral qualities which is absolutely necessary to secure both outward success, and a willing, harmonious discipline within the workshop. In the long run, a successful co-operative manager must always be a really first-rate man.

If the rarity of working men fit at all points for the duties of management be as yet the main hindrance to the spread of co-operative production, there is another valuable form of association in which the management is supplied by the very class hitherto used to exercise it. We must here recall an observation formerly made, that for productive purposes co-operation is now passing into the form of the Limited Company under the Joint Stock Acts, in which we for the most part fail to trace it, except in individual cases. Several co-operative mills and other bodies are thus registered as Joint Stock Companies. One group, however, of what may be termed co-operative companies has been brought into peculiar prominence, and to some extent into mutual relations, through the zeal of Mr. E. O. Greening, of Manchester. The rapid spread of the " Industrial Partnership," or " Partnership of Industry " system,* to which we allude, would have been impossible if the worker were not by this time admitted by his employer to be capable of being, as a shareholder, associated

---

* See, as to this, Mr. Holyoake's paper in the Transactions of the Social Science Association for 1865, p. 480; Mr. E. O. Greening's pamphlet on ' The Present Position and Prospects of Partnerships of Industry,' Manchester, 1866; the ' Industrial Partnerships' Record,' published monthly since March, 1867; and a paper by one of the present writers on "Some New Forms of Industrial Co-operation," in ' Good Words' for April, 1867.

more or less closely in the management of large concerns; or as a mere bonus-receiver, of being stimulated to greater exertions by the hope of a distant addition to the amount of his wages. This system is now, under various modifications, being applied by Messrs. Briggs and Co. and the South Buckley Company to mining; by Messrs. Crossley to the carpet manufacture; by Messrs. Fox, Head and Co., to iron-works; by Messrs. Greening to another branch of iron manufacture; by the Cobden Memorial Mills to the cotton manufacture; by Messrs. Blythe and Co. and by Messrs. Lloyd and Summerfield, to the earthenware and glass manufacture; by Mr. Goodall, of Leeds, to printing, etc. etc. The principle, as we have seen, is being adopted by the working class in their own undertakings, as by the Cabinet-makers, or by the Frame-makers and Gilders. Thousands* of working men are in these various establishments learning to enter into the position, to share the interests of the employer class. The commercial success of these undertakings is already patent to the world in the handsome dividends already paid by the older-established ones to their shareholders. One sample only of the efficacy of the principle, drawn from quite another quarter than those hitherto indicated, shall be given. The respected chief of the 'Tonic Sol-Fa' school writes thus:—"We have tried the 'partnership of industry' plan in our printing office at Plaistow for a year. Before that, the office yielded me either $2\frac{1}{2}$ or o per cent. Since we adopted the plan, it has yielded 5 per cent.

---

* The 'Industrial Partnerships Record' reckons at from 8 to 10,000 the number of persons employed under the system referred to.

and promises to yield more. *But better still, it saves me
no end of vexation and care.*"

Not the least remarkable feature of the Co-operative
movement, as well as of that of the Partnerships of Industry which has grown out of it, is its connection with education. The example set by the Rochdale Equitable
Pioneers, of a reading-room and educational fund, has
been followed by many co-operative bodies, in Lancashire
especially.* Thousands of pounds have thus been raised
by the working men, as a voluntary rate on their co-operative success, for purposes of self-improvement. And it is
from the example thus set them by the working classes
that the founders of the new " Partnerships of Industry "
have borrowed the provision embodied in the articles of
association of several of them, which authorizes their directors, before recommending a dividend, to set apart a
reserve fund, for the purpose, amongst others, of " creating
and maintaining a fund for establishing and supporting a
library, news-room, workmen's club or other educational
benefits for the servants of the Company.''

* Four societies figure in the returns of 1866 as contributing over
£100 a year to an educational fund, viz. Rochdale, £537, Bury,
£261, Oldham (King Street), £150, and Bacup, £144; three contribute between £50 and £100 (Northampton, Manchester, and Salford
Equitable, and Heywood) ; five, between £25 and £50, etc. It must be
observed, moreover, that the educational fund being often, according to the
Rochdale pattern, a rate of two and a half per cent. on profits, it goes
on always increasing with the success of the Society. The ' Equitable
Pioneers ' have bestowed a handsome ' free drinking-fountain ' on their
town. Several co-operative bodies subscribe to charities, and contributed
during the cotton distress to the relief fund ; the ' Equitable Pioneers,'
from £7 to £10 a week.

The Co-operative movement is, however, no doubt still in the main confined to our manufacturing, mining, and coast districts, though gradually creeping into the small towns of the agricultural districts; as in Essex, in the shape of co-operative stores; or even laying hold on agriculture, through the co-operative farms of Suffolk.* The spread of general education is, we believe, slowly paving a way for it on all sides.†

§ 3. *Spread of General Education.*

The race between Education and Population is, no doubt, far from being a neck-and-neck one. " Instead of the 800,000 or 900,000 now at school in England and Wales," said lately in the House of Commons a former education minister of this country, the Right Hon. H. A. Bruce, " there ought to be two millions " (April 5, 1867). The Manchester and Salford Society have declared that in 1862 the proportion of the population attending day-schools in Manchester and Salford had actually diminished since 1834, from 967 per 10,000 to 908 ;‡ that in 1865,

---

* See an interesting paper by Mr. John Gurdon, in the Transactions of the Social Science Association for 1864, p. 693.

† Efforts have been made more than once to bring the various co-operative bodies into some definite organization, or at least to promote mutual relations between them, as by the " Society for Promoting Working Men's Associations " in 1850, the " Co-operative League " in 1852, etc., but all organizations for such a purpose have died out hitherto within a few years. Various conferences of delegates from co-operative bodies have also been held, as in London in 1852, in Manchester in 1853, 1861, etc.; but as such conferences have always in importance fallen far short of those held by trade-societies, to which we shall hereafter refer, we need not dwell upon them.

‡ See Mr. Hole's ' Homes of the Working Classes,' Appendix J, p. 195 and following.

of 104,000 children between three and twelve, those attending day-schools of all classes were only 55,000. The Principal of Saltley College has stated that in Birmingham in 1866, out of 40,164 children between five and ten only 18,518, or 46·17 per cent., attended school; out of 34,495 between ten and fifteen, only 9226, or 28·78 per cent.* And yet, in spite of these and other disheartening statements, we venture to think that none but the most fanatical of educationists can sincerely deny the progress of education amongst our working class. It may be true, as was stated in the Commissioners' Report of 1861, that " the junior classes of schools, comprehending the majority of children, do not learn, or learn imperfectly, the most necessary part of what they come to learn,—reading, writing, and arithmetic." But it is no less true that the same Commissioners declare that, with the exception of the children of out-door paupers, or of parents viciously inclined, " almost all the children in the country capable of going to school receive some instruction " (Report, vol. i. p. 84). " The progress," they further say, " made by popular education in the course of the last ten years is measured by the fact that the proportion of day-scholars to the population was ascertained by the census of 1851 to be 1 in 8·36.† Our returns collected through societies connected with education and by other means show that in the middle of the year 1858 the proportion was 1 in 7·7.‡ The returns collected by the Assistant Commis-

---

* See a letter of the Rev. James Fraser to the 'Times,' April 16, 1867.
† In 1833 the proportion was only 1 in 11·27.
‡ Between 1818 and 1858, as Mr. Baines puts it in his speech of 1861,

sioners show that in their districts, which included one-eighth of the total estimated population of England and Wales, the proportion was 1 in 7·83. This result coincides so nearly with that of the inquiry conducted through the societies as to supply a strong confirmation of its accuracy " (p. 88). Between 1857 and 1865 again, the average school attendance at public schools for England and Wales had risen from 531,210 to 901,750 ; for Great Britain, from 626,696 to 1,057,745, the school accommodation being indeed sufficient for one-half more, or 1,677,808 (of whom 1,470,473 in England and Wales).* The quality of schools, again, has improved far more even than their number has increased. Thus, those even who, like the Rev. J. P. Norris, believe they have seen " little or no advance " in the proportion of the population " willing to avail themselves fully " of the education offered, declare yet that they have " seen a rapid increase in the number of good schools." Hence, as a fact, the decreasing proportion of educational marksmen in the population. Between 1841 and 1862, the proportion of male minors who signed the marriage register with a mark fell from 32·7 per cent. to 23·7 ; that of female, from 48·8 per cent. to 28·5 ; the rate of educational progress being, however, less in Scotland and Ireland than in England.

population increased 66 per cent., day-scholars 275 per cent., and Sunday scholars 405 per cent.

* The Rev. James Fraser, in a letter to the 'Times' (April 17, 1867), reckons the present total number of day-scholars between 4 and 12 in public and private schools at about 2,160,000, of whom "not much more than three-fourths," or say 1,620,000, would be in average daily attendance, out of a total population between those ages of 3,500,000.

If, indeed, we consult the evidence appended to the Commissioners' Report of 1861, the testimonies to the improvement in the character of the working population generally by means of education are so abundant, that in reference to them it is puzzling to know where to begin, or where to leave off. Mr. Edward Akroyd, one of the very largest employers of labour in the West Riding, says, in reply to the Education Commission, " Since the introduction of the factory system of education, I have observed in most of the districts to which I have alluded a great improvement in the condition of the working classes, both morally and intellectually. I have also observed that the manners and habits of the working classes have been proportionally elevated." The Rev. Samuel Earnshaw, M.A., Chaplain of St. Peter's, Sheffield, speaking of two schools with which he was connected, says—" The children are generally orphans taken out of the lowest class. After an average of about four and a half years' instruction they are sent out, the boys as apprentices and the girls as domestic servants. In these schools education, I consider, has a fair chance, and their results show what is the tendency of education in all cases. Now, it is a fact that the boys are eagerly sought after by masters as apprentices, because of their intellectual and moral qualities, and in after life many of them become eminent, all of them most respectable members of their class." The Rev. John Freeman, Rural Dean, Rector of Ashwicken, Norfolk, says :— " The Chairman of the Quarter Sessions at Norwich has repeatedly spoken of the steady and progressive diminution of crime, and the same remarks are continually called for at Swaffham, the cause assigned being the improved state of education. The Rev. Prebendary Penrose replies thus to the Commissioners : " There is certainly less vulgarity and coarseness, less rudeness and violence at our feasts and statutes, our fairs and markets. There is more good taste in dress and general behaviour. An interest is felt in a higher class of literature. The poorer classes are at least more civilized, and, I am willing to believe, more moral also. I know of no cause which can have had this effect, which is unquestionably good as far as it goes, but the influence of education. The interest which the Government has taken in the cause is universally appreciated, and has led our people to set a higher value on the institutions of our country."

Colonel Stobart, of Etherley, Darlington, a coal-owner resident amongst his workpeople, says : " The education of the poor has had great influence upon the general intelligence of that class,—first, on those who have been the direct subjects of education, and from them its influence has spread, to some extent, over all." Henry Sheats, Esq., replies as follows to the query in the Commissioners' circular as to the result of education amongst the poor :— " It has unquestionably added to the value of their labour, —an intelligent workman, other things being equal, being worth more to himself and his employer than an ignorant one. It has also helped them to accommodate themselves more readily to the great and frequent changes in the methods of labour necessitated by the constant discoveries of science." Rev. C. B. Wollaston, vicar of Felpham,

Bognor, Sussex, and inspector of schools, gives the following testimony :—" My experience has convinced me that
children brought up at our National Schools make better
labourers and domestic servants than the uneducated; and
I am certain they are more regular at church, and more
attentive to their religious duties." William Walker, Esq.,
of Bolling Hall, Bradford, manufacturer : " My whole experience enables me to bear witness to an immense improvement in the character of the population since the
passing of the Ten Hours Factory Bill in 1847, which gave
time to such workers, and indirectly has influenced some
other trades favourably." The Rev. F. B. Zincke, B.A.,
vicar of Wherstead, and one of Her Majesty's chaplains in
ordinary, speaks thus :—" In my own immediate neighbourhood, a purely agricultural one, the intellectual effects of
education now perceptible are that it has vastly extended
the mental horizon of the labouring classes. The labourer
now habitually looks beyond the parish and the market
town. It has also qualified the most intelligent of the
class for the numerous situations now to be had as porters,
etc., on railways and in towns. The moral effects have
been valuable. It has greatly exalted their ideas of re-
spectability, and enlarged and refined their ideas of home."
Mr. Cumin, Assistant-Commissioner, reports : " Unless the
evidence of every witness is unfounded, the working
people of this country have greatly improved; to use the
expressions of the Dean of Bristol, and no one knows the
common people better, ' For a shy, surly, dogged de-
meanour, there is now a frank, ready, loyal, free courtesy ;
for suspicion, confidence; for turbulence, docility.' I do

not pretend to be able to contrast the working classes as they now are with what they were thirty, or even twenty years ago, but wherever I went, I found them full of candour, intelligence, and civility, deeply grateful to those who took an interest in their welfare, and keenly sensible of any attempt to corrupt them, or to control their independence." Mr. Hare, another Assistant-Commissioner, gives this important testimony :—" Several large employers in Hull, as well as in the other parts of my district, concur generally that education gives additional value to labour." Such testimony as this might be extended almost indefinitely, but to what purpose? Dr. Adler sums the matter well up when he replies to the Commissioners' question as to results : "To prove the beneficial results of education would be to prove the advantages of light over darkness."

The above evidence, it will be observed, extends over the whole population, and affords some cheering glimpses into the progress of the agricultural class. Another hopeful fact must not be overlooked, viz. that we seem at last to be mastering ignorance, even in its stronghold of pauperism. The workhouse school, with some creditable exceptions, simply bred paupers; the modern District School raises its pupils out of pauperism. After five years' experience as chaplain of the North Surrey District School, the Rev. E. Rudge (as quoted by Mr. E. Carleton Tufnell in a paper on "The Education of Pauper Children," read before the Social Science Association in 1862*), declares his conviction "that there is not a boy in the whole school who would not shrink from a return to the work-

* Transactions, p. 278.

house as degrading, so long as it were possible to gain a livelihood by honest industry." The same happy results have been obtained in the education of girls. " At Anerley," says Miss Barbara Corlett in a paper read before the same association in 1861,* " they turn out the best little maidens that can be imagined, . . . and it is necessary to place your name on the books for three years to insure one of these much-prized Anerley girls." To say nothing of the noble " Ragged School" movement, our Industrial and Reformatory schools again are, to a certain extent, returning to society as useful producers some of those whom they received as vagabonds and criminals.

All this leaves us, no doubt, very far yet from such magnificent examples as those set to England by her former American colonies,—by Pennsylvania, spending in 1866 over £1,200,000 on her schools, which numbered outside of Philadelphia 725,312 scholars, with an average attendance of 478,066, besides nearly 100,000 for Philadelphia itself; even by New York, where, out of a total population between five and twenty-one of 1,354,967, 919,033 attend or have attended school. But if a sad proportion of our working-class remains still uneducated, let t be remembered that every single leading man in that class proclaims the want of education to be one of its greatest calamities; that the expediency of a system of compulsory education is almost a dogma with most of the thinkers in the class. And certain it is at least that there is nothing in the mental constitution of our working population which can justify our educational sloth. One

---

* Transactions, p. 338 ; see 343.

of the writers of this volume was asking a friend, formerly a National schoolmaster of varied experience (extending from Cornwall and Wales to Yorkshire), now a master in an old-established private school, what difference he found between his old scholars and his new ones. The reply was, " Very little. Of course my present boys have a training, in manners especially, which the National schoolboy has not. But place the latter under the same conditions for a few months, and there would be no difference at all. And of one thing I am quite certain, that the National schoolboys have to work very much harder than the ' young gentlemen.' "*

* We have said nothing, it will be observed, in this section, of Sunday-schools. We must candidly confess to the opinion that the educational value of these, as respects the children who are taught in them, is but slight. Observers of weighty authority have gone much further. In a sermon preached in York Minster at the service for working men, 17th March, 1867, to an audience of 4000, by the Rev. J. Erskine Clarke, of Derby, and published at the request of the working men who heard it, the following passage occurs :—

" I fear that we clergy and Sunday-school teachers have done harm, while we were working to do good. We have thought and taught that the right place for every working man's child, for a great part of Sunday, was in our school-room, or in the children's seats at church. . . . We have lost sight of God's law of parental responsibility, and have magnified instead a human institution which has sadly disappointed us in its results. For it must be admitted that Sunday-schools have failed to yield fruits in any proportion to the self-denying labour bestowed on them. Out of 10,000 inmates of prisons and penitentiaries, 6500 had been on an average three years in a Sunday-school. The Registrar, Mr. Horace Mann, says that ' most of the 4,000,000 or 5,000,000 who are constantly absent from public worship must have passed through Sunday-schools.' . . . If our Sunday-schools had made worshippers in any fair proportion, every church and chapel that had one for ten years ought to have become

§ 4. *Spread of Adult Education.*

We cannot however at present look forward to the period when the educational training of the working class will be mainly carried on in childhood. For many a long year to come, the self-education of the adult must supply the deficiencies of that given to the child. And whilst the education thus acquired is seldom the means of raising men from the very lowest depths of ignorance (in which the desire for knowledge itself too often is found to be extinct), it may often powerfully assist those who have acquired the rudiments of learning.

The question of Adult Education is an enormous one in itself, and has supplied ere this the matter for several interesting works, of which we need only mention Dr. James W. Hudson's ' History of Adult Education' (1857–8). As respects the working class, all we can do will be to indicate some of its main branches. We may first glance at those appliances for Adult Education, which partake more or less of a public character.

No great assistance, we may begin by observing, is given by the State towards the general adult education of the

far too small for its congregation ; yet there are hundreds of churches which have had for years half as many scholars as there are sittings in the church, and yet the congregation has shown no increase. Sunday-schools have failed to make church-goers or communicants. . . . We have taken the child under our vicarious wing on Sunday ; the father has remained at home ; *his* example is stronger than *our* precept ; so when the son or daughter is grown up, they follow the father's pattern, and think they are doing all that is required of them when they send their children to the same Sunday-school to which they went themselves, while *they* take the parent's place at home ; and so the evil is perpetuated."

working man. There is, however, a limited class of men, drawn almost exclusively from his order, in its service, for whose general education considerable pains have been taken of late years—our soldiers. The Fourth Report of the Council of Military Education, to March, 1866, showed that out of 177,430 British soldiers, 21,700 neither read nor wrote, 28,600 read but did not write, 116,000 did both, and nearly 11,000 had received a superior education; that within the then last six years the proportion of the uneducated had undergone great improvement,—least, however, in the cavalry, greatest in the military train. Regular examinations are held, certificates of education are granted to the men, and in some corps the possession of a school certificate is made an indispensable condition of promotion. There are special classes, meant in part for the carrying forward of those who seek something beyond what the ordinary school teaches ; and these, notwithstanding the dislike of certain commanding officers, are increasing in number, and in many ways proving their usefulness. The garrison libraries in 1866 contained 203,700 volumes, and issued 488,504, being an increase of more than 7000 volumes and 26,000 issues on the previous year. There are also recreation-rooms and lectures in connection with regimental schools, which cannot fail to be useful as agents of improvement, and must be a welcome variety in the monotony of barrack life.*

---

* The work of military education comprises also children's schools for three classes of children, in which 17,163 were educated, 1865-6. The model school at Chelsea and the Hibernian military school supply many of the teachers in the regimental schools.

But towards the education of the working man in particular branches of knowledge, State assistance has been freely and directly given.

(1) *Science and Art Education.*

The progress of the working class in Science and Art belongs, we consider, rather to the education of the man than to that of the child. The rudiments of both may, and should be, acquired in childhood, but it requires the matured powers, the developed taste of the adult, to make either study a reality. The public recognition of the claims of the working man to prosecute both belongs entirely to the period under review.

It was in the field of Design that such recognition first took place; not, indeed, from any appreciation of the working man's right as a man to enjoy all means of manly culture, but simply with a view to making him a more useful instrument in the battle of competition with foreign countries. Our first "Schools of Design" were established in 1837, in consequence of the report of a Parliamentary Committee in the previous year.* The work, however, languished till 1851, when the first "Great Exhibition," by the contrasts which it offered between our patterns and those of France or of India, woke up our manufacturers, and the public generally, to a sense of our deficiency in artistic education for commercial purposes.

---

* The following details are borrowed from a paper on "Schools of of Art," by D. Raimbach, 'Social Science Transactions,' 1862, p. 301; from the summary of another paper read at the same meeting, by Mr. Buckmaster (*ibid.*, p. 350); and from a paper by Mr. J. S. Wright, on "New Trades in Birmingham" (*ibid.* p. 826, and following).

Hence the formation, in 1852, of the "Department of
Practical Art." From this time the development of Art
education became rapid amongst us. In 1852 there were
but twenty-one "schools of design." In 1861 there were
ninety "drawing schools," or "schools of Art." The
whole progress of this branch of national education is exhibited in the following Table, supplied through the kind-
ness of Mr. N. Macleod, of the Kensington Museum :—

*Numbers under Instruction in Drawing in Schools of Art, and
in Public and other Schools.*

Year.	Schools of Art.	Public and other Schools.	Totals.
1852	4,868		4,868
1853	6,502		6,502
1854	7,030		7,030
1855	10,510	18,988	29,498
1856	12,337	22,746	35,083
1857	12,509	30,802	43,311
1858	14,008	65,465	79,473
1859	17,482	67,490	84,972
1860	15,214	74,267	89,481
1861	15,483	76,303	91,786
1862	15,907	71,423	87,330
1863	16,480	79,305	95,785
1864	16,555	94,083	110,638
1865	16,684	86,967	103,651
1866	18,176	86,492	104,668

Some curious fluctuations will be observed in the above
figures. They are, however, sufficient to show that within
the last ten years (1856–66) the number of art-pupils has
all but trebled. And no higher testimony to the success of
England's efforts to spread the knowledge of the art of design amongst her working classes can be offered than that

of the French working men delegates—keen, critical, jealous observers,—who were sent to our Great Exhibition of 1862. Nothing seems to have struck them more than the development of our system of art education, and the progress in design of our workers.* Thus the sculptors in ornament say : " The progress made by sculpture in England is immense since the Exhibitions of 1851 and 1855." The cabinet-makers : " Comparing the products of England in 1862 with those of 1855, one sees that she has made a gigantic advance." The shawl-designers speak of England's great progress, and envy her schools of design. The jewellers, who admit on several points England's superiority to France, regret that all competent men in the jewelling, carving, engraving, enamelling, and goldsmiths' trade should not have been able to go to London to see the Kensington Museum.. The painters on porcelain dwell on the vast progress of the English workmen within ten years, and attribute it mainly to the "immense extension given to the study of drawing," etc.

Quite apart, however, from the commercial effects of our public efforts for art-education, is the growth amongst working men of a real sense of the visibly beautiful. Those who have had the opportunity, as students in Mr. Ruskin's drawing-class at the London Working Men's College, of seeing the fascination exercised over many a working man by the gradual discovery of the hidden charms of form and colour in the works of God and of man, know that the artisan is as capable of appreciating

* See the interesting volume, entitled ' Rapports des Délégués des Ouvriers Parisiens à l'Exposition de Londres en 1862.' Paris, 1862-4.

art for its own sake, and pursuing it with disinterested love, as the most refined aristocrat.*

The claims of Science to national encouragement, as a subject of study for the many, were only recognized some years later than those of Art ; but both branches of education seem now happily married together in the " Science and Art Department" of South Kensington. The following memorandum supplies a view of the growth of our Science schools since 1859 :—

" Year.	No. of Schools.	No. of Pupils.
1859	4	
1860	9	500
1861	38	1330
1862	69	2544
1863	75	3111
1864	91	4666
1865	120	5479
1866	153	6835
1867†	220	10,231 "

* Do any of our readers know the remarkable engraving called " The Forge," by James Sharples, engine-smith, of Blackburn, a self-taught painter and engraver, who first spent three years in painting a picture of his daily scene of work, then five years in engraving that picture, made most of his own tools (some of them quite unknown to the trade), and never had seen an engraved plate till he brought his own to a publisher? The chief effect of light in the design may not be bold enough, but nothing can exceed the loving faithfulness of the work, the conscientious following out of form in the utmost depths of shade. It is a plate such as none but a true man could have wrought at.

We may here mention that we have hitherto wholly failed to obtain data towards solving the question, whether the working classes have availed themselves to any extent of the Registration of Designs Acts. In many branches of manufacture indeed these Acts are a dead-letter, or nearly so.

† These numbers, it is stated, are below rather than above the truth, but the exact statistics are not known at this period of the year.

From the above figures it would appear that the Science pupils do not number as yet 10 per cent. of the Art ones ; a result not to be wondered at, if we consider both the greater severity of the studies in point of character, and their generally far more remote relation to pecuniary profit. It is, however, expressly stated by Mr. Macleod, that whilst the pupils who attend the drawing classes belong " almost entirely " to the working class, " the proportion of ladies and gentlemen being very small," on the other hand, " those who attend the science classes belong entirely to the labouring class." We may thus reckon that 10,000 members of the working class are now yearly receiving scientific instruction.

There has been indeed, as respects science, and that science of the highest and severest character, one very remarkable attempt made to impart its acquisition to the working man, as distinct from the members of all other classes,—we mean the lectures for working men, delivered at the " Royal School of Mines " (perhaps better known still as the " Museum of Practical Geology"), in Jermyn Street. When this institution was founded, the Duke of Newcastle—all honour be given to his memory for so doing !—made it a condition of the professorships that each professor should deliver one lecture yearly to an audience exclusively composed of working men. It was found, however, that these occasional lectures were of comparatively little value. The professors could not sufficiently explain themselves—their subjects were not understood, They agreed between themselves to give each a course, instead of a single lecture. The most marked success has followed the experiment. We have the authority of Professor Huxley for stating that the attendance is only limited by the means of accommodation ; that for years there has been no increase in the numbers attending, simply because any increase is impossible. About six hundred only can find room, and the tickets that admit to these lectures are so eagerly sought after, that the applicants form quite a *queue* on the mornings when they are issued. It is added as the testimony of all the professors, that these audiences are the most satisfactory which any of them are in the habit of addressing. Those who attend submit themselves more completely to the lecturer ; listen more carefully to statements of fact, and follow with a more intent intelligence his argument from point to point to its conclusion, than any other class of persons. They seem thoroughly *en rapport* with him, and are quite free from that offensive dilettanteism which is so annoying to an earnest lecturer.*

(2) *Public Libraries.   The Penny Postage.*

We pass from the direct appliances for adult education to the indirect ones. The working of our public libraries established under 'Ewart's Act,' though these are free to all classes, must bear largely on the mental improvement of the working class. From some 'Notes on the Results of the "Libraries' Acts" of 1850 and 1855,' by Mr. Edward Edwards,† we may borrow a few facts as to the

* We are bound, indeed, to say,—and we speak from undoubted evidence,—that these audiences are not exclusively what they are supposed to be, and that clerks, shopkeepers, etc., find easy admission to them.
† Transactions of the Social Science Association for 1860, p. 855.

Free Libraries of Manchester and Liverpool. The former, the first established under the Act (in 1852), both as a reading and a lending library, had after seven years (together with its two branches) 27,000 volumes for readers, and about 20,000 for borrowers, and had issued from the reference department 602,000 volumes, from the lending department 592,000. The average daily issue in both departments together had risen from 455 volumes in the first year to 1042 in the seventh. The total number of individual borrowers had been 24,000,—"a large proportion of them working men in humble circumstances, and the families of such . . . consequently persons whose access to books was theretofore of a most restricted sort,"—and "the total amount of uncompensated loss to the corporation, through books lost or injured, over and above necessary wear and tear, did not exceed 60 shillings during a period of seven years." In the reference or reading department, again, "the attendance of persons hitherto possessing very small facilities for the acquisition or the cultivation of reading," had been "very considerable," and was "increasing." And whilst the issue of "Literature" in the lending department amounted to 57,000 out of 75,000, and that of "History and Politics ' together only to 13,000,—in the reading department, the issues of "Literature" were only 41,000 out of 115,000, and those of "History and Politics," on the contrary, 60,000.* The Liverpool Free Library, which had also two branches, and which was first opened also in 1852, had at the close of

* In 1864-5 the total number of volumes had risen to 68,210, of which 35,133 in the reference and 33,077 in the lending department. The

1859 52,000 volumes in all; and had issued in seven years, from the reading department, 1,110,000 volumes, and in six years, from the lending department, more than 15,000,000. A lighter taste, however, prevailed amongst its readers than that of the great factory capital. Thus, of the 203,000 volumes issued in the reading department during the then last year, about 150,000 were of " Literature," and only 27,000 of " History and Politics." The total uncompensated loss would be covered by £3 or £4.

The Birmingham Free Library, again, of which an account is given by Mr. E. C. Osborne,* is a much more recent institution, dating only from 1861. Within the first 287 days it had 6288 volumes, and its issues had amounted to 108,057 volumes, the number of borrowers being 5422. A classification of 310 borrowers, admitted during March, 1862, showed that nearly half of these (132) were working men, besides 24 ' office boys,' who can hardly rank much higher.

If the working man has shown himself not unwilling to read, he has equally shown himself willing to write. It would be cumbering this volume with superfluous figures to dwell on the results of the Penny Postage. Every one knows that it has led, and is daily leading, the postman into nooks and corners of city and village where he never had occasion to go before. It may be said that working

total number of persons holding vouchers as borrowers was 10,791 ; the number of readers was 71,065, of whom 60,000 belonged to the trading and working classes.

* Social Science Transactions for 1862, p. 783.

men who can write are great letter-writers. Of many letters from working men which lie on the table on which these lines are written, there are few which do not exceed a sheet.

(3) *Sunday Schools, Mechanics' Institutes, etc.*

If we turn to the services rendered to adult education among working men by purely voluntary bodies, we find ourselves in a veritable *embarras de richesses,* and are thereby compelled to pass cursorily over several agencies which, to those who are best acquainted with them, may often seem among the most important of any.

We spoke depreciatingly of Sunday-schools as means of infant education. We believe they are of far more value to the adult, where he is not kept away from them by the presence of children. For him their awakening power is, we are convinced, considerable. A correspondent, from whose communication we purpose quoting more largely hereafter, speaks of them in this relation from experience as "powerful educational agents, intellectually as well as morally." Their effect is no doubt greatest upon the very lowest class,—upon those who, through long hours of work in an ill-paid calling, have absolutely no leisure left them for self-improvement but upon the Sunday ; and hence a gentleman of large experience among the working classes of Norwich reckons " Sunday-schools above all" as having promoted a better feeling "amongst the lowest class" towards religion. Their highest value, however, we venture to think, has been mainly that of the training and discipline they have afforded to the teachers, a large proportion of whom has always belonged to the working class. " Nothing has kept me straight but teaching a Sunday-school in Fetter Lane," was once said to the writer of these lines by a most intelligent working man.

The ordinary Evening Class,* where men and boys can be kept separate, affords more consecutive teaching, and is thereby, we believe, a more effective means of adult education among the working class. Let us quote a single instance as a sample of thousands. The chief accountant at the co-operative store in a cathedral city was fifteen years ago unable to write a single letter, to read in the Bible, to do a simple addition sum. He began to learn in an evening class attached to a place of worship, and there, and still more through the help of a neighbourly shoemaker, teacher in a Sunday school, he educated himself. " I cannot puzzle him," writes the minister who was his first teacher, " in arithmetic ; he enjoys a tough job of that sort, and really has worried out the art for himself." And none, be it observed, feel education as a living, expansive power like those who have thus fought one out for themselves. " Sure am I," writes the working man in question himself, " that the real road to prosperity both in the Church and in societies is by education. I have observed, since I have been a member of the Co-operative Society, that as a rule a member without education is a complete bore, or troubles himself very little about the prosperity of

---

* By this we mean such classes as are constantly being founded in connection with churches, chapels, large factories or other establishments, or sometimes independently of such.

the Society; whereas an educated member will help the Society all he can, and when he sees an evil he will try to eradicate it."

But among the agencies which have been most influential in spreading education generally through the working class, and in raising its character generally, we must not overlook the Mechanics' Institute, and other institutions having similar objects, though various in name.* Although a considerable number of these institutes are to be found in most parts of England, they prevail most in Lancashire and Yorkshire. In these counties, scarcely a town or village exists which cannot boast of its Mechanics' Institution, and in the villages they are often supported with more energy and success than in the larger places, owing probably to the absence of rival attractions. In 1861, according to the calculations of Dr. J. W. Hudson, as quoted by Mr. E. Baines, there were supposed to be, in all, above 1200 of such institutions, with 200,000 members,—in 1831 there were but 55, with 7000.

The Mechanics' Institute has no doubt in many places become deserted by the working classes. But this is by no means true as a general rule. In Yorkshire, says Mr.

---

* The " Edinburgh School of Arts," founded in 1820, is claimed to be " at the head of all the Mechanics' Institutions in this country " (Scotland?) by Dr. George Lees; see Transactions of the Social Science Association for 1863, p. 376. " Workmen's Christian Institutes," " Temperance Institutes," etc., form other similar groups, which space forbids us to dwell on. See, as to the early history of these institutions, an article in the ' Quarterly Review,' vol. cxiii., on " Institutes for Working Men."

Barnett Blake in a paper on the Mechanics' Institutes of
Yorkshire,* the majority of the Mechanics' Institutions
" not only supply the educational wants of working men,
but are mainly supported, and in many instances managed
by them." A new life seems indeed to have been breathed
into these institutions, first by the system of evening
classes, secondly by the formation of the ' Unions of Mechanics' Institutes.' One very remarkable feature in the history of Mechanics' Institutes, says Dr. Pankhurst,† " is the
strong and universal tendency to subordinate all their
agencies and machinery to the promotion of class instruction. Viewed in relation to the progress of sound education, it is impossible to overrate the importance of this
feature." The " Unions " of institutes again, of which the
first was the " Yorkshire Union," founded in 1857, have
borne excellent fruit, springing up almost of necessity
wherever the spirit of association is strongly manifested. In
districts where this tendency is less felt, Mechanics' Institutions as a rule lack the vitality necessary to give full
effect to their operations. But in almost all our great
fields of productive labour the "Union" of Institutes
comes to their aid, and by means of its tabulated experience, of the visits of its travelling agent, and of the
lecturers which it sends out, enables them to accomplish a
work which, as isolated bodies, the separate institutes find
mostly beyond their power, especially at their first commencement.

* Transactions of the Social Science Association for 1859, p. 335.
† In a paper on " The Union of Lancashire and Cheshire Institutes,"
Social Science Transactions for 1864, p. 476.

At the date of Mr. Blake's paper before referred to there were in the "Yorkshire Union" 138 institutes, 90 of which had evening classes, attended by over 9000 students, of whom 5224 were taught reading, writing, and arithmetic, whilst the next most largely-taught study, geography, was only taught in 49 institutes out of the 90, to 895, —a fact conclusively proving Mr. Blake's position, that in Yorkshire it is really the working class whose educational wants these institutes supply. But the institutes in union, besides reading-rooms supplied with newspapers and periodicals, had above 140,000 volumes, and issued them at the rate of nearly 400,000 a year, or about 16 per member.*

The latest Report of the Yorkshire Union shows, indeed, some falling off of the number of institutes in union, which is stated at 122, 78 of which had 130,214 volumes, and which had together upwards of 20,000 members; whilst out of 13,920 members in 42 institutes, 5830 were members of evening classes. But as "the actual number of institutes in Yorkshire not in union may be estimated" —so we are informed by Mr. James Hole, the most com-

* The same volume of 'Transactions' from which the above facts are quoted, contains papers to the same effect on the "Bradford Mechanics' Institute," by Mr. John Godwin (p. 340), and on "Some Statistics of the Huddersfield Mechanics' Institution," by Mr. Frank Curzon (p. 345). Of the former it is shown that one-third of the Committee were, or had been, working men, and that from two-thirds to three-fourths of the members were either working men or the sons of working men. The latter appears in great measure to owe its success to the practice of taking weekly payments, under which the operatives actually appear to pay a larger sum per annum " than any similar institution in the kingdom," viz. at 3½d. a week, 15s. 2d. a year.

petent authority on the subject—"at half as many more,"
the decrease in the amount of education imparted is probably only apparent.   The Lancashire and Cheshire Union,
again, contains 131 institutions, 82 of which sent in returns,
upon which the Council reports that they number in the
aggregate 22,780 members.   71 of these institutions have
together an annual income of £24,186, 35,853 volumes
in their libraries, and an attendance at their evening classes
of 7342.   There are special prizes for essays having reference to important local branches of industry, and to
the relations generally of industrial life,* some of the subjects being as appropriate as they are important, though to
the students of such institutions, it is to be feared, rather
puzzling.†

Most of the Unions of Mechanics' Institutes, it may be
observed, offer prizes to their members ; and although
much may be said against educational competition, it cannot be denied that these have proved a powerful stimulus,

* The following are amongst the subjects for the present year :—
Social Economy; Biographies from English History ; Improvements in
Machinery; the Influence of Co-operation upon the Future of the
Working Classes ; Calculation of the Speed of Wheels ; Mechanical
Drawing ; the Wages Question.

† In the Rev. H. R. Sandford's paper on " Evening Classes, and the
Associations for promoting them," in the ' Social Science Transactions'
1864 (p. 426), will be found further details as to the " South Staffordshire Association for Promotion of Adult Education," the " Southern
Counties " and " North Staffordshire Adult Education Societies ;" and
see also Dr. Pankhurst's paper, before referred to.

The Birmingham and Midland Institute, though as yet a much smaller
body than the great unions, deserves also to be mentioned.   See as to
this Lord Harrowby's speech as President, at its annual meeting of
January 14, 1867, in the ' Times' of Jan. 18.

to the working man more particularly. " The working classes in Lancashire," says Dr. Hudson (we quote from Mr. Baines's great speech of 1861), " offer from their ranks competitors who invariably excel the middle classes. In mathematics, in chemistry, in French, nay, even in British history and geography, the clerks and book-keepers of Manchester are far inferior to the weavers of Oldham and other small towns." Out of 1067 advanced male pupils of the Lancashire Union of Mechanics' Institutes examined by him in the winter of 1860-1, 566 were mill operatives, 155 mechanics and persons employed in foundries, 75 journeymen employed in the building trades, 75 employed in other trades, 18 in field operations, the remaining 178 clerks, shopmen, etc.; whilst out of 136 female pupils, 86 were mill operatives, 17 dressmakers, hat-trimmers, etc., the remainder servants, shopwomen, etc. But the prize of Geometry was carried off by a shoemaker from Oldham ; that of History by a mechanic from Crewe ; of Colonial History by a weaver from Blackburn ; whilst out of the ten prize-holders the only two belonging to other than the working class were a mill-warehouseman, who carried off the prize for Arithmetic, and a clerk who shared with two joiners those for Decimal Currency.

In connection with the prize system, it would be unjust to overlook the efforts of the Society of Arts, which, indeed, through its examinations has sought to make itself a central regulator of working class education, and has served in this respect as a pioneer to the " Science and Art Department" of South Kensington. The Society of Arts' prizes are, next to the South Kensington ones, no doubt still the "blue ribbons" of the studious and aspiring young artisan.

(4) *Working Men's Colleges.*

Whilst the Mechanics' Institute has, we believe, in many places continued to be of the utmost benefit to the working men,—especially to the youth of that class,—it is unquestionable that in other parts they have gradually withdrawn from it, leaving it to be filled by the middle class. The causes of this change, where it has taken place, seem to be fairly indicated in an essay of James Wall, a journeyman printer, published in 1858.* "The objections to Mechanics' Institutes on the part of the working class," he says, "are—1. That the management is not in the hands of the mechanics. 2. That politics and religion are excluded. 3. That the institutes are only one in each town, and centrally situated. 4. That they are closed on Sundays. 5. That the instruction given is desultory, unconnected, and more scientific than elementary. 6. That weekly payments are not taken." It is obvious that three of these six objections,—as to the non-participation of the working man in management, the desultory and un-elementary character of the instruction, and the absence of weekly payments, are avoided by the Yorkshire institutes, or some of them. But the real fact seems to be that the "Mechanics' Institute," instead of being too good for the working man, is often beginning to be not good enough.

---

* Quoted in a paper by Dr. Elliott on "Working Men's Reading-rooms, as established in 1848 at Carlisle," in the Transactions of the Social Science Association, 1861 (pp. 676-9).

He wants to reach into the education of the classes above him in the social scale; he wants, above all, though he may not often explain his own wants to himself, to feel himself united with his fellow-men in some closer bond than that of merely meeting together in an institution. Hence the " Working Men's Colleges," of which many have sprung up of late years.

The oldest college of the kind is the " People's College " at Sheffield, now a quarter of a century old (founded 1842). For the first six years, its founder, an Independent minister, was almost the only teacher; but his teaching had such good fruit, that his pupils have become teachers, and have kept the college self-governed and self-paying. It was followed, twelve years later, by the London " Working Men's College," which has taken higher ground than any other, especially in its cultivation of a college social life, and in refusing to allow its students, as such, to attend any examinations but those connected with the Universities or the Privy Council, and has received, since 1854, over four thousand students; and soon after by the Halifax College, developed from a night school. In 1858, the Salford College was founded. The still later College at Ipswich has had remarkable success in point of numbers, there being now more than a thousand members. Besides the " City of London College," there are, we believe, one or two other Working Men's Colleges (Hull, etc.) of which we have no details. Several have ceased to exist after a short duration ; one at Manchester has merged into the Owens College, losing somewhat of its working-man element.

The government of these bodies is very various,—some being ruled by a self-renewed council, which in others contains representative students, whilst the Sheffield College is essentially democratic in constitution. Every College teaches more or less of each of the five great branches of study—Art, History, Languages, Mathematics, and Physical Science, but there are great differences in the extent and success of the work. Halifax may be called a very successful adult school of high character, doing its work in a thoroughly practical manner. Ipswich has, apparently, teaching of a somewhat higher character, and a more extended programme; while Salford has developed its work to the utmost extent, having attached to it two very large day-schools, and a preparatory class, and giving practical and successful teaching in art and physical science. The London College puts forward the most comprehensive programme of studies,* and has also a large elementary class, an adult school, and a middle class girls' school.

Notwithstanding their name, these bodies are not ex-

* The programme of the London Working Men's College for the commencement of its thirteenth year, beginning October 22nd, 1866, included, besides a Bible-class, classes in drawing, vocal music, history and geography, English grammar and literature, Early English, French, German, Latin, Greek, arithmetic, geometry, trigonometry, algebra, book-keeping, botany, natural philosophy, and zoology; with an elementary class for advanced reading and writing, elementary grammar, and arithmetic from division to practice, and an adult school. It is remarkable, moreover, that, of twenty-eight teachers whose names figure on this programme, no less than twelve have been students of the College, taking charge even of such classes as drawing from casts and natural objects, English grammar, elementary French, algebra, and geometry.

clusively composed of operatives, but even in those which are most largely attended by other classes (as the two London ones), the number of genuine working men who avail themselves of them is considerable. Speaking generally, the students may be said to be one-half genuine hand-workers, the other half belonging almost exclusively to the class of clerks, warehousemen, and others earning about the same wages as the artisans. If there be any preponderance, it is in favour of the mechanics, who certainly have gained at least as much distinction in the examinations. Perhaps from 3000 to 4000 may be reckoned as the number of working men who attend yearly the classes in these institutions, and are gradually feeling their way to the highest branches of education.*

(5) *Reading Rooms, Working Men's Clubs and Institutes, etc.*

Much humbler institutions than the Working Men's College have in other cases supplied the deficiencies of the Mechanics' Institute, where the latter has failed to meet the wants of the working man. At Carlisle, as Dr. Elliott's before-quoted paper informs us, " Working Men's Reading Rooms" have sprung up, which are controlled exclusively by working men, supply books and newspapers on party politics and religion, are open during the greater

---

* See further the papers on this subject of Mr. David Chadwick, in the 'Transactions' of the Social Science Association (" On Working Men's Colleges ") for 1859, p. 323; of the Rev. F. D. Maurice (" Working Men's Colleges "); Mr. E. G. Clarke (" The City of London College "); and Mr. R. B. Litchfield (" The Social Economy of a Working Men's College ") in the Transactions of the same Association for 1862, pp. 293, 297, 787.

part or the whole of Sunday, afford elementary instruction at appointed times (including the reading aloud of newspapers), and are supported by weekly payments. There are six of them, which, at the date of the paper, were as flourishing as ever, and numbered usually about twice as many enrolled members as the prosperous Mechanics' Institute of the city, which numbers from 400 to 500 out of a population of 30,000.

It is indeed only the intellectual *élite* of the working classes who can be expected, after growing to manhood, to undergo the drudgery of class-learning for purposes of self-improvement. A vast number look more either to individual self-improvement by means of the reading-room or the lending library, or to social recreation of a harmless kind. Hence the growth of the " Working Men's Club and Institute" movement, which has its focus in the "Working Men's Club and Institute Union."* The objects of such bodies are set forth as follows in a paper entitled " Hints and Suggestions for the formation of Working Men's Clubs and Institutes," published by the Union : "To provide a Club or Institute, as members of which the working men of the neighbourhood can enjoy rational social intercourse with each other, coupled with opportunities for mental improvement, recreation, and mutual helpfulness ; and further, to give them facilities for carrying on various plans of social improvement, such as Co-operative Societies, Friendly or Benefit Clubs, Mutual Im-

* The " Metropolitan District Association of Working Men's Clubs and Institutes " has been lately organized as an auxiliary to the central body.

provement Societies, Building Societies, and the like, in the prosecution of which working men are at present often obliged to resort to public-houses for the mere want of better meeting places."* Many of these bodies have evening (especially singing) classes, all reading rooms and libraries, and it is one of the expressed objects of the Union to lead men up from the club to the Working Men's College. The payments vary from $\frac{1}{2}d.$ per week to 8s. *per annum*, and it is considered by the Council essential that one half at least of the managing body in each institute should consist of working men. The number of these institutes is estimated at about 250, open in various parts of the kingdom. Many of these have large numbers of members ; the Sunderland one, for instance, now in the fourth year of its existence, 800, of whom two-thirds are weekly members only, *i. e.* presumably working men. If we averaged them at 50 only, the total number of members would amount to 12,500, but as there are many institutes not in connection with the Union, the real total does not probably fall far short of 20,000—a figure which must be considered in the main as additional to that of the members of Mechanics' Institutes. Various useful undertakings have already sprung out of the movement ; *e. g.* in London the before mentioned Co-operative Associations of Cabinet-makers and Dyers.

Beyond these institutes again, the various Mutual Improvement societies,† field-clubs, and other similar soci-

---

* See also Mr. Solly's paper on " Working Men's Clubs and Institutes," Transactions of the Social Science Association for 1863, p. 679.

† Among Working Men's Mutual Improvement Societies may be

eties existing amongst the working classes, defy all enu-
meration. One such body is probably unique in its
character. In Sunderland is a small book-buying and
lending society, composed of six working men—a cork
cutter, two wood-carvers for ship-work, a watch-maker, an
engine-fitter, who, having lost a finger, ekes out his livelihood by painting photographs, and another wood-carver
by trade, but now doing well as a photographic painter.
The taste of these men runs chiefly on old ballads, of
which they possess various collections. They have put
themselves in connection with the Early English Text
Society, to which they intend to subscribe " so soon as
work gets better." They have picked up a quantity of
curious books (including an edition of the Percy ballads,
unknown to Lowndes), and having sometimes to buy
several copies at a time of the works they wish to possess,
have a stock on hand of old " Song Garlands," Cumber-
land songs, and ballads, and other queer stuff in the way
of local literature, which they are glad to dispose of.

§ 5. *The Spread of Newspapers and Cheap Literature.*

Whatever may be the use made by the working man of
public and other libraries, the main attraction to him of all
institutions to which he may have access is the reading-
room, and, in the reading-room, the newspaper. To what
extent the higher-priced newspaper literature penetrates at

quoted the " Society of Wood-Carvers," whose existence spreads over
nearly the whole of the period under review (founded 1833). It has a
most valuable collection of books, casts, engravings, and photographs.

present to the working class, through the medium of such
reading-rooms as are attached to the Mechanics' Institute,
the Working Men's College or Club, the Co-operative or
Trade Society, etc., it would be difficult to determine;
though there are probably few of any character without a
'Times.' But the cheap newspaper is the one mainly
within the reach of the working man's purse and of his
influence, and it is at the same time one of those creations
of the period we have been reviewing in which he may
well feel a quasi-parental interest. For the existence of
the penny newspaper has only been rendered possible by
the relaxation of the fiscal laws affecting the press, and in
the warfare against these, as before stated, the working
man took an active part.

The cheap newspaper and periodical cannot perhaps be
defined strictly as educators. Yet, for good or for evil,
and probably on the whole for good, they are very powerful ones. The experience of the most observant in the
retail periodical trade is, that young readers from amongst
the poorer classes generally begin with some exciting illustrated story, catching the eye with its plates, which in the
lowest and worst of the cheap publications used to be
sometimes daubed with yellow, red, and blue. But the
main reliance of the publishers now is on unnatural and
violent incidents thickly crowded, and developed by dia-
logue that runs on with a rattle like the stick of a London
boy drawn along a row of area-railings. The title also
must be striking, and have connection with murder and
any additional number of mortal sins that can be conve-
niently crammed in. After a little, however, these strong

dishes pall upon the appetite, and gradually the reader finds his way to something better.   It is certain, moreover, that the very worst and most vicious of the penny publications have the smallest circulation.   Indeed they only maintain their ground at all by limiting the quantity they give.   'The Highwayman's Daughter,' 'Jenny Diver,' 'The Lady Highwayman,' 'Blueskin,' 'The Mysteries of the Past,' and several other atrocious and stupid publications give but eight small pages for a penny, whilst the general run of good publications give sixteen twice the size, and sell perhaps fifty times as many; so that one may almost look forward to the day when this literary filth may disappear altogether—if for no better reason, from its unprofitableness as a marketable commodity.

Thirty years ago 'Chambers's Journal,' the publications of the Society for the Diffusion of Useful Knowledge, and some few others, were the only weekly publications of any consequence to be found on the counters of newsvendors.   Then followed stories in numbers, many of them issued by a man named Lloyd, of London; such as 'Varney the Vampire; or, the Feast of Blood.'   They had a large sale, but were ultimately put out of the market by new publications of a better character, such as the 'Family Herald.'   They had been so profitable, however, while they were running, that a re-issue of them was tried about seven years ago, in the hope that a new generation had grown up which would buy them as eagerly as the previous generation; but the speculation was an utter failure, and 'Varney the Vampire,' with the majority of his disreputable companions, had to retire discomfited.

Now publications, so numerous as to put even naming them out of the question, flood the country; many of them conducted with great ability and brought out at a heavy cost, the vast majority decent in language and spirit, so that although they may do little towards the cultivation of a correct taste, they at least endeavour to avoid anything approaching to a corruption of morals. Mr. Abel Heywood, of Manchester, in giving evidence before the Select Committee appointed in 1851 to inquire into the operation of the law relative to newspaper stamps, is very decided in his opinion that the good publications put down the bad. " You are of opinion that the greater demand is toward the good papers, are you not ?"—" Yes." " The increase in circulation is the greatest, in your opinion, in the best papers?"—" Yes, decidedly." Further on, Mr. Heywood says :—" The bad publications are attempted, and they are carried on for a while under various methods; and after getting deeply into debt they are obliged at last to go out, and perhaps knock up the publisher at the same time." The following question put by Mr. Cobden, and the reply to it, are worth stating : " Is it the result of your twenty years' experience in this business that you have found that the objectionable publications are short-lived, and that those publications which are of the highest intellectual and moral quality have a tendency to increase in circulation ?"—" Yes."*

The newspaper press has undergone an expansion quite

---

* Mr. Baines, in his speech of April 10, 1861, quotes ' Chambers's Encyclopædia ' on the book trade, as giving the following classification of the circulation of periodicals :—

as extraordinary as that of the cheap literary periodicals. In an ably written article in the ' Westminster Review,' April, 1829, there is much information on the then condition of the metropolitan newspaper press. At that period there were six evening and seven morning papers, the former circulating 11,000 copies daily, and the latter 28,000, giving 39,000 as the full circulation of the daily London press. And this number is boasted of by the writer as being an increase of 5000 copies daily in seven years. Adding to these 110,000 copies of weekly papers issued on the Saturdays and Sundays, besides about 250 provincial papers, the circulation of which, except in a few cases, was not large, the writer, after consulting the latest stamp returns, computes the gross issue of the kingdom at 500,000 copies of newspapers weekly. And this,

Works of an improving tendency—monthly circulation 8,043,500
„   exciting, but not immoral   „   „   1,500,000
„   immoral and irreligious   „   under   80,000

Between 1850 and 1861 the issues of the Religious Tract Society had increased, from 11,090,259 tracts and books in the year, to 41,710,203, or 270 per cent. (Some further details as to similar publications will be found in Mr. H. Roberts's paper on " Pure and Instructive Literature for the Working Classes," in the Transactions of the Congrès International de Bienfaisance for 1862, vol. ii. p. 95.)

Since Mr. Baines's speech the development of periodical literature has been enormous. To quote one instance only, ' Good Words,' which was then only struggling for existence, sells now its 160,000 copies a month, besides about 8,000 volumes at the end of the year, or upwards of 1,900,000 in the twelvemonth.

The shilling magazines (now rivalled by the sixpenny ones) deserve a word of notice as having first introduced working men to this branch of literature. We could mention more than one London workshop in which one or the other is taken in and read aloud.

limited and trivial as it appears to us now, was at that time considered as exceeding anything on any other part of the globe, except in the United States of America.*

In the interval between 1832 and 1851, as will be seen by reference to the evidence of several of the witnesses examined before the Select Committee of that year to inquire into the operation of the newspaper stamp law, a considerable increase had taken place in the circulation of the London daily papers,—the 'Times' alone, according to Mr. Mowbray Morris, circulating nearly 39,000 daily; whilst Mr. W. H. Smith, the great newsagent of the Strand, estimated the aggregate daily issue of morning and evening London papers at 60,000. But so little were the most intelligent witnesses able yet to project themselves into the future, that Mr. Mowbray Morris, in answer to the question, " Is it your opinion that a penny newspaper would not succeed in England on account of the expense of bringing it out, the large machinery, and the necessity of large capital being employed on account of the expense of collecting the necessary news?" said: " I could not sepa- rate the one from the other ; the whole expenses of pro- ducing a good newspaper render it impossible to work at that price." On which reply take the following facts for comment. There are now, according to a parliamentary return, dated July, 1866, in England and Wales 1393 re-

---

* The figures quoted by Mr. Baines in his speech of April 10, 1861, differ somewhat widely from the above. He there reckons the total number of newspapers in the United Kingdom in 1831 at 295, of which 205 in England and Wales, and their total circulation at 38,807,055, of which 19,746,851 for the London ones.

gistered papers.* And not long ago one of these "impossible" penny papers of Mr. Mowbray Morris—the 'Daily Telegraph'—published a certified statement placing its daily issue at 138,700, thus giving for this one paper 823,200 per week, or 332,000 more than the whole newspaper press of Great Britain issued thirty-eight years ago.

We have few data for calculating the circulation of the other London daily papers, but taking the morning and evening 'Standard' and morning and evening 'Star' together at 900,000 a week, and the 'Times' and the rest of the high-priced dailies at 420,000 a week, we shall have a gross result of 2,118,000 as against 360,000 in 1851, to say nothing of the large circulations of daily papers published in the provinces, such as the 'Manchester

---

* The number in 1861 for the whole of the United Kingdom, according to Mr. Baines, was 1102, of which 819 in England and Wales; and the total circulation in 1860 of the London papers was 118,799,200.

The facts quoted by him as to provincial towns are no less remarkable.

In Manchester, in 1831, there were no daily papers, but four weekly ones, issuing not more than 12,000. In 1861 the total weekly issue in Manchester of daily and weekly papers was 346,000; the number of periodicals taken in, 200,000, besides the circulation of the London and provincial papers.

In Bolton, in 1831, there was one newspaper published, with a circulation of 1000; there were in 1861 two, with a circulation of 5000, besides a monthly journal circulating 2000.

In Birmingham there were in 1826 but two newsvendors, selling 7000 copies of newspapers and periodicals weekly; in 1861 there were over 300, besides booksellers dealing in periodicals, and the weekly sales were 83,200.

Such facts might be indefinitely multiplied.

Guardian,' 'Manchester Examiner,' 'Leeds Mercury,'
' Newcastle Chronicle,' and several other well-written and
widely-circulated daily journals, which exercise considerable influence on the public mind.*

Those who had doubts as to the experiment of the
cheap newspaper before it was fairly tried must be hard to
teach if by this time they have not discovered how ground-
less their fears were. There can be no question that in
every way our newspapers are better now than they were
in the days of monopoly, whatever room for improvement
may still remain. Notwithstanding the many sins and
shortcomings of the newspaper press, the working man of
to-day, with his broadsheet for a penny, is by its aid a man
of fuller information, better judgment, and wider sympathies than the workman of thirty years back, who had
to content himself with gossip and rumour, and whose
source of information as to public events was the well-
thumbed weekly newspaper of the public-house.† "I
think," writes a minister whose life has been devoted to
high Christian aims, "that the enormous increase of newspapers has been a great educational power,"—adding, in-

---

* The diffusion of political information amongst our masses is perhaps best judged of by the single fact that the total number of political
papers published this year (1867) in France is only 330,—*i. e.*, 35 more
than it was in the United Kingdom in 1831 ; whilst, as before stated,
England and Wales alone had in 1866 1393 such papers, or more than
four times the number of the French.

† " One bookseller tells me," writes a friend from Wolverhampton.
" that about fifteen years ago he sold 35 dozen weekly of Lloyd's publi
cations. These have all now disappeared, and a much more healthy
literature has taken its place. But the cheap daily press is revolution-
izing the literature of the country."

deed, these remarkable words : " and I also think that if
we could give men votes, they would read these newspapers with ten times more earnestness and ten times
more thought."

We have only to add that cheap literature has been
accompanied or followed, within the period under review,
by cheap science and cheap art, each of which would furnish a history, and an interesting one, of its own. The
writer of these lines well remembers the honest pride with
which a working man once told him that he had watched
the discharge of the pollen from the anther through a
penny Stanhope lens bought in the street, and described his
observations on fresh-water polyps (the finest of which, by
the way, he declared himself to have found in his own
water-butt—supplied, in the old days of unpurified water,
by the Southwark and Vauxhall Company). As respects
art, again, no reader remains to be reminded that engravings are now thrown in as mere adjuncts to the cheapest
literature, which would have fetched a price of their own
even after the ' Penny Magazine' had been started.

§ 6. *Recreations of the Working Class.*

One question remains to be considered in reference to
the results of improved legislation, both as respects the
facilities thereby given for harmless enjoyment and the
leisure for receiving it afforded to the working man. Not
to dwell at present on the public-house, we would not
venture to deny that the enjoyments of the working
classes are often baneful and degrading. We are aware
that the concert or 'harmonic meeting' is often made only

an incentive to debauchery; that the indecent *pose plastique* veils itself under a pretence of art, the filthy 'anatomical museum' under a pretence of science; that the 'penny gaff' has become almost proverbial as a school of vice; that the 'casino' is often little more than the ante-room to the brothel; that the example set in those respects by London is gradually spreading throughout all our towns. But not one of these forms of depraving pleasure, be it observed, is peculiar to the working man; wherever he resorts to them he is simply aping the example of other classes, claiming with them a sad fellowship of corruption and vice. The same may be said of the spread of betting habits among the working class,—a fact now greatly deplored by its most thoughtful members.

On the other hand, countervailing influences may almost always be brought to bear against those we have mentioned, when men know how to apply them. Read, for instance, in the 'Transactions' of the Social Science Association for 1860,* the paper of the energetic and popular vicar of St. Michael's, Derby, the Rev. J. Erskine Clarke, on 'The Working Man's Saturday Night, its Bane and its Antidote;' see his account of the 'Literary and Musical Entertainments' which have been so successful in the Potteries on the Monday, on the Saturday in Derby, and which, under the name of Penny Readings (given to them, we believe, first in Ipswich), have since then run all through England; of the village, local, and amateur bands which are brought together for the purpose, willing to perform for no other remuneration than " some slight

* Page 805.

refreshment during the evening." Such gatherings would have been literally impossible thirty-five years ago. The law, the conditions of labour, the habits of the people, would alike have prevented them.

But the popular interest in ' Penny Readings' is apt to flag after a few seasons. The one source of recreation which need never flag is music, especially when of a choral character. Although the taste for music has greatly diffused itself amongst all classes within the last thirty years, the opening of the working man's ear to its pleasures has been most marked. The consideration of that magnificent growth of popular musical teaching, which belongs exclusively to the period under review, might well have deserved to find a place in the pages we have devoted to the progress of education ; for we are well persuaded that music is one of the most powerful of all educational agents. But among all such agents, it enjoys one pre-eminent privilege, which, over and above its value as such, renders it, so to speak, the king of pleasures,—that of affording enjoyment to the absolutely ignorant. To the ignorant, the joys of science are absolutely shut out, as are those of literature properly so-called ; even form and colour require a certain education of the eye to be appreciated. Music alone, over and above all those treasures of enjoyment which it reserves for the trained ear and hand and voice, has charms for the child, even for the idiot. We do not therefore disparage it, when we treat of it rather as a pleasure than as an object of learning.

In recording here the names of those who have most contributed to train men to the fitting enjoyment of this

pleasure,—of Mr. Hullah, who first organized choral teaching on a large scale, obtained for it Government recognition and aid, and has latterly done so much to diffuse
a taste for the best music ; of Joseph Mainzer, who the
first boldly addressed himself, by means of a more moderate scale of fees for musical tuition, to a much lower
stratum in English society than Mr. Hullah had approached;
of Mr. Curwen, not indeed the originator of the tonic system, but the creator of the "Tonic-Sol-Fa" school of song,
the most popular of any ; of Mr. Martin, who by this
time has eclipsed the fame of his master, Mr. Hullah, as a
choral teacher,—space fails us to give even a summary
history of their efforts.   Confining ourselves, however, to
the Tonic-Sol-Fa system, as the one which more especially
addresses itself to the working class, we may say that in
the year 1862 returns were obtained of 94,371 pupils then
under instruction in the system ; that the total number of
such pupils (no returns being obtainable from a vast number of classes) was reckoned at 125,000, exclusively of the
many hundreds of thousands who had learned the system
and ceased to attend class ; that the yearly increase in such
number is from 5 to 10 per cent. ; that the addresses are
known of upwards of 1800 teachers.*   "You may notice,"
writes Mr. Curwen himself, " that nearly all our pupils
belong to the working class. . . . A number of our teachers,
especially in London and Glasgow, have engagements to
teach the schools of the middle class, and several of them
are the proprietors of such schools.   The universal testi-

* These figures seem all to include the colonial developments of the
system.

mony in these cases is, that the young ladies and young gentlemen, as they are called, are taught singing only with extreme difficulty and long patience. The disappointment and distress of a Tonic-Sol-Fa teacher (who has hitherto instructed Ragged schools, National schools, British schools, and ordinary evening classes), when he comes to a middle-class school, is something remarkable." *

" I do not at all agree," continues the respected writer, " with the writer in the ' Westminster,' who says that the majority of our working classes have no musical taste at all worth speaking of. It is true that they enjoy Christy minstrel songs, and German part-music, but it is also true that they appreciate the finest English glees and madrigals, that Handel calls forth an enthusiasm from the very depth of their souls, and that, although to a less extent, they are well able to appreciate the delicate musical feeling of Mo-zart and Mendelssohn. As far as my Tonic-Sol-Fa friends are concerned, I can easily prove the steady growth of this higher taste, by showing the increased sale of the best glees, madrigals, cantatas, and oratorios which I publish.†

---

* Compare this testimony with that of the School of Mines' Professors, *ante,* p. 164.

† The development of Tonic-Sol-Fa musical literature may be judged of by this fact, mentioned by Mr. Curwen in a paper which is briefly summarized in the Social Science Transactions for 1862, p. 357, that there had been purchased during the then past twelvemonth more than 450,000 penny sheets of Tonic-Sol-Fa music. Of late years publishers who possess no more than a trade interest in the matter have published more in the Tonic-Sol-Fa notation than Mr. Curwen himself.

Cheap music and musical literature, it should be observed, are also en-tirely a growth of the period under review. We have not space to sketch out here its history.

Quite recently, my class at Anderson's University, Glasgow, (who were chiefly working men) were listening with the greatest intentness to a fugue of Bach's, watching the treatment of subject and counter-subject, and showing by their eager looks during the performance, and their strong applause afterwards, that they fully understood the points to which I had drawn their attention, and thoroughly enjoyed the old Leipzig organist. And at the present moment we have Tonic-Sol-Fa string bands commencing to play, and that with a relish, Corelli, Pleyel, and Haydn."

Outside indeed of any musical school, wherever the price is low, working men now rank amongst the attendants at all popular concerts, even though the music should be of the most classical and severest character. Few London artisans of the highest class could perhaps be found at the present day who have not once in their lives listened to an Italian opera; a small minority have enjoyed it and repeated the experiment. Sacred music is, however, that which in general the working men best appreciate, helping efficiently other classes to appreciate it in turn; since it is a well-known fact that almost all large musical choirs in the provinces—those of Glasgow, Bradford, Manchester, etc., and even, though to a less extent, of London,—are in great measure composed of working men and women. The Bradford choir, which Mr. Costa, after conducting with it a performance of the Messiah, declared to be the best he had ever heard, consists, we are told, entirely of factory hands.* In Manchester, we are told by Mr. Curwen,

---

* See Mr. Baker's paper on the "Physical Effects of Diminished Labour," Social Science Transactions for 1859, p. 567.

"they call Mr. Hallé's well-trained and famous choir ' Charles Hallé's mill-girls.' "

For the young and strong, however, there are recreations more attractive, and physically more important, than music. No one can have overlooked of late years the revival, even amongst our town population, of healthy games and athletic exercises. The days are gone when skittles were well nigh the only game involving any amount of strength which was known to the working man. The spread of cricket has been most marked. The London co-operative gilders, when fairly afloat, shortened for themselves their Saturday labour in order to play cricket, and found themselves pecuniary gainers by the change. The interest excited by the Oxford and Cambridge boat-race is on the whole an exceedingly healthy one, and by diffusing the taste for rowing has probably saved many a young London working man from gross forms of temptation. Boating clubs, as well as cricket clubs, are now almost sure to spring up, wherever working men are brought together in any number within reach of a river.* Quoits, German gymnastic or ' Turner' exercises are also spreading, and afford the hope that another generation or two may see grow up a town population of far better *physique* than the existing one.

Lastly, we cannot but allude to those ' excursions,' so popular in our manufacturing districts especially, which have in great measure superseded the ' wakes,' ' fairs,' ' feasts,' etc., formerly the only means of enjoyment for the worker outside of his own town. Of the Lancashire wakes, at

* *E.g.* at the London Working Men's College, which boasts of both.

one time very numerous, Eccles wake alone retains much popularity. In Yorkshire, indeed, the feasts are said to have been more frequented of late years, and to give rise still to much disorder. But even from thence, how many working men, who formerly had never a chance of seeing London or the sea, and consequently were compelled to seek their diversion in such scenes, will now save their money for a trip to some distant part of the country, to the Metropolis, nay, even for a visit to a foreign country, to a Paris exhibition !*

The most interesting of such excursions, however, are

* Whilst these lines were being finally prepared for the press, we received a batch of papers relating to 'Working Men's Excursions to the Paris Exhibition, organized by the Metropolitan District Association of Working Men's Clubs and Institutes,'—"fare to Paris and back, with one week's lodging, including extras, 30s.; do. with meat breakfast and superior accommodation, 44s. 6d." The following passages from a circular sent by the Committee to large employers may be quoted:—

"At the meetings which have been held at this office, facts of very great interest have been adduced which tend to show that for want of a knowledge of some details in construction and finish, purchases to a vast extent are made on the Continent, in numerous branches of industry, which would otherwise be made in England. Articles which, as regards substantial workmanship, can be made better in England, are purchased in France for the English market, because of some superiority in finish and appearance. It has been stated that in many cases of this kind, an intelligent artisan would be able by a visit to exhibitions like that at Paris and to the French establishments (many of which are now open to foreign visitors), to understand in what points our workmanship was deficient, and how to remedy that deficiency. The advantage to be derived by a superior workman from the inspection of new designs, processes, mechanical inventions, in the cultivation of his taste, and in the industrial information he would thus obtain, is so obvious, as hardly to require mention."

those of whole establishments at a time. There is now scarcely one of our great houses of business in any trade or business which does not give its yearly treat—'way-goose,' 'bean-feast,' etc.—to its workpeople, generally at some country place of resort. It is the great event of the year,—looked forward to from the morrow of the last preceding one. Every co-operative workshop has one almost as a matter of course. The excursions of the London gilders form an Odyssey already. At the London Working Men's College, again, though the general 'college' excursion is a somewhat tame affair, and seldom ventures out of call of 'Big Ben,' yet when autumn arrives, an ever-increasing number of students scatter themselves in small bands, sometimes of only two or three, sometimes of seven or eight, far and wide over the country, crossing even the Channel now and then, bringing back with them, with invigorated health, a store of new memories and new ideas, and a power of assimilation to other classes which could never have been acquired within the four walls of the workshop.

Apart, however, from all forms of social enjoyment, from the most refined to the most boisterous, we must bestow a word on that very hopeful, and at the same time very curious, revelation of the varied modes in which the English artisan finds solitary recreation from his toil, which has been supplied of late years by the so-called ' Industrial Exhibitions,'—already, be it remembered, a recognized institution of the country, since they have obtained the protection of a special law.*

* See *ante*, p. 62.

In the ordinary occupations of the workshop, numbers of men clearly find that they possess tastes and aptitudes not satisfied by the routine tasks in which they are regularly engaged. Don Quixote was convinced that had he not been called to the relief of distressed damsels, and the general redressing of wrongs, he would have excelled in making mousetraps and birdcages. As it was with the illustrious Manchegan, so it is with the men of our factories and workshops. Of the poets amongst them nothing need be said ; neither the pains of poverty nor the drudgery of labour can still their voices ; but until these industrial exhibitions opened their doors, it was scarcely suspected how much of the leisure of working men was given to pursuits which, if they answered no higher end, preserved those who followed them from the contamination and wasteful extravagance of the public-house. We may be somehow reminded of a masquerade when we find high art cultivated by butchers and engineers, shoemakers, tailors, and hatters figuring away as constructors of watches, clocks, and steam-engines.* Still, whether the result be that of exhibiting the worker's proficiency in his own trade, his capacity of producing what in the old guild days would have been technically termed a master-piece, or his power of mastering perfection in some branch of labour more or less alien to the sphere of his daily toil, it must be confessed that these exhibitions have developed a wonderful amount

* The " Art Workmen's Exhibition" in Manchester was not open to these strictures, but was unfortunately not a pecuniary success.

It may be pointed out that ' Industrial Exhibitions ' are expressly enumerated among the purposes for which the " Hall of Arts and Sciences" is authorized to be used.

of latent powers in the working class, not only of invention and ingenuity, but still more of thoughtful perseverance, and of spontaneous adaptation to new conditions of toil.

Take things all in all, we believe that the progress of the working man has been greater in nothing during the last thirty-five years than in learning to enjoy harmless, wholesome, and rational forms of recreation.

PART V.

WHAT THE WORKING CLASSES HAVE DONE WITHOUT THE LAW.

WE have seen a little of what the working men have done since 1832, the law favouring them. Something must now be shown of what they have been able to do, the law not favouring them, or at least affording them but the most niggardly measure of protection in their undertakings.

§ I. *Trade Societies.**

Prominent among such are, of course, the Trade Societies. Without entering into any discussion as to the

---

* The principal sources from which the following details are taken are:—The Report of the Trades' Societies' Committee of the Social Science Association, 1860; the 'United Kingdom first annual Trades' Directory for 1861' (not, we believe, continued); the 'Report of the Conference of Trades' Delegates of the United Kingdom, held in the Temperance Hall, Townhead Street, Sheffield, on July 17, 1866, and four following days;' the 'Minutes of Proceedings of the United Kingdom Alliance of Organized Trades' Conference at Manchester, Jan. 1, 2, 3, and 4, 1867'; the 'Report of the Trades' Conference, held at St. Martin's Hall, on March 5, 6, 7, and 8, 1867;' and the 'Minutes of Evi-

origin of these bodies, we may say that in 1832 their objects generally were to keep up wages and limit the influx of apprentices. Now, however, they frequently support their members in sickness, pay burial fees in case of death, assist those who are out of work, and, in some cases, give considerable sums to such of their members as are incapacitated by accident, as well as annual payments to such as are unfitted for labour by age.

The largest individual Trade Society is reckoned to be that of the "Amalgamated Society of Engineers, Machinists, Millwrights, and Pattern-makers,"* founded in 1851. This Society, the year before the great lock-out, which occurred in 1852, had 11,829 members, and a balance in cash of £21,705. 4s. 11½d. That fierce fight with the employers brought the number of members down to 9737, and the reserve fund to £17,812 in 1853. At that time it was thought that trade unionism had received its death-blow. This calculation was premature. Last year this giant Society numbered 30,984 members, with an income of £75,672. 6s. 2d., and a clear balance in hand of £115,357. 13s. 10½d. It had 229 branches in England and Wales, 32 in Scotland, 11 in Ireland, 6 in Australia, 2 in New Zealand, 5 in Canada, 1 in Malta, 8 in the

dence before the Royal Commission appointed to inquire into the Trades' Unions and other Associations,' up to April 30, 1867.

* According to the 'Report of the Trades' Conference, held in St. Martin's Hall, on March 5, 6, 7, and 8, 1867,' the 'Miners' National Association' now numbers 36,000 members, and has thus shot ahead of the Amalgamated Engineers. But the constitution of this body is much looser than that of the Amalgamated Engineers; it is only a federation of distinct societies.

United States, 1 in France (total 295). The total amount expended by it had been, during 15 years :—

For " donation," *i. e.* assistance to those out of work,
   including strikes £279,840
For sick benefit. 115,127
Superannuation. 26,935
Accidents, etc. 12,400
Funeral benefits 34,600
During 13 years for assistance to other trades . . 9,415
Benevolent grants (12 years) 6,400

                 £484,717

It is growing still, for Mr. William Allan, the secretary, on his examination before the Trades' Unions Commission, stated (19th March, 1867) that it had now 33,599 members, in 308 branches.

The " Amalgamated Society of Carpenters and Joiners" (a history of which has been given by Professor Beesly in the ' Fortnightly Review') affords another instance of these vast trade organizations. Much younger than that of the Engineers, having been established in 1860, it has yet grown rapidly, as is shown by the following table, given in its seventh annual report :—

	Branches.	Members.	Funds in hand.
Dec. 1860 . .	20 . .	618 . .	£321. 3s. 2½d.
„ 1861 . .	32 . .	650 . .	593 12 0½
„ 1862 . .	38 . .	949 . .	849 8 10
„ 1863 . .	53 . .	1718 . .	2,042 11 3
„ 1864 . .	81 . .	3279 . .	4,566 10 0½
„ 1865 . .	134 . .	5670 . .	8,320 13 7
„ 1866 . .	187 . .	8002 . .	13,052 4 3½

the last twelvemonth, it will be observed, showing an

increase on the previous one of no less than 53 branches, 2332 members, and £4731. 10s. 3½d.* Its expenditure during the last twelvemonth had been—

		Per member.
For Privileges	£2,524 17s. 9d.	or 6s. 3¾d.
Sick benefit	2,246 1 2	or 5 7¼
Donations and travelling expenses .	1,334 10 8½	or 3 4
Tool benefits	362 0 9	or 0 11
Funerals	423 10 0	or 1 0¾
Accident benefits	360 0 0	or 0 10¾
Grants from contingent fund . .	379 18 2	or 0 11½

Total . . . £11,808 9 0½

Another and much older society in the same trade, the "Operative House Carpenters' and Joiners' Society," which has been established forty years, was stated by its Secretary, Mr. Last, on his late examination before the Trades' Unions Commission (9th April, 1867), to have 10,000 members, 150 branches, and to have admitted 2504 new members during the past year.

The "Friendly Society of Operative Masons" was in like manner stated by its Secretary, Mr. Richard Harnott, (March 26th, 1867,) to have had in November, 1866, 17,762 members, 278 branches, an income (1865–6) of £17,746.4s. 11½d., and a general fund of £12,334.0s.8½d. in hand.

The "Operative Bricklayers' Society" had in December last 5700 members (being an increase of about 700 in a twelvemonth), 96 branches, an income (1865–6) of

* In March, 1867, according to Mr. R. Applegarth, the secretary, on his examination before the Trades' Unions Commission (18th March, 1867), it had 190 branches, and 8261 members.

about £2700, and a fund in hand (December, 1866) of about £3200 (Evidence of Mr. Edwin Coulson, Secretary, 2nd April, 1867).

Another bricklayers' society, the "Friendly Society of Operative Bricklayers," of Sheffield, has 5254 members, an income (1866) of £5964. 5s. 2½d., and a fund in hand of £3649. 15s. 8d., by its last report (Evidence of Mr. George Housley, Secretary, 9th April, 1867).

The 'National Association of Plasterers' was stated by its Secretary, Mr. Charles Williams, (2nd April, 1857,) to have 8000 members, £1200 a-year income, and a general fund of about £2000.

Other societies of 5000 members and upwards, represented at the Sheffield Conference of Trades' Delegates last year, or the Manchester and London Conferences of the present year, are :—

The Amalgamated Tailors of England (Manchester), 11,060 members ;

The Friendly Society of Ironfounders of England, Ireland, and Wales, 10,669 members ;

The Boiler-makers and Iron Ship-builders, 9000 ;

The Tailors' Protective Association (London), 7000 ;

The East Lancashire Power Loom Weavers, 6000 ;

The Northern Association of Cotton Spinners, 6000 ;

The Amalgamated Iron Workers, 5000 ;

The Associated Carpenters and Joiners of Scotland, 5000 ;

The Power Loom Weavers (Blackburn) 5000.

Another large and interesting body is the " National Association of Coal-mine and Ironstone Miners of Great

Britain," or " Miners' National Association," the ' Transactions' of whose " General Conference" at Leeds in November, 1863, form a volume of 147 pages, published in
London (Longmans) and Leeds. No more valuable document can be consulted as to the spirit of self-help which
is stirring amongst our working classes. The districts represented were Northumberland and Durham, Middles-
borough-on-Tees, Scotland, West Yorkshire, South Yorkshire, Wigan, East Worcestershire and South Staffordshire
(West of Dudley), South Staffordshire, North Staffordshire, West Bromwich, Worsley, Farnworth and Kearsley,
South Wales, North Wales, Willenhall and Wednesbury,
and Darlaston. Among the officers elected was even a
chaplain, the Rev. J. H. Stephens, and amongst other
resolutions passed was one " That the Executive be empowered to make levies from the members to carry
on the business of the Association; the sum in hand
at one time never to be less than £100 or more than
£1000." This body, as already observed, is in the nature
of a federation of trade-societies, and its present figure of
36,000 members (which we are assured is far within the
mark) includes bodies of considerable magnitude in themselves, such as the " South Yorkshire Miners' Association "
and the "Derbyshire and Nottinghamshire Miners," both
represented at the Manchester Conference, the one for
6000, the other for 7000 members.

Again, the ' Engine-Drivers' and Firemen's United Society,' a body which has lately risen into prominence,
numbers now 64 branches, about 15,000 men, and has
over £1800 a-year income.

The eighteen bodies above enumerated will be found alone to comprise 201,690 members, and besides these many large societies exist, which were represented at none of the Conferences referred to, nor have yet come forward for examination before the Trades' Unions Commission. At least 100,000 men belonging to the smaller societies were represented at one or other of those Conferences; and yet the great bulk of these smaller bodies must have remained unrepresented throughout. No temptation to exaggerate the number of members existed, since the expenses of such Conferences are defrayed by a capitation levy.* The trade-society men themselves estimate their number at 700,000; we shall certainly be under the mark if we reckon them at 500,000.†

But even the amalgamated societies themselves do not

---

* Hence frequent discrepancy between the numbers given in at the Conferences and those deposed to before the Commission. The fact is, that at the Conferences delegates only take credit for paying members, and a vast number of members do not pay if they can help it. But these bad paymasters have not the less to be taken account of in estimating the strength of the movement.

† It is to be regretted that the ' United Kingdom Trades' Union Directory,' published in 1861, has not been continued. This contains a list of Trade-Societies, in the alphabetical order of the towns to which they belong, giving their club-houses, with the names of their secretaries, and times of meeting, where these can be ascertained; but without statistical details. 408 towns are enumerated, and the list was certainly far from complete, even at the time. It is not, however, possible in many cases to distinguish from it between distinct local societies and mere branches. A supplement, however, introduces us to a few important societies not named in other publications, *e.g.* the " Amalgamated Society of Tobacco Manufacturers," with 31 branches in England, 11 in Scotland, and 13 in Ireland.

give a measure of the power of organization, the capacity for social action, manifested by the working man in this his own peculiar province. Many towns have local associations, formed of distinct societies. Such are the London Trades' Council, representing 60,000 men; the Sheffield "Association of Organized Trades," comprising 5000 men,* and 33 trades; the "Amalgamated Trades of Preston," the "Associated Trades of Hyde," the "Association of Organized Trades of Derby," the "Bristol Associated Trades," the "Halifax Trades' Council," the "Organized Trades of Nottingham," the "Tailors, Shoemakers, Bricklayers and Plasterers" of Barrow-on-Furness, the "United Trades Protection Association" of Liverpool, the "United Trades of Warrington," the "Wolverhampton Trades' Council,"—all of them represented at the Sheffield Conference. Some of these bodies are of old standing; thus we have before us the twelfth annual report, for 1857-8, of the "Liverpool Trades' Guardian Association," which we presume to be the same as the present "United Trades Protection Association of Liverpool" above noticed. Another old-established body of the same description, not represented at the earlier Conferences, the "Glasgow Council of United Trades" (6000 members), which rendered efficient service to the Trade Societies' Committee of the Social Science Association in its investigations, made its appearance in St. Martin's Hall with ten others, mostly named already, but including the important "Manchester and Salford Trades' Council" (10,000 members).

These Conferences, whether of single trades as a whole,

* 6000, according to the Report of the London Conference.

or of many trades together, which are held, sometimes at stated intervals, sometimes only on specific occasions, are no less interesting than their standing organizations. Besides the Miners' Conference above referred to, the report of the Committee on Trades' Societies of the Social Science Association above quoted tells us of a Conference of Shipwrights which met in London from the 23rd to the 27th June, 1858, to form the " United Kingdom Amalgamated Society of Shipwrights," at which fifty-four delegates attended from thirty-five ports, representing in all 11,766 members. The " Flint Glass Makers' Friendly Society's " rules were revised at a Conference held in June, 1858. Still more remarkable, however, were the three general Conferences above mentioned ; at Sheffield (July, 1866), where accredited delegates attended for societies comprising from 180,000 to 200,000 men, and where a " National Association of Organized Trades," at present termed the " United Kingdom Alliance of Organized Trades " was founded ; at Manchester (January, 1867), held by the last named body, at which 59,750 men were represented ; the Trades' Conference in St. Martin's Hall (March, 1867), at which upwards of 192,000 were represented ; the figures, as above pointed out, being probably in general rather below than above the mark. Whether the general federation of the " United Kingdom Alliance of Organized Trades " will be able to hold its ground (similar attempts in former years having failed), remains to be seen. Compared with the figures with which we have been dealing, it is not yet of great importance, since by February 13, as we learn from the preface to its rules, just published, it comprised only 68 trades, and 61,203 members for whom entrance fee had been paid.   Still the fact remains that about 1 in 10 of the 5 to 700,000 society men of this country belongs by this time to a larger federation embracing the body of which he is by his trade a member.   Nor can we overlook a still further development of the Trade Society's work.   At the Sheffield Conference, above mentioned, the " International Association of Working Men," comprising 12,000 members, was represented by two delegates ; and a " Workmen's Congress " was held in Geneva (November, 1866), at which the English delegates took a decided lead, gave form to the proceedings, and carried most of the resolutions proposed by them, showing themselves the most practical and business-like group in the strange assembly ; at which the French in turn, enervated by fifteen years of despotism, gave evidence of having sunk below the level of capacity for business of the other Continental workmen.

In the face of the figures we have quoted, of the publications we have referred to, of the evidence that has been given before the Trades' Unions' Commission, the accusation of secrecy so commonly launched of old against these bodies, —and no doubt justified whilst the law proscribed them,— must (the Sheffield case, indeed, remaining in suspense) disappear.   It is difficult for the delegates from 100,000 or 200,000 men to conspire secretly at any time ; certainly not when they meet in conference at public rooms and halls under the eye of newspaper reporters, and publish their proceedings afterwards to the whole world.   Nor can anything be franker than the testimony of the officers of these societies before the Commission. The Secretary of the Amalgamated Engineers has brought forward the unprinted bye-laws which are read to candidates for admission, and whether these may be considered bad or good political economy, they have certainly nothing criminal about them. The details given by him and others relating to the constitution of the societies are most copious, as well as most interesting. It is true that all this power of organization, instead of being accepted as an evidence of social development, is treated by some only as a cause of alarm to other classes. " I shall not refer to the subject of strikes," said Mr. Lowe, in his speech of May 3, 1865, on Mr. Baines's motion for Reform, " but it is, I contend, impossible to believe that the same machinery which is at present brought into play in connection with strikes, would not be applied by the working classes to political purposes. Once give the men votes, and the machinery is ready to launch those votes in one compact mass *upon the institutions and property of the country.*" As if the Amalgamated Society of Engineers, with its 30,000 members, which, in 1865, spent £14,070. 4s. 9d. in " donations, sending members to situations, and beds for non-free members ;" £13,785. 14s. 9d. for " sick benefit, stewards, and medical certificates;" £5184. 17s. 4d. for "superannuation benefit;" £4887 6s. for " funeral ;" £1860 for " accidents," etc. were not an " institution " ! As if the working man's labour were not as truly " property " as that capital which it enables to accumulate ! As if it were likely that the great Trade Societies should have accumulated their capitals of thousands of pounds,—tens of thousands,—nay, in the case of the Engineers over £100,000 —invested them, as many of them have, in Post-Office Savings-Banks at $2\frac{1}{2}$ per cent.; rendered tens of thousands of widows, and of sick men, of the aged and disabled, dependent upon those funds, in order to " launch " votes in a compact mass at institutions or at property ! The calumny is one so preposterous that it surely needed an unreformed House of Commons to listen to it, and it goes far to justify the Trade Societies in claiming such a measure of political reform as will render the like impossible henceforth to be uttered.*

We do not mean to say that Trade Societies always make a good use of their money—what class of men, nay, what individual, always does? We do not mean to deny that the possession of a large accumulated fund may often tempt a society to a strike ; does not many a man make ducks and drakes of his money when he has too much of it ? We do not say that strikes are always wise or successful—any more than lock-outs. Both we look upon as public nuisances, and generally damaging to both parties engaged ; for fighting is generally folly, and costs

---

* As a matter of fact, the Trade Societies of London especially, instead of being ready to be launched " in a compact mass " at anything at all, are at present torn to pieces by a dire internal feud between the rival organizations of the " London Trades' Council " (more or less represented by the ' Commonwealth ' newspaper), and the " Working Men's Association " (whose organ is the ' Beehive '). The former body, although represented at the Sheffield Conference, absolutely refused to take part in the proceedings of the one in St. Martin's Hall, which had been convoked by its rival.

more than it earns. We do not pretend to dispute that trade-society rules may often sanction or even enjoin mischievous or unjust practices; are employers always actuated by unerring wisdom and the purest benevolence in their dealings with their customers? In the present state of English society, however, we cannot wish that such bodies should not exist; we believe that the evils which they produce—and they are often undoubtedly great—are outweighed by the advantages which they confer on the worker, and through him on society. Some of these we will briefly enumerate.

The number of Trade Societies which are connected with ordinary benefit purposes is very great. The figures above given for the Amalgamated Societies of Engineers and Carpenters may give an idea of the extent to which such bodies perform the work of an ordinary Friendly Society. Generally speaking, one contribution covers all the objects of the society. In other cases there are separate funds, and even without actual separation the payment for either class of purposes may be optional; as in the "Friendly Society of Operative Masons," in which, to belong to the sick fund, a man pays $3\frac{1}{2}d$. a week more than to belong to the trade fund only. The payments for Friendly Society purposes may altogether exceed those for trade purposes; as in the "Friendly Society of Operative Bricklayers of Sheffield," where out of a yearly expenditure of £4500, about £2800 go to "death" and "accident" benefits, though there is not even a sick fund; and in the "Manchester Operative House-Painters' Alliance," where (in the parent society) £24 are paid for strikes, to £199 for funerals, accidents, and other benefits.*

The list of benefits varies greatly,† but they include generally the cases of sickness, accident, and superannuation,—sometimes emigration, or insurance of tools; besides travelling and ordinary want of work, which last, it will be remembered, are purposes not recognized as provident by the Friendly Societies' Acts. The whole of these contributions must be considered as acting in diminution of the poor-rates and of the burthens on voluntary charity.‡ Many of the societies, indeed, subscribe directly to various charities; the Amalgamated Society of Carpenters and Joiners has even started a life-boat fund. The ' South Yorkshire Miners' Association,' it was lately stated by Mr. Normansell, its secretary, at a dinner at Dodworth, the second day after the Oaks Colliery Explosion, "were able to send their trustees to the bank for £1500 to supply the wants of the poor widows and orphans who were bereaved by that catastrophe. And now they were paying not less than £50 a week towards the widows and children of this district, . . . and they meant to keep up the £50 a week payments. Surely," he added, with a pardonable pride,

* Evidence of Mr. William Macdonald, Secretary, 9th April, 1867.

† See, for instance, in the Trades Societies' Report of the Social Science Association, 1860, pp. 144–45, a tabulated list of societies, with the benefits allowed by them.

‡ "The unions do more than merely raise the wages, they are a great benefit in this respect, that they are the means, I believe, by their sick funds, by their accident funds, by their death funds, by their funds for supporting men when out of employment, of keeping men off the poor-rates." (Lord Elcho's speech at Dalkeith, ' Times,' Jan. 29, 1867.)

" £50 a week would not break the back of 7000 members."

But in addition to mere appliances for the relief of their members, many Trade Societies have reading-rooms for the use of members, or publish circulars, or even newspapers. "In connection with the Typographical Societies in large towns," says Mr. J. W. Crompton in a report on Printers' Strikes and Trades Unions since January, 1845, "there are generally libraries and institutes. . . . In the circulars published monthly by the Provincial Typographical Association, any case of fraud, or attempted imposition, or other unworthiness committed by a member, is published to the entire trade. The Scottish Typographical Association also publish a monthly circular, and a Journal of Typographic Art is published in London."* The London Consolidated Society of Bookbinders has issued since 1850 the instructive 'Bookbinders' Trade Circular.' The Chain-makers have their 'Chainmakers' Journal and Trades' Circular.' The Potters have a 'Weekly Journal,' price one halfpenny, with a circulation of 2000.† The 'Engine-Drivers and Firemen's Society' has since July 14, 1866, published the 'Train,' a weekly journal of no inconsiderable ability, which may be had at every railway book-stall. Again, the 'Amalgamated Society of Engineers' has repeatedly given prizes for Essays on subjects connected with its business. The 'Manchester Operative House-painters' Alliance' gave £5 to the 'Art Workmen's Exhibition.'

Again, it should be observed that Trade Societies are

* Report of Social Science Committee on Trades' Societies, p. 90.
† Report, p. 28.

very generally feeling their way towards co-operation; and though their attempts in this way have been rarely successful, owing perhaps chiefly to their inability to realize the conditions of business from the employer's point of view, they may point with pride, amongst other instances, to the "Union Wheel" of the Sheffield grinders, which, from Dr. J. C. Hall's paper on the "Effects of Sheffield Trades on Life and Health," read before the Social Science Association in 1865,* appears to reckon second only to that of Messrs. Rodgers and Sons as respects the average age at death of the workers (49 at the latter, 46 at the former, whilst at other wheels it falls from 43 to $38\frac{1}{2}$). "Both these wheels," says Dr. Hall, "are first-class, and, . . . as a rule, it is only the more prudent and better class of grinders who belong to such provident societies." At the Sheffield Conference of Trades' Delegates last year, a resolution was passed "That this Conference recommend every trade represented to encourage, and if possible adopt, the principles of co-operation, with a view of enabling working men to obtain a more equal share of the benefits resulting from their labours." The co-operation referred to, we need hardly observe, is co-operation in production,—that form of co-operation of which Mr. J. S. Mill has said, in his evidence before Mr. Slaney's Committee of 1850 on the Savings and Investments of the Middle and Working Classes:—"I think there is no way in which the working classes can make so beneficial a use of their savings, both to themselves and to society, as by the formation of associations to carry on the business with which they are

---

* Transactions, p. 382; see p. 396.

acquainted, and in which they are themselves engaged as workpeople." Co-operative Stores have, however, been also largely promoted by Trade Societies, especially those of trades which are cursed with the truck system, as mining and the iron trades.*

The training in self-government is, however, we venture to think, the most important result produced by the Trade Society, and one which no other form of organization as yet evolved among the working classes can develope on so large a scale. No greater mistake can be made than, as journalists and politicians are apt to do, to treat the mass of members of Trade Societies as dupes, idlers, drunkards, or incapables,—their leaders as knaves,—strikes for higher wages as their common object. The more these societies are examined, the more apparent it will be that they represent almost invariably the bulk of the able, industrious, and provident workmen in each trade; that they are habitually well governed† by men fairly elected by the members as the most trustworthy,‡ respectable, and intelligent amongst

---

* "I can assure you," writes the President of the Amalgamated Ironworkers' Association, "that no trade has been cursed by the blighting influence of the truck-shop more than the Ironworkers'; but in many places the truck-shop has disappeared, and co-operative stores have taken its place."

† Where the men in a trade generally are given to drink, or any malpractice, of course the society men will not be free from such tendencies. But what we have said above as to the choice of officers is strikingly illustrated by a fact within our knowledge, viz. that in a Sunderland Trade Society a member was elected secretary within a fortnight after joining, simply because he was a sober man.

‡ A friend, a member of the Bar (at one time secretary to the committee of a Conservative candidate for the City of London), who has been

them; that they prevent far more strikes than they encourage.

No Trade Society could maintain itself, of which the members were not habitually at work, and sufficiently thrifty to put by something for their contributions; of which the leaders were not careful to keep their men at work as far as possible, honest enough and judicious enough themselves to be able to reckon in turn on the punctual payment by others of the moneys required to carry on the operations of the society.

Employers often complain of the difficulty of dealing with working men, whilst nevertheless they have in their hands the terrible argument of dismissal, whilst their dealings are confined to a few dozens, hundreds, very rarely thousands of workmen. How much more difficult must it be for the officers of Trade Societies to deal with those same working men, when numbering as many thousands often as a large establishment might employ hundreds, where they can use no other arguments than those of their

much connected with the working class, writes thus on the subject of trade societies:—" Though a Tory in politics, I am a strong supporter of trade unions, and think that every member of a union ought to have a vote as such, precisely the same as the members of the trade-guilds had in former years, and the members of the City companies (which originally were nothing but Trade Unions) have now. . . . I believe the respectable working man would like it better than any other enfranchisement, and we should obtain the cream of the working classes. According to the rules of Trade Unions a man is liable to fine and even expulsion if not steady, sober, honest, etc., so that it would be impossible that any man of disreputable character could have a vote as a Trade Unionist. A franchise of this kind would be far better than a brick and mortar one."

own honesty, ability, good sense, and good temper! Sometimes the temporary leaders of a Trade Society may be hotheaded and unwise; but the permanent officers will almost invariably be found picked men of their kind,—now subtle, imperturbable diplomats, now men of the worthiest and most sterling character. An examination of the accounts of the leading societies will show that their business is managed with great economy. If any charge can be brought against their management, it is that they cost too little, not too much; and if those who take money for public services are to be denounced as "vampires," it may be said that the Trade Society vampire is the most ill-used creature of that species in existence.*

A strike is as much a calamity to a Trade Society as it is to any one else. It is in time of peace, when work is plentiful and wages high, that the society flourishes; the immediate effect of a strike is necessarily to deplete its coffers and circumscribe its resources. The provisions as to strikes which occur in trade society rules show clearly that they are viewed only as necessary evils. "When a strike for an advance of wages," say the Operative Masons, "is contemplated by any lodge, the secretary is to report

* Mr. Odger, well known as secretary of the London Trades' Council, receives for his services to that body 2s. 6d. per week. In the Amalgamated Society of Engineers, "the highest salary that is paid to a branch secretary is £10. 4s. a year, and he must have 300 members before he can get that amount, and it comes down to as low as 25s." (Mr. W. Allan's Evidence, *ubi supra*.) In the Bricklayers' Society, Mr. Thomas Connolly, examined before the Commission, April 2, 1867, "had only 30s. a quarter for keeping the accounts of from 200 to 300 men, which just amounts to paying a man a farthing an hour for all the time it is necessary for him to devote to it."

the same to the central committee, showing the number that would be out, the number of payable members, the state of trade, and the position of the society in the neighbourhood, also the number of members belonging to such lodge that voted for and against the application being made. The secretary to summon each member of the lodge who may reside within three miles of the lodge-house to discuss the application; votes to be taken by ballot; majority to be binding; no proxies allowed."

The Coachmakers say : "No shop or town shall be allowed to turn out on their own responsibility; but, in the event of any oppression or dispute, the secretary of such town, in conjunction with the members, shall furnish the executive committee with all the particulars of such grievance, who shall determine whether it be expedient to summon delegates; and if found necessary to do so, the executive committee shall send one delegate, and the town secretary where the grievance takes place shall summon one delegate from each of the two nearest relieving towns. Should the delegates fail to settle the matter amicably, they shall represent the case to the executive committee, who shall determine whether it be necessary to call the men out or not; and if two grievances at once, the executive committe shall decide which shall have the preference; and when it is practicable, only one strike be allowed to take place at one time."

The Amalgamated Society of Carpenters and Joiners head their monthly report with a reminder to members of the following resolution :—"That in the event of the members of any branch of this society being desirous of soliciting their employers for any new privilege, they must first forward to the council full particulars of the privilege required. The council will immediately consider the same, and, if circumstances warrant, grant the application. But should the employers fail to comply with the request made, the branch so applying must again consult the council as to their future course. And under no circumstances will any branch be allowed to strike without first obtaining the sanction of the council, whether it be for a new privilege, or against an encroachment on existing ones."

Surely it is impossible to surround a declaration of war with more precautions and formalities. Would to God it were as difficult for an English Ministry to involve the empire in hostilities as it generally is for a Trade Society to enter upon a strike! Let it be observed, moreover, that strikes are expressly discountenanced by many Trade Societies in their rules; that one of them (the Smiths) boasts of being the "Original Anti-strike Society;" and literally every one which can do so, of the length of time during which it has carried on its operations without striking.* "The executive council does all it possibly can to prevent any strike," says the secretary of the Amalgamated Engineers; "we endeavour at all times to prevent strikes. It is the very last thing that we would think of encouraging."† And the Secretary to the Operative Plasterers

---

* "I do not remember a strike in our society," said Mr. W. Macdonald of his own society of 400 members, the "parent society" of the "Manchester Operative House-painters' Alliance." (Evidence, *ubi supra.*)

† Evidence, *ubi supra.*

showed that their Executive Council had positively stopped a strike by supplying other men in place of the strikers.*

But the most remarkable evidence on this subject is afforded by the proceedings of the Sheffield Conference. A resolution having been proposed by Mr. Odger, to the effect that the various Trade Societies of the United Kingdom should be invited to join the proposed amalgamated society of all the trades, "for the purpose of resisting lock-outs in any trade so connected, and in rendering pecuniary and moral support to such branches as are necessitated to seek the same," several amendments were proposed, in effect for the purpose of empowering the association to aid strikes, but were withdrawn, or rejected by large majorities, the vice-chairman saying : "You will observe that we came here not to form a trades' combination for the advancement of wages either one way or the other, but to resist those great evils of lock-outs, and to discou rage strikes." "If they led trades to believe," said another speaker, "that they would get the support of the trades of the country on all occasions of strike, strikes would be precipitated by the action of this organization, and it would be a complete failure in a short time."†

Conferences like the Sheffield one, at which working men belonging to Trade Societies are represented by the hundred thousand, and the very object of which is to draw

---

* Evidence, *ubi supra.*

† Eventually, at the Manchester Conference, the second rule of the "United Kingdom Alliance of United Trades" was adopted in the following form :—"Its object shall be to render pecuniary aid and moral support to all trades in connection with the Alliance who may be exposed to the evils resulting from lock-outs."

their mutual organization closer, are of themselves sufficient proof that the working men at least must consider the Trade Society beneficial to their own class. Let us see in a few instances what they claim to have, or what their friends claim them to have achieved by its means. "It is said," we read in a speech by Lord Elcho, at Dalkeith,* "that the unions led to the abolition of serfdom in 1799, when in Scotland men were transferred like chattels with the pit. Through the action of these unions, it is said that women work no longer in pits, while children's labour has been limited; that education below twelve years is prescribed for every boy before he is admitted into the pit; that the truck system has been abolished; that inspection has been obtained; and that the payment of wages at public-houses has been stopped. Further, I am assured that it is through the action of the unions that there is less violence attaching to strikes; and that, among other things, workmen do not have their ears cut off, as they used to have them last century, by their fellow-workmen; *and I believe it is so.*"

"Trades' Unions," writes again a Yorkshire friend (not a working man) of large experience in the subject, speaking of the class, "are becoming important influences for social improvement. No union committee-man could be tolerated now if a drunkard. Without sobriety, intelligence, and wisdom, no such man advances to influence. The action of the unions at Barnsley has been productive of almost miraculous improvement. Details are told of the brutality of the Barnsley roughs, even within these

* See 'Times,' January 29, 1867.

ten years, that could not now be tolerated by the lowest of
themselves. And yet there is a marked difference between
a district in the neighbourhood not in union and the others
which are. In the one, the men get the same pay as the
unionists, but waste it uncontrolled. In the union districts,
with better pay and shorter hours of work than heretofore,
the men are turning their attention to garden-plots, to pig-
feeding; joining Co-operative and Building Societies. They
are saving in Penny Banks, and the Post-office has many
hundreds of pounds of their money. It is found that
though the men work shorter hours daily they do more
work and earn more money, because they work more regularly, do not break time, and have no ' Saint Mondays '
or ' play-days.' There is a very decided improvement,
both physical, moral, economic, and social, in the whole
Yorkshire district where union prevails. But where there
is no union discipline, we have dog-fights and man-fights,
riots, and manslaughters at every assize."

In South Yorkshire indeed, whatever may be the case
in other quarters, the effect of the Miners' Trade Society
has been rather to draw the employer and the employed
together than to keep them asunder. "Strikes in the
South Yorkshire Colliery district," says a writer in the
'Barnsley Chronicle' of April 13, 1867, " are fast becoming matters of history, and in their place we have gatherings, demonstrations, dinners, or whatever one may choose
to call them, at which masters and men vie with each
other in their expressions of mutual goodwill and esteem."
He proceeds to report the proceedings of the latest among
several such reunions during the last few months, a dinner

had by the workmen in the employ of the Strafford Collieries Company, to which the proprietors had been invited, and which was attended by the viewer, commercial manager, and other officials of the company, as well as by several of those of the South Yorkshire Miners' Union. Mr. Normansell, the secretary to the latter (an extract from whose speech we have already given), said "that it was becoming the rule of the district to meet with employers and managers on one common platform. It was the association which had brought this about. The association had got to that position now that it could do more good without resorting to strikes and play-days than it could do by resorting to them. . . . It was not their interest to create strikes; it was their interest and bounden duty to prevent them if they could."

Take again the case of the Scotch bakers' reform, as given in a letter of Mr. John Bennett, Secretary of the Operative Bakers' National Association of Scotland, to Mr. Ebenezer Stevens, a London master baker, and published by the latter in 1859.* " It was in 1837 that the journeymen bakers in most of the towns and cities throughout Scotland memorialized their employers for a strictly cash remuneration, instead of the then existing system, whereby they received board and lodging in the houses of the employers, in part payment of wages. A great number of employers acceded to this request voluntarily, and such as did not were ultimately compelled to do so, being in part

---

* See Dr. W. Neilson Hancock's paper on the Journeymen Bakers' case, Transactions of the Social Science Association, 1861, (London, 1862,) pp. 599 and following.

operated on by the strength of the operatives' association, and partly by the force of public opinion. This gain was certainly a great boon, and enabled journeymen bakers, like other citizens, to have homes of their own selection, which worked a great improvement in the morals of the men ; and in no form was this more remarkable than in the number of marriages which took place in a very short time. Previously a married man among journeymen bakers was a rarity ; if married, he would find it difficult to get a situation, being almost invariably told, when making application for employment, that only single men were wanted, and such to board and lodge in the house. Our success in the matter of wages, etc., begat another aspiration. Through our excessively prolonged hours of labour, we were still debarred from many privileges which were enjoyed by other operative classes. We had established reading-rooms and libraries in most of our towns, but they were of comparatively little use, excepting for journeymen out of employment, as the length of hours almost generally wrought by bakers prevented the men from either attending the reading-rooms, or making use of the books in the libraries. . . . It was also found that although, since our success in the matter of wages, there had been a much greater attendance on religious exercises, both of married and single men, yet their drowsiness in church was so great as to prevent them joining in the services in such a manner as would be seemly, and which drowsiness was purely to be attributed* to the undue prolongation of the time of labour throughout the week. We determined . . . to

* What a compliment to the Scotch ministry !

get a limitation of the hours of labour. In 1845, when Mr. Fielden introduced his Bill into Parliament for a restriction of the hours worked in the factories of the United Kingdom, there came this question, ' Is it practicable for bakers to work to ordinary time ?' To the credit of some of the employers, they gave the twelve hours system a trial. The result was the setting to rest all doubt as to the practicability of working to ordinary time. . . . Conferences were held with the employers, and it was agreed upon, almost universally, to restrict the hours of labour, from 5 A.M. to 5 P.M." The system has established itself to this day, and with such success, that a memorial of 150 master-bakers of Edinburgh and Leith, addressed in April, 1860, to the master-bakers of London after referring to the alteration, declares that " the whole experience of the masters since that time has been more and more strongly to confirm them in the opinion that the step they then took, though at the time it was taken by many of them with doubt and reluctance, was most beneficial, not only to the workmen, but to themselves. . . . From the improved condition of the men, the masters receive no small share of the benefit. They are more diligent and active in their work, more regular and trustworthy in their habits, so that at least an equal quantity of work is done by them . . . under the new day system, as under . . . the old night, or rather night and day system. In a word, the masters do not hesitate to say that even in a commercial point of view, the change has been to them a great advantage. . . . And . . . in no single respect have the customers of the Edinburgh bakers been put to any inconvenience by the alteration, nor have they been obliged to forego any of the advantages which they formerly enjoyed."

The above remarkable narrative shows how a great social improvement in a particular trade has been effected by the workers, against the prejudices of their employers, but to the entire ultimate benefit of both classes. And whilst it shows the power of the Scotch working man to carry out such a reform without the aid of the law, it shows also how beneficent legislation may act by example in quarters which it does not attempt to reach directly. The occasion of this Scotch baking reform was clearly Mr. Fielden's Factory Act.—The Bakehouses' Regulation Act, 1863, it may be observed, although applying to all three kingdoms, does not touch either of the two points of the Scotch reform.

We could multiply such narratives *ad infinitum.* Suffice it to say that the convictions of the great bulk of the working classes on the subject of these societies are, we believe, summed up in the following passages of a paper read by Mr. W. Dronfield (now Secretary to the " United Kingdom Alliance of Organized Trades"), at the Social Science Congress in 1865, not published in the " Transactions " of the Association, but since printed by the " Association of Organized Trades of Sheffield," as an Appendix to the Seventh Annual Report of the Executive :—" The opponents of Trade Societies often tell us that Unions are not only mischievous and dangerous to the community generally, but inimical to the interests of those for whose benefit they are intended, and that they fail in accomplishing their objects . . . It is manifest to those who know anything of their working, that the very reverse is the fact; and as well might such parties attempt to make working men believe that the light of the sun is less than that of the moon, or that night does not succeed day. Numerous cases might be pointed out in trades that are organized, where either advances in wages have been obtained, the old rates maintained, or the hours of labour shortened, while we defy our opponents to prove that in trades not in union, or that have become disorganized, similar advantages have accrued."

We are far from being mere partisans of Trades' Unions. They are at best one-sided and one-eyed. Existing simply to protect or further a single class-interest, they appear to us far inferior to Co-operation, which seeks to harmonize warring interests; aiming only at improving the condition of the wages-receiver, they are lower in conception than whatever tends to abolish the thraldom of wages-receiving itself. And yet we believe, not only that they constitute the most powerful of all the self-evolved agencies operating upon—energizing, if we may use the term—the working class, but that their improvement and development afford the most convincing proof of the progress of the artisans of England.

Paradoxical as it may seem, there is indeed no form of social activity which does not do more than it aims at, even when it does less than that. The Building Society secures a man more than his house, even when it fails to give him a title to the latter; the Co-operative Society more than the profit made on his weekly purchases, even when it pays no dividend; the Benefit Society something more important than a sick allowance and burial fees, even though its tables should be altogether faulty. But above all, the Trade Society confers quite other benefits than those belonging simply to improved wages, even when it strikes for these and fails. The house, the business profit, the help in sickness and death, the higher wages, may all be worth striving for ; but besides these, and in their future results, far beyond these in value, are the individual strength revealed, the forethought and sobriety developed, the growth of mutual trust and confidence, as well as of that wholesome distrust of the noisy, the plausible, the violent, the self-seeking, which only bitter experience enforces ; the gradual acquisition of those powers of organization which, when rightly controlled and directed, make the will of the mass like the will of one, and its might as that of millions. We believe that there is no school like that of the Trade Society to teach the working man the value of these things; that it has taught and is teaching it to them.

It was said seven years ago by the Trades' Societies Committee of the Social Science Association : " The Committee wish to record their opinion distinctly that improvement in the management of Trades' Societies has been most marked and satisfactory." Since that period the progress of improvement has been still more rapid. Not only have those trade-outrages, which thirty years ago were to be looked for in almost any trade, become confined almost exclusively to the town of Sheffield, but the Trade Societies of Sheffield itself have come forward and solicited an official investigation, in order to clear themselves of the guilt of such outrages. In fact, the main ground of complaint against Trade Societies seems no longer to be their violence, but simply their power. Is that power, however, one which acts as a mere disturbance to the cause of trade ? Has not experience shown that no class of men on earth are more prone to rush headlong into speculation, to have their heads turned by exorbitant profits, to give way to panics, than British manufacturers and merchants ? Now the habitual action of the Trade Society, as the organ of the workers' interests, is to operate as a drag upon rash speculation, to curtail excessive profits, and by acting generally as a moderator of production, to lessen the risk and mischief of panics. Parliament has occupied itself with debates as to the probable exhaustion of our coal-fields ; but what healthier check can be imposed on that process than the action of our Miners' Associations, in limiting the hours of labour, and raising the cost of extraction ? And what is true of coal-mining is true of the iron-trade, and of every other. The stock of iron in the bowels of the English soil is a limited one ; and is it really a ground for decrying Trades' Unions, if by their means we should come to retain a portion of it a century or two longer in our own power than we might do, if our iron-masters and manufacturers in iron were allowed full scope to flood the whole world with the cheapest conceivable iron, wrought at Belgian or French wages, in order that our Continental rivals may cut our throats, whether physically or only figuratively, with cheap goods, all the sooner ?

What effect Trades' Unions are likely to have on the commercial prosperity of the country is no doubt a question regarded with much anxiety and apprehension by large numbers of thoughtful people. But as the question is approached and examined, its gravity decreases, because it is seen that it rests with ourselves to find such a solution of it as will be safe and satisfactory for the country. Blind and obstinate class antagonisms cannot fail to bring results of the very worst description; but we need not anticipate a continuance of these after the old evil fashion. Whilst the workmen's Trade Societies have been becoming more moderate and larger in their views, the offensive spirit of mastership which sought to carry everything with a high hand, and settle all matters without considering the wishes or interests of the workers, has also greatly softened within the last few years. The capitalist is beginning to acknowledge the propriety of considering the welfare of the worker whose help he needs. He has almost ceased to insist upon his right to do all things in his own way simply because the capital is his. We yet at odd intervals hear threats that he will leave the country, take his capital with him, and invest it where his operations will not be interfered with by the committees of Trades' Unions, but these menaces are usually uttered in the press or in Parliament by indiscreet friends of employers, not by employers themselves. England is still the great central field of the world's industry—the field where, with all its drawbacks, capital yields the most certain and the largest profit, and where trade almost continuously increases, notwithstanding the obstacles thrown across its path by the quarrels of kings and governments. From one part of the country or another we may hear from time to time outcries about declining trade; but the Government returns are at hand,

and in place of despondency as to our impending ruin, the figures in our blue-books beget tranquillity and confidence.

The present outcry about foreign competition is one which, when by going back twenty, thirty, forty years, one verifies its identity with the outcries of those various periods, really provokes a smile. Of course, under a free-trade system, we cannot expect to undersell all the world. The foreigner must do better than we in some things. Surely we have no right to complain if he learns to manufacture the raw product of his own soil cheaper than we can do that same product imported; or if he manages to secure markets to which the cost of transit is less for him than for us. Is it really a thing dreadful and alarming, for which Trade Societies are to be belaboured, if the Norwegian, with vast forests at his door, sends ready-made doors and window-frames to us, instead of the mere wood out of which they are shapen? The only wonder is, that he should not have done so before 1866 or 1867. But the case of the Belgian iron-trade has been lately made so much of against trade societies, that one or two facts relating to it may be offered to our readers. In 1806 the produce of the iron furnaces of England and Wales was 250,000 tons of pig-iron; in 1820, 400,000 tons; in 1840, 1,395,900 tons; in 1848, 2,008,200 tons; in 1865, 4,819,254 tons. This may be regarded as a rather rapid growth in one particular branch of business, sufficient to prevent despondency. To meet this quantity in the markets of the world, Belgium —taking the figures of Messrs. Creed and Williams as correct—has a gross produce of 392,178 tons. And this is the production, amounting to less than 1-11th of our own, which is made a bugbear to us! But that Belgium is not really underselling us in foreign markets may be seen by the following passage, quoted from Messrs. G. B. Toms and Co's. Circular in the ' Public Ledger,' December 31, 1866 :—" For rails of high quality, such, for instance, as the Brighton or East India Railways would lay down, we have nothing to fear at present from Belgium, because the tests employed are declared insupportable at the foreign works, and it is only in common iron that their prices even approach those of Wales. They *have not* secured the 40,000 tons for Russia as stated." (The ' Times,' which made so much of the latter statement, has not contradicted it.) And after the late riots in the Belgian mining and iron districts, we must really wish Messrs. Creed and Williams joy of their Belgian workers, frugally rejoicing in their wages of 1s. 10d. a day, of a temperance so exemplary in meat as well as drink, that when those gentlemen wished to go down a Belgian coal-mine they could hardly find a collier's dress wide enough for their English bodies. The burning of mills, the sacking of property, the bloody encounters with the soldiery, are facts which, with us, belong to the past history of labour, not to the present. If any wish to revive them amongst us, by all means let them try to put down Trade Societies.

But there is another aspect to the question. It is quite true that wages pushed to a point of exorbitancy would interfere with trade. But such a danger is not close upon us ; whilst the danger—far greater and more immediate— of losing our skilled artisans by emigration, is at our doors.

America and the Australian Colonies are the points to
which our emigrants are almost exclusively attracted, and
the numbers of our working people going annually to
these places may, at no very distant day, lead to a rivalry
in manufacturing enterprise far more dangerous to the
old country than anything that can result from an investment of English capital in Belgium or France. From
1820 to 1832 emigration from the United Kingdom to
the American Colonies, the United States, Cape of Good
Hope, and Australia, fluctuated between 8000 and 49,000
annually. Since then the passage to these countries has
been shortened and cheapened, its dangers and disagreeable
incidents have been abated ; chances of success in his new
home for the emigrant have increased, and variety of employments has greatly augmented. As a natural consequence
the tide of emigration has greatly swelled, varying from
100,000 to nearly 400,000 a year ; whilst the United States
of America, teeming with the raw material of every great
branch of industry, and animated by a most daring spirit
of enterprise, absorb nearly two-thirds of this outflowing.
This emigration is not a speculative supposition, but a fact.
It is not a threat to intimidate employers, but a veritable
portion of our daily experience as a nation.

Take for instance the very minutest thread of that emigration of labour,—so much of it as trickles over into the
Continent of Europe. No cotton or iron manufacturer,
carrying his capital to France or Belgium, can do anything
to sensibly affect our position either in war or peace, so
long as he does not carry his workmen with him. But
the workmen are being carried there without him, not to

receive those lower Belgian or French wages which seem to be the *beau idéal* of a certain class of employers, but *higher* wages than in their own country. Mr. William Allan's evidence before the Trades' Unions Commission shows us that the English engineers who have been taken over to France " are getting from £2 to £2. 10s. per week," whilst " the same class of men in all probability would be getting here 36s. a week." Can anything prove more conclusively that the Englishman's labour is really cheap, although his wages are high (shall we not rather say, *because* his wages are high?), and that therefore no real economy in production is to be derived from lowering his wages to that Continental level, at which the Belgian or French workman's labour must evidently be dearer than his own ?

But there is yet another aspect to this question. Assume that the competition of the American or Australian, even of the French or Belgian producer, becomes a formidable one ; assume that the high rate of English wages caused by Trade Societies, or the agitations in trade which they occasion, is a drawback to us in that competition. Is there no other remedy than that of forcing down wages at home, reducing ever lower the condition of our workers, limiting more and more the purchasing power of the most numerous class of our population ? The working man at least thinks that there is, and he of the Anglo-Saxon race especially is diligently applying one. And it is simply the use of that very process which the English employer so complains of—combination. The ' Times' of the very day on which these lines are written (April 29th) is full of details of strikes and disarrangements of trade through the working men's combinations in the United States. The network of Trade Societies is spreading over Australia, as almost any newspaper from thence will show. We have at this moment a strike of working tailors in London. It has only followed the like in Paris. And the short interval which has elapsed since the relaxation of the French combination laws has sufficed to teach the French workmen that strikes have but little chance of success, without the funds and the organization of a Trade-Society to back them; and when these shall have been realized, they will learn, what has been learned by the English working men in trade after trade,—that after a first great contest, the trade-fund and the trade organization are in most cases sufficient to fulfil the needs of the workers, without a strike.

Now a little reflection will suffice to show that, admitting, for argument's sake, to the fullest extent, the hindrance of a Trade-Society to the employer at home, the moment its machinery begins to be applied in a foreign country, it benefits him to an exactly equivalent amount. If it acts as a drag upon production here, so it must there. Every American, Australian, French, Belgian strike is *pro tanto* a strike in favour of the English employer. Nothing in this point of view can be more noteworthy than the actual ramification of our largest Trade Society into the Colonies and foreign countries, the fourteen Colonial branches, the eleven American, the French branch of the " Amalgamated Society of Engineers." The Sydney branch, for instance, was formed in consequence of the

lock-out of 1852, by a number of society men who emi-
grated to New South Wales,—a remarkable evidence both
of the dangers to England of a victory by the employers,
and of the mode in which those dangers are neutralized
in turn by the working men through their combinations.
And Mr. Allan stated lately before the Commissioners
that among the few strikes his society had had of late
years, had been one in Australia for eight hours a day, the
cost of which was indeed defrayed by the men themselves,
but which entitled them at the end of the year to the benefit of that equalization of funds among the different
branches, which is a distinctive characteristic of the great
amalgamated societies.   Clearly every penny spent in that
strike, was laid out in effect by working men to keep
up the profits of English master-engineers, as well as the
wages of English workers.

What really the working man is feeling his way to,
more or less consciously, more or less openly,—what was,
indeed, avowedly urged as desirable at the Geneva Conference, especially by the English delegates,—is a general
assimilation of wages in the various trades.   By which,
indeed, is not to be understood the introduction of equal
money wages, but, as is well explained by the secretary to
the Amalgamated Society of Carpenters and Joiners, in
the preface to their last report, an equalization of the conditions of labour ; so that, taking into account the price
of lodgings, food, and other necessaries, and other local
advantages or disadvantages, the pay of all workmen of
equal standing in a given trade shall be equivalent, wherever they may be employed.   We need not here discuss

the feasibility of the attempt, nor its wisdom. Suffice it to say that, so far as it succeeds, it must tend to equalize the conditions of trade for all employers, to introduce an element of stability into contracts, and thereby to moderate competition at home; that, from the moment it begins to be carried out, if we may use the term, internationally, it must tend, in like manner, to moderate competition between country and country.

Considered, therefore, under their most general aspect, the tendency of Trade Societies is not to disarrange trade, but to steady it in the interest of the workers, and if steadiness of trade be a blessing, and not a curse, then in the interest of all. You say that this is but a form of class selfishness. Granted; but where is the class, as a class, which is ruled by anything higher? And, after all, class-selfishness in its worst form is surely better than individual selfishness. A mass of working men seeking to get as much pay for as little work as they possibly can without ruining their employers, is certainly not a very elevating subject of contemplation. But the individual employer, not caring whom he may crush of those below, of those around, in the battle of competition, if he can get a profit for himself,—at arm's length with his workmen, at arm's length with every other employer,—is a still more depressing one. The task of the former will require, as among themselves, much forbearance, much endurance, much self-surrender; the task of the latter requires nothing but a clear head, a good digestion, and (whilst within the reach of law) a strictly legal conscience.

But is there no escape from the tyranny of self-interest,

whether expanded into a class, or concentrated in an individual? The working man at least thinks there is.*

§ 2. *Arbitration in Trade Disputes.*

A war between employers and employed, which tends to drive capital out of the country, or to make the country an undesirable home for honest industry, is perhaps more than any other, an evil to be discountenanced and condemned. But no possible good can arise from any attempt to decide between these rival interests which is in the least one-sided. No plan to enable the masters to triumph over the men, or to assist the men in overcoming their employers, can be otherwise than injurious to the interests of the nation. In such strikes and lock-outs as those of the Amalgamated Engineers, the Preston factory workers, and the London building trades, we have had an opportunity of seeing how much of ill-will may be generated, and how much suffering and loss may be in-

---

* We have devoted so much space to Trade Societies as such, that we have none to assign to a number of different organizations which either aim at some of the objects of the Trade Society without adopting its machinery, or pursue really different objects by similar means. A number of early-closing associations, or societies for promoting the welfare of working men in particular branches of employment—among which the " Association of Foremen Engineers " is the most prominent, and has reached a really high standing in mechanical science—to say nothing of the before-mentioned " Society of Wood-Carvers "—belong to the former group. Among the latter we may instance the " Workmen's Lord's Day Rest Association," and other bodies for better observance of the Sunday. Much interesting matter could no doubt be supplied as to these various fields of working-class activity, however subordinate in their economic importance to the one we have been attempting to survey.

flicted. As a nation, we are bound to discover some method of reconciling these contending interests, to seek out how much of gain may lie in their reconciliation. Strikes and lock-outs are indisputably the worst agencies that can be employed for the settlement of trade disputes. Those who despair of Arbitration as a reconciling power, do not see how much there is in the situation of masters and men to favour it; nor do they comprehend the many methods of reconcilement that would suggest themselves, were the sensible and moderate of both parties brought into frequent and friendly contact. It is of advantage to employers as well as employed that the operations of trade should be carried on with as little interruption as possible. Steadiness in the price of labour as well as in the cost of material is desirable; unlooked-for fluctuations frequently interfere with the legitimate profits of trade. Now one great cause of such fluctuations lies in this, that amongst employers in every trade there are persons whose anxiety to get on in the world makes them utterly unscrupulous. They try to possess themselves of every order, and to gain possession of all markets. For this purpose they resort to every trick by which they can reduce the cost of production, so that they may undersell their more honourable rivals. Cheap labour is one of their favourite methods, and when men are out of employment, either by slackness of trade, or by their own imprudence, they invariably pit them at lower wages against the better paid workman. This reacts again on the more honourable employer, who has to meet his unscrupulous rival in the market, and to do so must also have wages reduced to a common level, or brought up to an equal standard; hence many of the strikes that take place throughout the country.* This great disturbing cause could, the working men consider, be best made inoperative by Arbitration. Honourable employers, and good, steady workmen, are equally interested in overcoming it; when these thoroughly understood each other, the respectable masters would encourage and support the steady and clear-sighted amongst the men, whilst the well-meaning workmen would in turn support them, and thus a spirit of goodwill and mutual respect would take root, more effectual for haronizing rival interests than anything that can possibly be done by legal enactment, or by any growth of power on one side or the other, for the purpose of fighting out these miserable conflicts.

Certain it is at any rate that, beyond his cherished Trade Society, the working man has been perseveringly feeling his way to that which one school of political economists treat as impracticable—Arbitration in trade-disputes. It is impossible to mistake the strong, and of late years rapidly growing desire of the working classes for legalized arbitration as a substitute for strikes. In how many instances has arbitration been offered by the men, and rejected by the masters—by the engineers in 1851-2, by the Preston

---

* Dispassionately looked back upon, the great lock-out in the London building trade and the introduction of the hour system seem to have been in the main a blow aimed by the great contractors,—whose chief interest it is to be able by turns to procure and throw off, with the greatest ease and celerity, large supplies of labour not of the highest quality—against the old master-builders, whose interest it was to do their work well, and keep good workmen when they had got them.

weavers repeatedly in 1853, the West Yorkshire miners in 1858, etc. etc.! In how few—the Staffordshire ironfounders' case seems the only prominent one in point—has it been offered by the masters, and rejected by the men! In many instances arbitration is required to be resorted to by the rules of societies. "The committee will use all reasonable means," say the rules of the "Protective Association of the Joiners of Glasgow and West of Scotland," "either by conferring with the parties, or by means of arbitration, to obtain an amicable adjustment of the matter in dispute." "If at any time the workmen therein find it necessary to strike for an advance of wages, or from any other necessary cause," say the rules of the Scottish Miners' Association, "the district committee shall refer the matter to a working arbitration; . . . should the men refuse it, they place themselves beyond the pale of the Association."

Sometimes the societies have even succeeded in obtaining legal means of settling disputes by arbitration. Thus, in the London printing trade, a scale of prices was agreed to at a general conference of master-printers and compositors in 1847, which was embodied in a deed, and has formed the subject of legal decisions ; disputes are settled by an arbitration committee, consisting of three masters, nominated by the master in whose office the dispute has arisen, and three journeymen, not employed in such office, nominated by the journeymen, with a barrister for chairman, appointed annually, and holding a casting vote. In the Potteries, the written agreement contains a clause that "if any dispute arise between the parties as to the prices or wages to be paid by virtue of such agreement, the dispute shall be referred to an arbitration board of six persons, to consist of three manufacturers chosen by the masters, and three working potters elected by the working men " —a system, we are told, which " has been much tried, and worked most successfully in ninety out of a hundred cases."*

Similar boards or committees have been attempted in many other trades. At Macclesfield, a court of conciliation was formed, in 1848, between the silk-weavers and their employers ; and during the four years of its existence no strikes took place, until it was broken up by an employer refusing to abide by the award; and " no sooner was the board broken up than strikes commenced."† At Sheffield, amongst the carpenters and joiners, a code of working rules was drawn up between masters and men, in May last ; and on the employers' own proposal, a committee, composed of an equal number of employers and workmen, meets monthly, to discuss and decide by a majority all differences that may arise on the one side or the other ; and many cases on both sides have been satisfactorily decided by it. " I may add," writes the intelligent secretary to the Amalgamated Society of Carpenters and Joiners, from whom we learn the above fact, " that in at least twenty towns our members have succeeded in getting codes of working rules mutually agreed to by the employers and themselves, each binding themselves to give two, three, four, or six months' notice of any alteration either may require, and if they are unable to agree, to

---

* Report of Trades Societies' Committee of Social Science Association, p. 282 ; see also Report of Special Committee of the House of Commons on Masters and Operatives, 1860, Mr. G. Humphries' evidence.

† Mr. Humphries, *ibid.*

settle all their differences by arbitration. For all practical purposes, strikes are impossible in such places."*

The Board of Arbitration of the Nottingham hosiery trade states,† that " having now had six years' experience of the practical working of the system of arbitration, as opposed to strikes and lock-outs, it is thoroughly convinced that in a free country, where workmen and capitalists have a perfect right to enter into combinations, the simplest, most humane and rational method of settling all disputes between employer and employed is arbitration and conciliation. The Board is strengthened in this conviction by the fact, that during the past two years the demand for hosiery has been, in several branches of trade, of an exceptional character, and labour, in some departments, unusually scarce; and notwithstanding the workmen have preserved their trade unions, by having a central authority to appeal to, composed equally of employers and employed, all questions calculated to produce irritation and lead to disputes have been promptly settled, all inequalities in the rates of wages have been adjusted, the manufacturer has been enabled to accept his contracts without apprehension and execute them without delay, and the rights of workmen have been zealously looked after and strictly preserved." A similar Board exists in the hosiery trade of Derby; the establishment of one in that of Leicester has been resolved upon; and the operatives in the lace-trade of Nottingham are seeking to follow the example set them by the hosiers.

* See further as to this, Mr. Applegarth's evidence before the Trades Unions Commission, given since the above was written.

† See ' Times ' of January 29, 1867.

Again, the Bill, originally brought in by Mr. Mackinnon, of late taken charge of by Lord St. Leonards, and now passing through Parliament, " to establish Equitable Courts of Conciliation to adjust Differences between Masters and Workmen," has been, as is well known, warmly supported by the Trade Societies. In the Report of the Select Committee of the House of Commons on Masters and Operatives, 1860 (p. 36), will be found a list, delivered in by Mr. T. Winters, formerly secretary to the " United Trades," of above sixty trades (many of them composite bodies, such as the Glasgow United Trades Council), which had in 1859 expressed a desire to have such Courts. But not long ago a letter was published from Lord St. Leonards, stating that delegates, representing upwards of 100,000 working men, had expressed themselves in favour of his Bill. This is itself only half the truth ; for at the Sheffield Conference, at which, as before stated, from 180,000 to 200,000 workmen were represented, a resolution was unanimously passed " highly approving" of the establishment of such Courts, " exceedingly regretting" the withdrawal of the Bill, and " pledging" the delegates present to "use every exertion to obtain the establishment of such Courts." The Bill in question may not, even if adopted, realize all that its partisans expect. But it is impossible to mistake, in its popularity with the working class, the evidence of a growing desire for the peaceable adjustment of trade differences, for the substitution, as their ultimate arbiter, of calm discussion for blind force or blind endurance.

PART VI.

GENERAL MORAL PROGRESS OF THE WORKING MAN.

OUR task has been hitherto comparatively an easy one, for it has been bounded on all sides almost by figures. But we come now to a region where figures are generally but of small avail,—where they are unsafe guides too often. No human arithmetic can ever separate the good from the bad, the faithful from the unbelieving. We can do little more therefore than skirt, as it were, the borders of the realm of conscience, keeping within the reach of visible land-marks, and giving for what they are worth the results of our own experience as to the mistier lands ahead.

§ 1. *The Temperance Question.*

The question of temperance amongst the working classes is one of those that lie on the border-land between social and purely moral progress. Intemperance is the vice of all others which is the most readily cast in the teeth of the working man. No study of his progress can be thorough which does not grapple with this fact. And were one to believe the orators of the various Temperance bodies, drunkenness within the last thirty years has increased instead of diminishing ; whilst if they can point to an increased ascertained consumption of alcholic liquors per head of the population, it is deemed an incontrovertible proof of their allegations.   Beyond this, however, Temperance Societies are generally chary of historical statistics, and their reports are singularly meagre in their record of actual work done. It would be very unsafe, on the other hand, we believe, to trust in such a matter to the " Judicial Statistics" of the Home Office.   Mr. Scott, in his able 'Statistical Vindication of the City of London,' has conclusively shown how unreliable these are generally.   Besides, drunkenness is perhaps of all legal designations of an offence the one which varies most in its application.   A man would easily be held quite drunk in one county who would be considered only gay in another.   Yet, allowing to the fullest extent the frightful reality of the evil, the vastness of the sums squandered away by the working classes on drink,—even when this form of self-indulgence is not carried to the pitch of actual drunkenness ;—one striking contrast offers itself, to those who can look back to the days before 1832, between that time and this.   Drunkenness was not then felt as an evil thing by the working class ; the active war upon it, which is now being carried on everywhere within the bosom of that class, was not thought of ; moderate men there might be, but the energetic, aggressive abstainer was not to be found. The Temperance movement, though it may be traced further back, had its true birth for this country in the awakening of the people at the time we started from, and its development belongs entirely to the period which has occupied us.* That movement is now powerful enough to have split into two, each section energetically carrying on its own work. And although it may be difficult to estimate the total number of abstainers†—which number itself would, thank God! give no idea of the habitually sober—certain it is that thousands of enthusiastic men have been labouring for years in this cause, chiefly among the working classes; and though not satisfied with the result of their labours, they know they have not been labouring in vain.

In the 'Temperance Year Book' for 1867, many interesting facts are recorded, as to the progress of Temperance in the provinces, carried on by public meetings and publications; whilst the fourteenth Report of the " Executive Committee of the United Alliance" for 1865–6, exhibits the proceedings of the most " advanced " section

---

* The Rev. Alexander M'Leod, in a most able paper on " Methods and Obstacles in the Repression of Drunkenness among the Poor," read in 1861 before the Glasgow Meeting of the Social Science Association (Transactions, p. 525), traces the origin of the movement in Glasgow to "about a quarter of a century ago," say 1836. And Mr. T. Beggs, in a paper on " The United Kingdom Alliance and the Permissive Bill," read before the same Association in 1862 (Transactions, p. 452), speaks of the " first movers of the Temperance Reformation " having begun their labours in 1835.

† Mr. Baines, in his speech of 1861, reckons the number of Temperance Societies at 4000, that of Teetotallers at " not less than" 3,000,000, of whom, however, perhaps more than half were under fifteen. There were thirteen large associations, employing forty paid lecturers, with an annual income of £22,000, three weekly newspapers, circulating 25,000 copies weekly, six monthly magazines, circulating 20,000, etc.

of the party. When it is considered that the requirements of the opponents of drunkenness have risen from mere Temperance to Total Abstinence, from Total Abstinence to the " Maine Liquor Law," or the " Permissive Bill," *i.e.* the power of a local majority of ratepayers to deprive their neighbours of the use of spirituous liquors; from the " Permissive Bill " to " the total and immediate legislative suppression of the traffic in intoxicating liquors," which the " United Kingdom Alliance " sets forth as its object (though meanwhile advocating the Permissive Bill), it will be seen how fierce the warfare has become. And although one or other section of the party may now boast of Peers and M.P.s, Baronets and Magistrates, Deans and Dissenting luminaries, M.A.s and D.D.s among its patrons, it is unquestionable that the strength of the movement has always lain among the working class; and that it was at first so greatly confined to that class, that it was long difficult to find gentlemen of position who would hold office in connection with the various societies which have grown out of it.   Even at the present time, when the question of political Reform is that of the day, a " Permissive Bill " meeting lately called together in one of our largest towns (Leeds) a far more crowded audience than a Reform meeting, notwithstanding the absence of London political " stars " at the one, and their presence at the other.

The strength of the Temperance movement, then, in all its forms, though by no means a proof in itself of the growth of sobriety, and indeed implying, on the contrary, the reality and magnitude of the evil it exists to combat, yet affords also a most cheering evidence of the development of moral power for the purpose among the working class. On the other hand, our Temperance friends require to be reminded that Excise returns as to the consumption of intoxicating drinks, though no doubt correct enough in themselves, are very frequently misread. Drunkenness may be diminished, without Total Abstinence, by a more regular consumption of the quantity taken. A family may consume, as a dinner beverage, what the head of it at one time swallowed down in occasional drunken outbreaks. Indeed, in many ways, though the quantity remain the same, the mode of its consumption may greatly diminish. Such an argument, we are well aware, is of little weight with the fanatical abstainer, who holds it for an axiom that "when a man begins to drink he begins to be drunk;" but we are convinced that, viewed in connection with the greater accuracy of revenue returns, and the diminution of illicit distillation, it has to be seriously taken into account in estimating the bearing of averages of individual consumption.

Nor must it be considered indeed that the various Temperance bodies are the only organizations directly warring against drunkenness among the working classes. Whatever may be thought of its policy, it is unquestionable that the " Sunday League" is largely supported by working men, and that the main ground of their support is this, that the opening of public museums, gardens, and places of entertainment will be a powerful check to drunkenness. The same consideration operates to enlist their support in favour of Working Men's Clubs and Institutes, and of other places or forms of popular entertainment. The bearing of the question of popular entertainments on that of drunkenness is fully admitted by the Temperance bodies themselves. The Abstainers' Union of Glasgow, the Rev. Alexander Macleod tells us, " has organized a system of sermons, ' lectures, concerts, and excursions. From September till May, they supply the attractions of the lectureroom and the concert hall to tens of thousands at a merely nominal price. And from May till September, by omnibuses, and trains, and steamboats, they take large companies every Saturday afternoon to fresh country scenes and recreations at extremely moderate fares."

The free opening of parks, libraries, galleries, whilst operating as a check upon drunkenness, affords also a powerful argument in proof of its decrease. The Crystal Palace, again, to whatever extent it may be frequented by all other classes, could never have maintained itself without the working class, which in turn, thirty years ago, would have been incapable of enjoying it. They now resort to it, in their days of leisure, by the thousand ; they crowd thither in tens of thousands on the occasion of a Foresters' Fête, or other like holiday of their own. Mr. F. Fuller, in a letter addressed to the 'Times' on December 31, 1866, and since largely circulated, declares that " ever since it has been opened, about a million and a half of persons have profited by it in each year ; and in the present year no less than 2,067,598 persons have visited the building, . . . and out of the 18 or 19 millions of people scarcely 18 cases of drunkenness and disorder have appeared in the police reports." In presence of this single fact, is it possible to believe in a general increase of drunkenness ?

But the most convincing proof against the assertion, that our working population has been growing more addicted to drink within the last thirty years, lies really in all the facts, pregnant with social progress, which we have been endeavouring to set forth. The growth of Friendly Societies, Benefit Building Societies, Land Societies, Industrial and Provident Societies, Industrial Partnerships, Working Men's Colleges, Working Men's Clubs and Institutes, etc., is absolutely incompatible with such a fact.* It is not the drunkard who borrows books from the Free Library. The Licensed Victuallers may have their high-priced journal, pledged alike to piety and the pint-pot, but it is neither the public-house nor the beer-shop that supports the cheap newspaper or the cheap periodical. Say, if you like, that all these things would have begun sooner, would have developed themselves far more rapidly, but for the drinking habits of the people ; prove by figures the sums still wasted annually in drink ; yet the generation which has seen all these benefits realized cannot be one that is growing more and more steeped in intemperance.

The circumstances indeed of different localities, not necessarily far apart from each other†—of trades even closely

---

* It should not be overlooked that many of these bodies are directly connected with the Temperance movement, which has besides an Insurance Office, two or three Friendly Societies (one of which, the "Temperance Provident Institution," had in 1861, according to Mr. Baines, an annual income of £114,000), several Building Societies, etc. Thus the "Temperance Permanent Land and Building Society," which began in Dec. 1854, had received in contributions, up to Dec. 1865, no less than £930,000.

† In Rochdale, Preston, and other places in Lancashire, Mr. E. Chadwick

connected*—vary widely in this respect. The more common experience is, we believe, that of the Rev. Alexander Macleod, in his paper above referred to, where he says that the "real problem" lies in the lowest classes; that whilst in others "there may be individuals, even families and little *coteries*, entangled in the evil, the only *class* in society where the evil does not seem to be yielding to the influences which have been brought to bear against it, are the very poor." I do not mean," he emphatically adds, "the industrial poor. I do not mean the class which would be admitted to the suffrage if the £5 rental were made the condition of the vote. I mean the classes which underlie these." After referring to the "great changes" which have taken place, "within a comparatively recent date, in the drinking customs of the better classes,"† he goes on to say : "These softenings of a social evil have made no impression on the drunkenness of the lowest classes. Down

tells us in his address on Economy and Trade to the Social Science Congress in 1864, drunkenness diminished during the famine year; in Manchester and other places it increased. (Transactions, p. 89.)

* *E. g.* in lithography, the "draughtsman" is almost invariably sober, the "pressman" too often given to drink.

† An English friend writes : "If drunkenness had in the last generation been a cause of political disqualification, the 'gentlemanly interest' would have had but few votes. In my father's time, about 1800, in the — Foot, the colonel used every day after dinner to lock the door, open the window, throw the door-key to the orderly, and tell him to unlock the door and send the officers' servants up for them at nine o'clock. My father had to pour his wine down his high boots and on to the floor, in order to get rid of his share of the liquor. In my own young days, all the gentlemen of the old school in our country neighbourhood were two-bottle men. The race of hard-drinking gentry was followed by a race of hard-drinking workmen. Fashions then descended more slowly than

there . . . it is neither disreputable nor unusual. The old sneer at sobriety, the old power to annoy the sober neighbours, the old drinking customs, still sustain the cruel supremacy of intemperance. The maudlin sentiments, the wretched toasts, the insidious drinking songs, once in vogue in the fashionable circles of the past, have descended into these lower regions. . . . The *real evil* we have to deal with, therefore, is not simply drunkenness, but drunkenness among the very poor.''

There is a tinge of local colour about this description which would not make it applicable in all its details to England. But the writer of these lines must assert, on the strength of his own personal knowledge, that the drinking habits of his youth have died out in whole trades in Lancashire; that in workshops where the hardy drinker was formerly a hero, drunkenness is now held a thing to be ashamed of. Sheffield, again, is a town which has acquired an unenviable notoriety for the prevalence of drunkenness among its skilled artisans; but when at the Social Science Congress of 1864, it was asked of Mr. John Watson, a fork-grinder, whether he thought that drunkenness was diminishing amongst his fellow-workmen, his answer was " Most assuredly."

From Wolverhampton again a trustworthy correspondent writes, speaking from personal experience : " Thirty years ago, a ' tinman ' was another name for a drunken, blackguardly, worthless fellow. As soon as a man went to work

crinoline has of late years; but the speedier adoption of upper-class ways that now prevails will, I believe, bring back the workmen from their excesses even more quickly than our gentry recovered from theirs."

at a fresh place, he was set upon in a few minutes for a 'footing' of 3*s.* 6*d.*, which was spent in drink. I am happy to say, this is all changed. The men in the tin-trade are not behind any class in sobriety, and those qualities which make good citizens. The 'footing' of 3*s.* 6*d.* is still charged, but is not levied immediately a man comes to work, and when received is not spent in drink, but goes to a fund for the relief of the sick. No 'footings' have been spent in drink for nearly twenty years. We have fines for fighting in the shop, being intoxicated, or using bad language. The latter is not strictly enforced, but the fine against fighting is, and for a period of ten or twelve years I cannot think of more than two cases. This will be seen to be very creditable, if we bear in mind that there are about 140 men, who are mixing together, using the same tools, and in many ways likely to come into collision, unless mutual forbearance is exercised. There are many teetotallers, many who attend places of worship, and very few drunkards. I should think you might be in company with 50 per cent. for months and not hear an oath from them, whilst of perhaps 90 per cent. you would rarely hear one. There has been a gradual improvement, which does not seem stayed yet." The writer goes on to speak of a day's excursion at the cost of the employer, in which nearly 200 persons of both sexes took part, and though " there was no stint as to drink," he never heard of one being incapable of taking care of himself. He adds that " the rules relating to shop-fines, for fighting, etc., are made and enforced by the men. If the master were to interfere in the matter, it would be felt that he was outstepping his bounds." The 'japan-men' are not behind the tinmen. In the iron trade, the mill men are " a respectable body of men, many teetotallers, and many attending places of worship; some of them members and even preachers. They often own their house or houses, and are educating their children, some of them very liberally; 10 per cent. is thought sufficient to deduct for men who are not respectable members of society." The improvement among the miners has already been mentioned. The hollow-ware men are in bad repute, and thirty or forty years ago "none of them ever thought of saving anything. Since then about twenty or thirty have built a house or houses of their own, drunkenness has decreased, and the men as a body have greatly advanced," though " still below most other classes, except the puddlers."

A Leeds friend, from whose communication we have already quoted, who has been for many years in close relations with the working class generally, and has perhaps a wider acquaintance with the miners especially than any man in the kingdom, writes: " Upon the subject of drunkenness, I am very clear that for the last ten or twelve years there has been a decided improvement in general among the working classes, and especially among coal-miners. In the general stream of improvement, there are little whirlpools where the current for a moment appears to go backwards, but the real progress is decidedly onwards." Even among the lowest class, he considers," the idea has been banished, that a man is a good fellow in proportion as he can drink. We have, alas! yet human brutes who measure enjoyment by drink, but in ratio to either population or class they are fewer. They are more observed than formerly, and their notoriety now is a proof of improvement upon the time when beastly drunkenness was so common as to be unnoticed. In large towns, and even in some country places, drinking has to be covered over with music, songs, and tricks of legerdemain or feats of bodily strength, skill, or endurance. I have no sympathy with your Blondins and Ethardos; but even these, with a peculiar class of comic singers and performing brothers and families now rising into notoriety, are the evidence of a slight stage of advancement. From Coal-hole and Cider-cellar we have now got to Highbury Barn and the Alhambra Palace,—a bad elevation, I grant, but still an advance. And the same process is extending throughout the country districts. Among the miners I know women yet who worked naked in the pits, in places worse considerably than where the ponies now pull the corves, and these are still ignorant and unmannerly. They often don't send their children to school, cannot teach them good habits at home, and are a positive source of deterioration to them. Under such mothers, and with such wives, the colliers naturally went to the ale-house, and many do so still. But we have a growing and glorious band of men, women, and families growing slowly into better habits and estimation, from the fact that they have leisure to acquire and means to enjoy both."

From Derby a by no means sanguine friend writes: "Looking back over ten years in Derby, I think the tide seems running the right way, though it takes a long time for the waves to make any very perceptible upward advance on the beach. I think there is rather less drunkenness even within the decade of my cognizance, though there is still a terrible amount. . . . There are very many more sober workmen than there were." This last testimony, it will be observed, is remarkable, as showing that though the general improvement in sobriety may be slight, it is yet great in the very class which we are specially considering.

On the other hand, it is undoubtedly the fact that in many instances it is not the worst-paid trades that are most given to drink. The Sheffield trades, almost generally, are a case in point. The Spitalfields weavers, glad to earn 8*s.* a week, are habitually temperate ; the coal-miners, earning nearly or quite four times that amount,— the puddlers, who, in turn, easily double the miner's figure of wages,—are too often drunkards. Those of Wolverhampton, for instance, we are assured, " have not advanced one bit these twenty or thirty years. There are very few teetotallers, readers of newspapers, or [persons] that attend any place of worship amongst them, their homes being miserable dens."* The cork-cutters are a tolerably well-paid trade, yet a friendly correspondent

* There is, however, improvement even in this group of workers. " I am ready to admit," writes the President of the Northern Ironworkers' Society, " that there is a large number of ironworkers who are as be- nighted to-day as they were twenty years ago." But whilst " thirty years ago, the prevailing opinion was, that it was impossible for a puddler or any other kind of ironworker to perform his daily labour if deprived of his beer, now . . . there are very many total abstainers amongst them. Great numbers of ironworkers are members of Building Societies, and hundreds of them live on their own property."

from Sunderland, from whom we have received much valuable information, writes of them thus :—" Out of twenty men in one shop I worked in as a journeyman (at twenty-one years of age) there was not a single man that did not expend from 2*s.* to 5*s.* a week in drink ; and I was offered the situation of Secretary to the Society when only a member fourteen days, simply because I was thought a sober man." In short, there are, it must be admitted, " conditions "—to use Mr. E. Chadwick's words*—" in which high wages mean only excess in drink." And he quotes the instance of a retailer of coals near Manchester, " who refused to give credit to any man who earned more than 24*s.* per week, because he found from experience that if he did so, he never got paid." So far is the theory from being universally true, that the lower you get in the social scale, the more you will find drunkenness and improvidence to prevail.

But it is never fair to dwell on the mere fact of intemperance in any person or class, without also adverting to its predisposing causes. The Rev. Alexander Macleod most truly says that " the view that drunkenness is a voluntary evil, something men deliberately choose to yield to," is " daily becoming less satisfactory," and is " especially" inadequate " when offered as an explanation of drunkenness among the poor." The " polluted atmosphere" in which large masses of the poorer dwellers in towns have to live, he points out as one such explanation; the absence of comfortable dwellings as a still more weighty one ; besides the absence of good food,

* See Social Science Transactions for 1865, p. 89.

and of means of temperate refreshment; not to speak of ignorance, that check upon all improvement. In many other cases the nature of the work pursued affords some special stimulus to drink. We believe that if the catalogue of all the occupations could be given, in which drunkenness is most prevalent, they would be found to include all that are most unhealthy and most exhausting, and to be in great measure confined to these. Among the former must be included the great bulk of the Sheffield trades,* among the latter, mining and the iron trade generally.† The prevalence of drunkenness in such cases, therefore, mainly calls for the application of sanitary measures, and for a diminution of the hours of labour,—in other words, for a further development of protective legislation.

The moment we admit that foul air, filthy dwellings, unhealthy toil, may drive a working man into drunkenness, we admit also that part at least of the guilt of such drunkenness lies at the door of others than himself; that, —to say nothing of the publican or beerseller,—the building speculator, the landlord, the employer, have to bear a share of it. There are instances in which it is

---

* See Dr. John C. Hall's paper on "The Effects of Certain Sheffield Trades on Life and Health," read before the Social Science Congress in 1864; Transactions, p. 382.

† The puddlers' work, we are told, commences at 4 A.M., and if the metal is excessively "grey," requiring a greater amount of work, it may be thirteen or fourteen hours before he returns. In summer "the heat is almost more than the men can bear. . . . Water is frequently drunk in such quantities that the stomach at last rejects it. The men's food comes to the works, and often remains untouched for hours; or it may be that alcoholic drinks are taken, to spur the jaded system and assist the appetite."

positively forced upon him ; in which he is literally sold by others to sin ; in which he may be shown to have done his best to rescue himself from thraldom to it, when opportunity offered. The strongest case in point is that of the London coal-whippers and ballast-heavers. Of this the following account is supplied by a friend, Mr. F. J. Furnivall, who has been much in contact with the classes concerned, the ballast-heavers especially :—" Not a sight easily forgotten was the first meeting with the ballast-heavers at Radcliff Cross,—their sodden faces, pale lips, and ragged clothes. These men were in 1852, and before, employed by thirty-nine truckmen or contractors, of whom twenty-seven were beershop-keepers ; the others, butchers, grocers, etc., who made the men pay whatever prices they asked for goods, and employed foremen who kept lodging-houses, and made men pay their half-crown a week for beds, though they were married and lived at home.

" ' But this,' said the appeal issued at the time on their behalf, ' is the least evil of the system. It was stated before that twenty-seven out of thirty-nine middlemen were publicans : the sure way, therefore, for men to get work, is to go and drink at the beershop, where credit can always be had, and when they have run up a score they are set to work :—while they are at work, more beer or spirits are sent them, which they *must* take ; and when they come back from work, they are kept waiting at the beershop for two to five hours, during which the drinking thus necessarily commenced is voluntarily continued, till half, and sometimes two-thirds, of their wages, are spent. The effect of this on the men themselves may be easily con-

ceived ; of their wives and families, one who knows them
well has said, " a large proportion of their wives and children are half-starved and in rags—their children grow up
untrained and vicious—whilst any of the casualties of life
immediately throw their whole families upon the parish,
or drive them to obtain their bread by infamous practices ;"
—they are reduced to a pitiable state of destitution, the
homes being a scene of desolation, while the father's time
is almost entirely spent at the public-house.'

" The men sought relief in a system which had been successfully applied to their brother workmen, the coal-whippers, who had been in exactly the same bondage ; namely,
by inducing the Legislature to pass an Act giving them a
Registry Office, at which they could make their own contracts with, and take their own wages from, the captains
and ship-owners who need their services, after paying the
expense of the office.

" Every one who worked with the men to get their system of employment changed, can bear witness that they
did work for it ' with all their heart.' But nothing effectual was done till Prince Albert was made Master of the
Trinity House. He inquired into the men's case, asked
Mr. Cardwell, then Vice-President of the Board of Trade,
to take it up ; and as he was then altering the regulations
of the Trinity House, he put the ballast-heavers under
the control of the Brethren of the House. All truck-
drinking was at once stopped. The change in the men's
condition at the end of the first year, when they held their
first annual dinner, was something marvellous. Healthy
brown faces and good clothes were seen all over the room ;

the men's homes were more comfortable, the children better clad, and kept longer at school; some of the men had turned teetotallers, and cases of drunkenness were comparatively rare. The improvement still holds good.

" The case of the coal-whippers has not ended so happily for the men; but even now they are better off than they were. Before 1843 the whippers were sweated by publicans under the truck-drinking system, and had drunkenness forced on them as a condition of employment. They bestirred themselves, and with the help of friends in the trade and the House of Commons, obtained an Act (6 & 7 Vict. c. 101), mainly through Mr. Gladstone's goodwill, for the establishment of an office to which every employer was bound to give the first offer of his work, at his own price. This set the whippers free from the publicans. But unluckily the Coal-whippers' Act was a terminable one; and after two renewals, in 1846 and 1851, the Coal trade, thinking the office employed servants after their prime, and kept up prices slightly, induced the Government in 1856 not again to re-enact the Coal-whippers' Act—it was Mr. Lowe himself who cut the men's cable—on the trade undertaking to establish an office under their own management, which they would induce employers to resort to, and so protect the men from the publican's clutches. To a certain extent the trade have carried out their pledge; but a Government office for the protection of men, and a Masters' office, are two different things, as workmen well know; and some of the old evils have been creeping in again, though not at all to their former extent."

We may add, in conclusion, that Mr. T. T. Flynn, the

intelligent "ruler" of the Ballast-heavers' office, writes that having been intimately connected with large numbers of working men on the river Thames since 1845, he con- siders them "greatly improved, both morally and men- tally. . . . Not 10 per cent. of them are drunkards; indeed drunkenness has very much decreased among them."

An instance of the same evils on a more extended scale is afforded by the mining trade of South Staffordshire, where the abominable "butty" system prevails. "The butty," says Mr. Tremenheere, at the opening of his report on the Mining Districts, 1859, is a contractor or middleman between the master and the man. He has under him an agent, the 'doggy,' who superintends the work in the butty's absence. It is a complaint of long standing that these contractors and under-agents take advantage of the men in various ways,—by stopping money from their wages, which they are obliged to spend in drink; . . . by sending drink to the pits in the middle of the week, and making the men pay for it, whether they want it or not; by pay- ing the men late on Saturday night, and keeping them waiting in or about the public-houses in which the butties are interested, in order that they may spend money in drink. . . . These and other complaints against the butty system were urged at various meetings, attended by from 1200 to 3000 and 4000 of the men (as at the one at West Bromwich, on the 17th August, 1858); . . . and it was added by one of the speakers, 'the man must pay whether he has the drink or not, and if the man does not drink there is little or no work,' meaning that those who do not drink are soon got rid of." "A large number of butties,"

he says elsewhere, "either keep or are interested in public-
houses; and although many evade the Act by paying the
men not actually in a public-house, but somewhere near,
the men are expected to go there, and to drink the recognized quantity; and if any do not attend, their quantity is
drunk by the rest."

By "the Act," Mr. Tremenheere evidently meant the
5 & 6 Vict. c. 99, then in force, which forbade the payment of wages "at or within any tavern, public-house,
beer-shop, or other place of entertainment, or any office,
garden, or place belonging thereto, or occupied therewith."
To meet such evasions as he describes, the 23 & 24 Vict.,
c. 151, provided that wages should be paid at an office appointed for the purpose in the special rules for the mine or
colliery, which should "not be contiguous to any house
where spirits, wine, beer, or other spirituous liquors are
sold." This provision, it must be observed, must be considered as the result of the men's own agitation; nor are
they content with it. At the general Conference of the
miners of the United Kingdom, held at Leeds in November, 1863, it was recommended amongst other things*
"that in no sense should a ' butty,' ' doggy,' underlooker,
viewer, or under-viewer, etc., be allowed to keep a shop
or public-house, either directly or indirectly." And we
shall be surprised if some provision to this effect does not
find its way into the next Mining Act.

It would be a mistake, finally, to suppose that these
evils are confined to mining. "How is it," writes an intelligent correspondent from Wolverhampton, "that the

* See Transactions of the Conference, p. 26.

men in some works are so much superior to the men in others? The answer, I think, will often be that the employers have . . . not sufficiently discountenanced drinking and vice, but have allowed public-houses to exist close to their doors. Perhaps they could not often prevent it. But *they may prevent their own foremen, managers, and chief men from keeping them and their situation.* I believe many employers reap a sore harvest of trouble through allowing this system.' In the iron-trade, indeed, we are assured " the truck system is in full and vigorous operation in Wales, in the West of Scotland, and in some parts of South Staffordshire, in open violation of the law ; and in many of these truck-shops you can purchase anything and everything for eating and wearing, and can be supplied with any kind of alcoholic drink :" whilst " the long pays, often monthly, (in several works in Wales they have only four clear reckoning days in the year,) . . . make the workman a slave."

If we now recall the fact that large numbers of working men rank as advocates of general measures against drunkenness, which either (as the Permissive Bill) would place the local suppression of public-houses in the hands of a body— the ratepayers—but partially, and in some cases to a very trifling extent, composed of their own class; or would suppress the trade authoritatively everywhere (the Alliance), we shall perhaps see grounds for viewing in a different light from that in which it has been hitherto presented by Mr. Lowe and other politicians of his stamp, whatever amount of drunkenness does still exist among the working class, and for considering that the political enfranchisement

of that class is likely to afford one of the most effective
means towards checking that vice, so far as it can be influenced by legislative enactments.   Indeed, the United
Kingdom Alliance, in their Report for 1865-6, declare that
" a Reform Bill, from whatever Government it may be
ultimately accepted, must strike at the root of publican
domination, and must therefore be an important Alliance
gain."

God forbid that by anything we have said we should in
anywise impair the moral responsibility of the working
man !—that we should lead him to believe that because
many causes may conduce to intemperance, therefore he
is not to be held accountable for giving way to it !—that, in
a word, temptation can whitewash the sin !   To sin without temptation is devilish, not human ; but to be virtuous
without temptation is not human either, for it is less than
human.   Virtue is nothing if it be not a struggle ; the man
is not a man if he know not what it is to fight against the
evil without and the evil within.   When all due weight
has been assigned to outer influences, it is yet the infirmity
even where not the depravity of will in the man himself
which yields to the temptation ; and the most unwilling
slave to the publican, in what we may term the drink-ruled
callings, might yet burst his fetters, if he were determined
to starve rather than degrade himself.

Still, the true conclusion on the subject of the drinking
habits of the working class, we believe, is this,—that whilst
intemperance is undoubtedly yet the cardinal vice of the
working man, and one to which he succumbs far too often,
on the whole he is not increasingly giving way to it, but

in almost every quarter fighting manfully against it. It is indeed admitted by working men who are most unsparing in their denunciations of this scourge of their class, that now "beastly drunkenness is the exception, not the rule —we have, in fact, become respectable drinkers." And whatever amount of culpable self-indulgence that fact may still represent, surely it is a momentous one, since the step is that from the brute to the human being,—stooping, it may be, earthward yet, but capable henceforth of rising to his full height,—"unto a perfect man, unto the measure of the stature of the fulness of Christ."*

§ 2. *The Workmanship Question.*

Having dwelt at such length on the working man's cardinal vice of intemperance, we need not tarry over any other, as being characteristic of his class. Let the sinless cast the first stone at him. There are, however, one or two other questions which deserve to be considered before we pass on to certain positive indications of moral progress in the class.

---

* Serious complaints are indeed made from several quarters as to the increase of drunkenness among children. There seems to me," writes our Derby friend, " to be a decided increase in the number of our drinker-boys, and even little girls, at great holiday times. The Liverpool Sanitary Report, which was suppressed, dwelt also on the number of drunken children in the streets.

This was one of the evils of the old factory system ; and as drink cannot be had without money, and the bulk of children in the less affluent classes only get money when they have earned it, the inference seems to be that the growth of the vice among children must be connected with some undue absorption of infant labour for productive purposes, upon which an extension of the factory inspection and educational system, such as is now proposed by the Government, would supply the best check.

A complaint is heard well-nigh from all parts of the kingdom that the working man does not work so well as he used to do. To put it in the words of a Derby friend already quoted, there is a "difficulty in getting work fairly and honestly done. . . . Men do not stick to their work with that stedfast industry which used to mark the British workman. . . . The masters in many trades here are sick of their work. . . . Small masters, I know, are getting out of their trade where they employ a few men, and either living on their means or taking to working for others for wages." A Liverpool friend, very favourable to the working man, speaks of the difficulty now of getting "a day's work for a day's wages." An architect of the highest character considers that one great secret of the enormous rise in the cost of building lies in this, that the men do not work as they used to do. The blame of this alleged deterioration in the industry of the country is generally laid on the men's Trades' Unions ; and so far as one can judge from the hitherto printed evidence before the Trades' Unions Commission, almost the sole object of one or two members of that Commission seems to be to fix its stigma upon them.

But it remains to be seen, 1st, How far the reproach is true ; 2nd, how far, if true, it is peculiar to the working man ; 3d, how far he is responsible for incurring it.

We must say, in the first place, that we do not believe the reproach to be by any means so generally true as it is alleged. England's proud prerogative of solidity of work has surely not quite departed from her. In the valuable volume already referred to, of reports by the French working-men delegates to our great Exhibition of 1862, we meet continually with such judgments as these on the part of our rivals: English work "offers generally greater guarantees of solidity," says the shoemakers' report. English sewing is of "incontestable solidity and perfection," say the glove-makers. "English goods . . . are generally well made, better set up than ours, and leave very little to be desired," say the harness-makers. The engineers are struck with the "perfect workmanship" of Penn's engines, "the finish, the polish of the pieces leaving nothing to be desired," all of which they find to be equally characteristic of the ordinary trade machinery of the firm; they praise the good quality of English cast-iron, etc. The tinmen speak of the superiority of English tinning; the lithographers, of the "fine and solid" English workmanship, which allows the printing off of very large numbers of copies. The cabinet-makers say that English furniture is made "very neatly and solidly," well finished outside and in; the printers, that English printing is "careful even in the most trivial works, and particularly in newspapers." The jewellers only go so far as to admit that English workmanship "is incontestably equal to our own," and the cases are few in which superior solidity is claimed for French in any department. These criticisms are indeed now five years old; but if any similar report be published as to the Paris Exhibition of 1867, we have not a doubt that its conclusions will be similar.

The credit of English workmanship, then, does not stand quite so low as might be supposed. Grant, however, that it is falling; that—to generalize an expression well-known in the tailoring trade—slopwork is becoming more and more common. Is this peculiar to our handicrafts? Is there no slop-journalism, no slop-literature, slop-art, slop-science, slop-education, slop-law-making, ay, and slop-religion? Are not all these growing upon us? Has 1867 seen no slop-Reform-Bills? Does the working class deserve more than its proportionate share of blame for that weakening of national morality which no doubt is manifested on all sides, in the tendency to substitute the crude, the showy, the dishonest, for the mature, the substantial, the conscientious? Has the most careless of working men any chance of surpassing the carelessness of a set of Unity Bank directors? or has the most fraudulent anything to teach the promoters, solicitors, chairmen, managers of many another corporate body, dead, dying, or yet alive? No doubt every working man is morally responsible for every wasted minute, for every piece of consciously bad workmanship, still more for every direct fraud. But who are his instructors? When the Merchandise Marks Act made penal both the use of false trade-marks and the marking of false quantities, weights, measures, etc., was this directed against the tricks of workmen, or the tricks of employers—many of them, it is well known, wealthy and influential? Was the Act for preventing the adulteration of articles of food and drink aimed at the worker, or at the class which claims to be above him in the social scale, and almost to keep him out of political power? As a matter of fact, what is the main, direct cause of bad workmanship in every branch of human activity, but the excessive pressure of competition, whether that pressure exhibit itself in the contract system, or in purely speculative production,—economic phenomena in many respects very different, but in both of which everything comes to be subordinate to time and cheapness? Nothing can be more instructive, as an instance of the evils thus generated, than the evidence before the Trades' Unions Commission of Mr. Edwin Coulson, Secretary of the Operative Bricklayers' Society, who, after detailing various kinds of frauds practised for the benefit of foremen and contractors, declares that a century ago work was better than it is now, not because there are not men capable " of doing superior work to what has been done in the olden times," but because " we often have no encouragement to do it as well as it might be done."*

And so far from Trades' Unions causing the deterioration of work, if there is one thing more axiomatically certain than another, it is that the worst work is and must always be done by others than the members of such societies. For the worst work must always receive the worst wages ; and

---

* Other details of frauds on the part of contractors, as practised upon railway companies, will be found in a little work called the ' Life of a Navvy,' edited by the Hon. Eleanor Eden—one of the most valuable bits of genuine working-class biography ever published. The chapter on ' Contract Work,' for instance, will show how twelve-feet planks are turned into twenty-four-feet planks ; how a contractor taught the writer to sink posts faster by sawing off six inches from the bottom ; how contractors may sometimes gain a hundred pounds by getting a navvy to raise a level-peg a few inches, etc. Let it be remembered that navvies, though they often strike, have seldom organized trade-societies.—The evidence of Mr. George Smith, contractor, in opposition to Mr. Coulson, should also be referred to.

the worst wages cannot admit of the exercise of so much providence as the putting by of a few weekly pence in a Trade Society. The cases in London, for instance, are many, in which, in a given trade, the only society or societies which maintain themselves are those of the West-End; the East-End workers being either entirely without organization, or their attempts at organization proving repeatedly abortive through the lowness of their wages and the demoralization thereby produced among them. It may be true, no doubt, that in some cases,—many fewer probably than are supposed,—Trade Societies do tend to discourage pre-eminent excellency of work, to keep workmanship to a certain level. But in all cases it will be found that the great difficulty of every society lies in the inferior workers,—those who are not capable of earning enough to be worth having as members, but are capable of damaging the members by the competition of their inferior but cheaper workmanship.

We believe, then, that Trade Societies, although not by any means likely to carry workmanship to its highest point of excellence, offer yet the most powerful barrier still existing against mere slop-work in every branch of trade. But behind the Trade Society stands another form of organization, which does tend to promote the highest excellence of work. Such is, beyond question, the character of Co-operative production.* Such must be, in proportion to

---

* See *ante*, p. 143. Even Co-operative consumption tends indirectly to the same result. It is notorious hat the great Co-operative stores will have the best article they can have for their money,—the best teas, coffees, etc., and consequently also the best shoes, clothes, drapery, and the like.

the extent in which the workers of the establishment are interested in the undertaking, that of every partnership of industry.

We venture to think, therefore, that a careful investigation of this question will show :—1. That, admitting the falling off in many cases of English workmanship, the working class cannot be justly charged with having done more than share in the general lowering of tone in what may be called the morality of production. 2. That bad work is the necessary result of excessive competition (fostered indeed itself by the maxims of a buy-cheap and sell-dear plutonomy). 3. That the working man's trade-organizations are the main obstacle to the prevalence of mere slop-work. 4. That his Co-operative Associations, and his admission to profits in other establishments, afford the best hope as yet open to us of raising anew the standard of English workmanship.

§ 3. *The Religious Question.**

The decay of religious feeling among the better educated working men again is proclaimed with sorrow by ministers of religion in the Metropolis and in other large towns, and was made a few months ago the subject of a remarkable Conference with working men at the London Coffee-house (21st January, 1867).† Very hard things were certainly said of churches and ministers by working

---

* Mr. Ludlow is solely responsible for the contents of this section.

† A " full and extended report of the speeches " at this Conference, under the title of " Working Men and Religious Institutions," has since been published. (London, A. Miall, 1867.)

men on that occasion. And yet those who, like one of the writers (who was present at the afternoon sitting of the Conference), could look back nineteen years in their intercourse with working men, could not but feel what a change had been wrought in the interval, even to make the bringing together possible for such an object of so large a body of working men, many of whom could only attend at the loss to them of half a day's wages.

It is true that at this Conference objections to the truth of Christianity were, by the terms of its calling, excluded from discussion, and that its doors were thus morally closed against the positive opponents of religion. A few able men may thus have been estopped from making their voices heard. Possibly the exclusion of such was a mistake ; possibly their presence would have provoked testimonies of active adhesion to Christianity on the part of the working men, which for want of such an occasion failed to manifest themselves.

On the other hand, it is not the less true that this Conference exhibited the spectacle of a vast number of intelligent working men, representing a great variety of trades from the lowest-paid to the highest, many of them leaders in their class, coming forward one after another to assign reasons why they did not attend the public worship of God. No sense of shame or self-reproach seemed in their minds to attach to the avowal. In what they said there might be much ignorance, much presumption, much injustice. One bookseller's porter and late costermonger, for instance, in his benevolence towards his clerical brethren, actually went so far as to evolve for their benefit out of the depths of his consciousness—like the German philosopher the camel—a whole system of district-visiting by ladies, in utter self-complacent blindness to the fact that such a system has been at work for years in all our large towns, and well-nigh throughout the length and the breadth of the country. Still the fact remains of this acknowledged not-attendance; nor is it of any avail to say that the same prevails throughout other classes—that in almost every congregation women and children outnumber men by often five or six to one, sometimes in a much larger proportion. Those who, like the writer, believe that the working class is the very heart and hope of the nation—that no class should feel, if he may so speak, so thoroughly at home in Christ's gospel as this—could well dispense with the joining in public worship of a few Pall-Mall loungers, if their places were filled by the intelligent toilers of the country.

But unfortunately the expression just used—" joining in public worship "—indicates precisely that from which the working man, so far as the Conference shows, seems farthest. Scarcely ever, if at all, does the sense of worship, as a duty, still less as distinct from the hearing or following a preacher, appear in any of the reported speeches. And here, possibly, lies the kernel of the difficulty. Owing to the suppression of a fixed liturgy in the bulk of the dissenting bodies, and to the perversion of the principle of religious freedom into a sort of canonizing of human self-will, on the one hand,—on the other, either to neglect of the teachings of a "Common Prayer" by Low-Churchmen, or to its prostitution by High-Churchmen to purposes sometimes avowedly histrionic, the worship of God has been too much degraded amongst us into the hearing or seeing of a man,—in some cases, latterly, of a stage effect. The very elementary idea of all worship, Pagan as well as Christian, that of a communication between God and man, between a weaker being full of needs, and a Mightier Being who is able to supply those needs, has in great measure died out; still more the Christian idea of public worship, as the united offering by the members of a Divine Family of their repentance, their praises, and their prayers to a Heavenly Father, in sure hope of acceptance in a spotless and self-offered Elder Brother. Could that idea once flash upon the mind and heart of the working man, full as he is of the strongest yearnings for fellowship, it is probable that not only the duty of public worship would be felt by him, but its privilege courted. But whilst the idea of public worship is for him only that of "sitting under" Mr. So-and-so, or, it may be, repeating certain formulas and postures, the sense of duty first naturally disappears, then that of satisfaction in its fulfilment. He feels, for instance, and feels rightly, that to sit under Mr. So-and-so is not in itself by any means a matter of duty. And then the social aspect of worship disappears in turn; it becomes merely a matter of personal advantage. The question comes to be, not "How am I, as a member of the Christian family, to worship God my Maker and Father?" but "Is this or that man worth my going to hear or to look at?" And, attending church or chapel under the influence of such ideas, he has come quite naturally, almost necessarily, to the conclusion that the men who get up into pulpits are not, after awhile, of themselves worth going either to hear or to see. The restoration amongst us, then, of that elementary idea of worship, as a direct communication between man and God, to which the officiating minister may give words and form, but nothing more,—which is absolutely destroyed from the moment that he affects or seems to stand between God and the individual worshippers who compose the congregation,—seems a necessary prerequisite to the return of the working classes to our religious services. So long as that idea remains unrestored, the chances are that every other class which learns to think will desert them in turn. For until it is, the so-called worship of God is but a worship of man. Priest- or preacher-following is only a mild form of idolatry, conscious or unconscious.

But, on the other hand, the restoration of public worship needs something deeper yet in ministers and people,—the re-awakening of the sense of fellowship as the very ground of Christian life. When that is once rekindled, it will be found that its sphere is all-embracing. There will be no more complaints—as were so frequent at the Conference—that ministers do not enter into social questions. All questions will be felt to be social, and all human society to be constituted in Christ. The minister will not, as the working man perhaps expects, take the side of the latter in all disputes with his employers. But the minister will feel and declare and show, by word and by deed, that, as the faithful servant and soldier of Christ, the King of kings and Lord of lords, he has to wage a life-long warfare against all that opposes itself to His sovereignty, against all claims of trade, or politics, or any other form of human activity, to regulate themselves without Him, and to form, as it were, independent realms of heathendom in God's world. He will utterly abominate, and to the best of his power put down, that pseudo-political economy which would make self-interest the ruler of human society, which would erect man's covetous desires into authoritative laws, and justify by its maxims any amount of oppression and starvation. As the disciple of a God who bids us " break every yoke," he will be ever ready to combat every form of political, or moral, or social slavery. As the follower of a God of truth, a God who is light, and in whom is no darkness at all, he will fear no form of truth, however strange, quench no light, however flickering. He will have faith that God's truth will vindicate itself, if he does not overlay it with his own fancies ; that God's light will shine forth into men's hearts and minds, if he does not bar it out with the walls and shutters of his own systems. He will not degrade the Bible into a manual of chronology or of geology, knowing that God's Fatherhood, Christ's Incarnation, the Redemption of mankind by His life and death, the Indwelling of the Holy Spirit, are truths absolutely and entirely independent of the question whether the earth has lasted 6000 or 60,000 years, or how the first chapter of Genesis is to be interpreted. Because he believes it to be the book of God, he will also believe it to be the book for man ; because it reveals God's truth, he will know that it is the great well-spring of freedom for mankind.

Just in proportion as we may be yet far from such a view of Christ's gospel, just so far, the writer ventures to think, are we far from seeing the working class embrace that gospel. But their complaints may help other classes to do so. No other class, probably, could have been drawn together on such an invitation to express so frankly its reasons for forsaking religious ministrations. And at the bottom of those reasons there may be felt, not dislike or indifference to the Gospel itself, but, on the contrary, a deep yearning for some mighty manifestation of it. The complaint is, not that Christianity is given, but that "priests and parsons" have given of it "short weight and short measure;" not that it is practised by its professors, but that their practice falls so far short of their professions; not that clergymen and ministers intermeddle with the working men, but that they do not come among them and show practical sympathy with them in their undertakings. Surely a temper like this, even when speaking out through hard and scornful words, instead of discouraging Christian ministers, should brace and quicken them to their work,—ay, though that work should consist partly in the shaking off of their most cherished traditions and habits of religious thought.

But—without wishing in the least to undervalue the weight of the testimony afforded by the Conference as to the indifference of many of the more intelligent working men to public worship—it must now be pointed out that there is also another side to the question. It is far from true universally that such indifference prevails. The Conference, it must never be forgotten, was held in London, the head-quarters of English *poco-curante*ism, —the place where a man of any class may most easily float through life without having to exercise any earnest effort of intellect or of conscience, where a fickle and soon-sated curiosity too often takes the place of all deeper interests and higher purposes. And although the example of London is more or less followed by our larger cities generally, there are very many important towns—whole important districts—where attendance at religious services is the rule and not the exception among the educated working men. Nay, thank God! so far from religious faith and growing intelligence being incompatible, the very reverse is proved to be the case by daily experience. The records of almost every religious organization will tell of minds awakened, intellects steadied and enlarged, by the reception of religious influences; every one who has taken part, however humbly, in any work of a religious character, *knows* of such instances. One only testimony to this effect shall be quoted; it is that of a minister for many years largely acquainted with the working class :—

"I spent my youth, as a minister's son, among the manufacturing population of the West of England. I visited their homes with my father, and knew their characters. I have myself been a minister nearly thirty years, and chiefly in agricultural and surburban districts. I have seen that the common religious meetings, and especially the great Sunday schools, were powerful educational agents, intellectually as well as morally. If you have ever noticed the utter stupidity of a farm-labourer of middle age, and then marked the wakening up of his whole being when he began to read (or began learning to read) his Bible, to attend religious meetings, to repeat hymns, and to think of God as his Father, and of Jesus as his Saviour, you have seen something very wonderful. And yet that wonderful thing has been continually occurring, and very extensively, indeed, in this land of ours. You will see thus,"—he adds, " that I have observed a rapid improvement in the working classes, and that I ascribe that improvement chiefly to religious agency, and to the various educational agencies connected with it."

And indeed, so far from its being generally the fact that hostility or indifference to Christianity among the working class is increasing, the very reverse is, the writer of these pages believes, more and more frequently the case. Many districts could be quoted in which open hostility to religion formerly prevailed among working men, and has been replaced by a friendly feeling,*—various towns in which the leaders of the working class were formerly infidels, and are now devout, God-fearing men.† Christ's gospel, let us be assured, has not lost its power over the masses since the days when it was said of its First Teacher, that " the common people heard Him gladly." If the churches are deserted by the working men in any quarter, it is because they have no " good news" to tell him. But they *are* learning that they have good news to tell him, as well as to hereditary pew-holders and paying seat-holders ; and he is hearing, or at least opening his ears to catch, the

---

* Such was the testimony given to the writer a few years since by the present Dean of Chichester, respecting the working classes of Yorkshire. Dr. Hook's own popularity amongst the Leeds working men, indeed, is a fact which hardly needs recalling.

† See, *post*, some evidence of this as to Norwich.

message. Indeed, the probabilities are, not that we are
on the eve of an era of greater religious indifference than
in the past among working men, but of a great religious
awakening among them.

§ 4. *Indications of Positive Moral Progress in the Working Class.*

Let us now pass, however, to some less controverted
questions,—to facts which offer more positive evidence of
moral progress in the working class, than those which we
have been considering.

One of these,—but which is scarcely less noticeable in
other classes, and indeed could not show itself unless re-
ciprocated,—is the gradual approximation of the working
man towards his fellow-countrymen of different ranks and
stations from his own.   Less than twenty years ago, there
lay between him and the men of any other class—except
in a few special instances—a sort of fog of distrust, which
almost prevented either from discerning the true linea-
ments of the other.   That fog has now in a great measure
rolled away.   In almost all large trades and towns, the
man of another class who wishes and deserves to have
working men for his friends, need not search very long
for those who are in turn worthy of his friendship, and
will bestow theirs upon him.   Benefit Societies, Building
Societies, Industrial and Provident Societies, Working
Men's Colleges, Working Men's Clubs and Institutes, etc.,
form an ever-increasing number of meeting-points, material as well as moral, between class and class, which are
gradually binding each to each by closer links of fellowship.

Into the ranks of authorship working men are passing—
not always rising—continually. They have taken part repeatedly in the proceedings of the Social Science Association, either by contributing papers to its transactions, or
by joining in its discussions.* The Secretary of one of
the great Amalgamated Societies has made his appearance
in the rooms of the Statistical Society ; and perhaps the
day is not far distant when even the Political Economy
Club may deign to invite some working man to tell his
views and experience on some of those economic questions
which so deeply affect him.

The growth of loyal national feeling among the working class is another remarkable fact of the period. The
positive disloyalty which was so prevalent in 1832, in

* We cannot resist the pleasure of referring to the candid and pathetic
paper, on "The Chain- and Trace-makers of Hadley Heath and its vici-
nity, and their employers ; or, Union and Disunion, and their Consequences ; by Noah Forrest, a chainmaker," in the "Transactions" of the
Social Science Association for 1859, p. 654.

On the other hand, it has been made a matter of complaint by the Sheffield "Association of Organized Trades," that Mr. Dronfield's paper, entitled "A Working Man's View of Trade Societies," read at the Sheffield
Congress, October 5, 1865, was not only not printed in the Transactions
for the year, but not even mentioned in the Summary of proceedings ; that
the discussions which had special reference to the questions more immediately affecting the working men's interest are omitted in the Report,
except as respects Courts of Arbitration, and that no mention is made of
what was said by the trades' delegates on the occasion. Mr. Dronfield's
position in Sheffield, and among the working class at large, should
alone have secured to him more courteous treatment ; nor can the writer
of these lines forbear to express his opinion (as a member of the Social
Science Association, and formerly on its Council), that Mr. Dronfield's
paper would have been a valuable addition to the slender volume of the
year's Transactions.—[J. M. L.]

1839,* in 1848, which even fifteen years ago was wide-spread, has almost universally disappeared. The Queen's reception at Wolverhampton last year—Mr. Bright's re-buke to the able but unlucky member for the Tower Hamlets a few months ago—are events which would have been impossible in the last generation. Among the most striking evidences of this altered change of feeling has been the participation of the working classes in the Volunteer movement. Though their hearty co-operation has too often been damped by official red-tapery, or the snobbishness of lords-lieutenant and commanding officers, on the one hand, and, on the other, by the ill-judged op-position of one of the chief organs of working-class opinion ; it is nevertheless certain that, whenever they have been en-couraged to do so, working men have largely entered into the Volunteer corps, and are continuing still so to do, and that working-men officers have shown themselves capable and efficient.

The improved conduct of political agitation amongst the working classes is another most remarkable fact. In London at the present day are two rival political organiza-tions, both largely, one nearly exclusively, composed of working men—the " Reform League " and the " Work-

---

* How many men of middle age will almost credit their memories when they recall to mind certain letters, very celebrated at the time, of Lord John Russell, in May, 1839, to the Lords-Lieutenant of certain English counties, suggesting the formation of associations for the protection of life and property, and to the borough magistrates in certain counties, directing them how to proceed for the preservation of the peace in disturbed districts? Yet these things stand duly recorded in Blue-books.

ing Men's Association." Yet,—allowing for occasional extravagancies of individual language or conduct,—the contention between the two seems rather which shall be the more orderly and moderate.* Contrast the behaviour of either, as representing the most 'advanced' political opinions of the day, with that of the followers of Cartwright and Burdett, of Cobbett and Hunt, of Feargus O'Connor and Frost, and it will be seen how enormous has been the advance in self-respect, in true manliness of feeling and purpose. Listen to an old Chartist prisoner (Mr. Mantle) speaking to a Conservative Chancellor of the Exchequer on a deputation from the Reform League, April 2, 1867 :—

* The Hyde Park disturbances of 1866,—the only disorderly incident as yet of the present Reform agitation,—were in part provoked by official blundering and police-insolence, and were at any rate wholly unintentional on the part of the working men who assembled for the purpose of the demonstration. Compare these with the London riots of a hundred years ago, as described in Mr. Jesse's recently published 'Memoirs of the Life and Reign of George the Third,'—with the "Weavers' Riots " of 1765, when "for three days London may almost be said to have been in the hands of the mob," and "during the three days referred to, Bedford House was not only garrisoned with soldiers and subjected to a state of siege, but at one time so bold was the attitude of the rioters, that while the military were engaged in repelling an attack on the front of the mansion, another detachment of the rioters very nearly succeeded in effecting an entrance at its rear ; "—with the "Wilkes riots " in 1768-9, soon complicated with a sawyers' and a sailors' strike, lasting with intermissions for only six days short of a whole twelvemonth, causing the loss of several lives, and ending with direct personal insult to the Sovereign ;—and it will be seen that in those days the pushing down of Hyde Park railings would have seemed a mere trifle. The Bristol Reform riots, again, a little before the opening of the period we have been considering, will show under how different conditions a Reform agitation was carried on less than forty years ago.

" In by-gone times " (he said, in speaking of the opinions and principles he was expressing) " they have consigned some of us, myself among the number, to a prison. To-day they bring us, through you, to the foot of the throne. We offer to the throne the homage of our loyalty; we offer to the Government those objections, those weapons, which those of us called agitators have used against you; we respectfully ask you to disarm us, and to leave us without the opportunity to rally the country against the Government. We have as keen an appreciation of our country's honour as any other class of men; we are as incapable of doing wrong to it as you are yourselves. The blood of working men, in times of trouble, has flowed as freely as that of the proudest peer of the realm. I have been twenty years engaged in the work, and am weary of it; I wish it were settled. We come with the dignity which conscious right gives us, and ask you to do us justice. . . . If the bill is passed in its present form, we shall look on the signing of it as a signal for a renewed agitation, but an agitation strictly within the limits of the constitution. If you do us justice, you will do yourselves justice, you will do your Sovereign justice, and history will do you justice."

Surely words like these,—apart from the gleams of real, though rather studied eloquence which distinguish them, —mark the growth of that which is most precious in a free country, the spirit of citizenship, of true patriotism.*

* Mr. Holyoake has said somewhere that " Pride in his country . . . is a dead sentiment in an English working man." Mr. Mantle's speech would be a sufficient refutation of the statement at the present day. It

No less remarkable, however, than the improvement of their political temper as respects home-questions, has been the development amongst the working class of what, if the term were not becoming a cant one, we might term international sympathies. During the great Continental war, a foreigner could hardly go abroad in our streets without being mobbed, simply because he was a foreigner. One signal instance of such mobbing occurs in the period which occupies us ; but, however unjustifiable legally, what a progress in the moral sense of the worker does it exhibit, when English draymen could deem themselves called upon to avenge on an Austrian general the floggings of Hungarian women ! But there are facts of a far less questionable nature, which will occur to the mind of every reader. The sympathy shown for Kossuth, and in a still larger degree for Garibaldi, show the growth amongst our working class of an interest in the politics of the world which is limited by no considerations of birth or language. That, after the vast emigration to America, Lancashire operatives should have learnt to sympathize with a kindred nation, and through newspapers, written in their own language, to understand its politics, is not surprising. But what ties with them had this Hungarian, this Italian, that they should surround either with

---

was true less than twenty years ago ; it is true no longer. Perhaps one of the causes which have most powerfully altered the feelings of the English working man towards his own institutions has been the growth of the French Second Empire. Placed face to face with that gigantic despotism, he has felt by contrast the value of English freedom, however insufficient in his eyes might yet be his share of political power.

such enthusiastic popularity? Surely a class which can appreciate the simple manhood of a Garibaldi has risen itself to a true, wise manhood. Surely the men who can take so genuine an interest in the destinies of foreign nations are fit henceforth to share in ruling their own.

§ 5. *An Instance of Moral Progress beginning amidst Diminished Prosperity.*

Let no one suppose from what has been said above that we consider the working classes of this country to have anywhere attained to the social and moral standing which they might have reached long ere this; that we wish to encourage them in any lazy self-complacency with results often in themselves very inconsiderable, and of which but a small proportion is often due to their own exertions. One of their own number—who tells us he married at twenty, and had to keep a wife and house on from 18s. to 20s. a week—says most truly, "When I contrast the advantages possessed now by young men with those we had when I was a lad, I do consider that there has not been that progress made that we should have had, vast as it is at present." And he compares sadly, in his own town of from 90,000 to 100,000 population, the 346 public and beer-houses to the 17 stationers, booksellers, and news-vendors. Whatever advance may have been made since 1832, it is certain that the turning of the tide has been in some instances comparatively recent; that in many its flow has been as yet but small. Such an instance we now propose to give. It will serve usefully to show how far from

satisfactory may still be the working man's moral condition in a large English city. But it will show something
more.

We have hitherto mainly confined ourselves to such
evidences of social and moral progress as have accompanied
the development of material prosperity. If we can supply
similar evidences amidst decreasing welfare, it will afford
us the strongest proof that such progress is genuine,—that
the tide is irresistibly rising, however tardy and slow its
advance. The declining city of Norwich will afford us
such an instance as we need. We offer to our readers, as
entirely trustworthy, the following sketch of its condition,
from the pen of a respected minister, who for many years
has mixed largely with the working classes of that city.
We have preferred not to distribute its contents under
separate heads, but to transcribe it as a whole, leaving its
details to speak for themselves, in confirmation of many of
our previous positions :—

" When I came to Norwich, the Chartist movement
was at its worst (1849), and this city was in a disgraceful
state, morally and politically. All classes had been trained
and educated in bribery. If you look into the reports of
the Commissioners of Inquiry into Norwich charities and
Norwich manufactures of that period, you will find that
nearly every public charity was made habitually an instrument of bribery and corruption by the highest gentlemen
in the city, and that one great cause of the decline of our
manufactures was the party spirit which led each side in
turn to egg on the mob of operatives to destroy machinery,
if set up by an opponent. I was continually told by gen-

tlemen how impossible they found it to trust their most confidential clerks and foremen with any secret, because no one could resist the touch of bank-notes on the palm; and when I say I know one man who refused £75 for a vote, you will believe that it was not small sums that were asked or offered in those times, on any occasion when bribery seemed available. My first experience of public men here was at an examination of a Chartist public-house keeper named ——, who had made or ordered pikes, before the magistrates. He openly challenged the mayor: 'Mr. Mayor, you know I have done worse things for the Whigs when you paid me than ever I have as a Chartist.' The mayor hid his face behind a newspaper, saying, 'Such observations do you no good.' Afterwards, on one of his fellow-magistrates observing that —— hit hard when he used those words, I heard the mayor say half-aloud, 'By G— it was true.' The man afterwards nominated a Chartist candidate in order to get up an election contest. He was settled with for £50 by a Whig baronet, and kept at the Guildhall till dark, that the mob might not take revenge, which, however, they did during the evening, and nearly killed him.* It was then the regular phrase of a working man, wanting to get his father into an almshouse or his child into a school, to begin, 'Please, sir, I have always voted with *the* party, but have had nothing done yet for any of my family,'—leaving the definite article to be applied as the hearer might be inclined.

"Soon after I came, one of our best and worthiest

---

* "This man's son is now one of the best of our local preachers, and a Sunday-school teacher."

manufacturers died. He had been, I verily believe unin-tentionally, the means of inducing, by a change in trade, a reduction of wages. He meant the reduction to be only on certain goods and for a time only, but it proved perma-nent. The mob of operatives now determined to stop his burial, and only by a clever device of the police in mis-leading them as to the route of the funeral did they miss pitching the coffin into the river, as they had intended to do. In the London papers there was a full account of this affair, but none in our local ones. I gave some sermons on the ' Relations of Masters and Men;' a crowd came, and as I touched on that scene, more than one pewful of men sprang to their feet, excited but silent. They bore what I said, and then went after service to a public-house and drank my health.

" I have known several reading-clubs got up and fail ; also several co-operative stores, but generally to break down through dishonesty of the agents or distrust of the men in each other. And so matters have gone on, mak-ing this city a nest of corruption and immorality, and dis-trust of class against class and man against man.

" *Yet of late a change for the better has come on.* The Co-operatives have had a large store, with branches, for eight or nine years, very successfully carried on,*—though just at this moment in a crisis from distrust, again created by

* A summary of its accounts, with which we have been supplied, shows that in the interval the number of members had increased from 20 to 852 ; the amount of business done from £170. 2s. 11d. to £12,894. 4s. 1d., and that of profits from £9. 19s. 1½d. t £488. 5s. 8½d.—the last figure, indeed, owing to official defalcations falling nearly £250 short of that of the previous year.

dishonest agents. The societies of Odd Fellows are very large. Building Societies are successful, but I think mostly among the upper artisans and small shopkeepers, the average of low wages preventing the ordinary workman from using them. There have always been clever, shrewd men among the weavers, and there are so now ; but the manufacture is steadily declining in all its branches, and shoe manufacturing is taking its place, with low wages and fluctuating employment, and a production of often very inferior goods for export.

" *Still the Co-operatives and other clubs are reading far more than formerly*, both books and papers. Very few indeed trouble us 'parsons' with their presence on Sundays, though the women go to missionary-rooms and Sunday-schools. But great changes for the better have taken place in some of the worst districts, *e.g.* ' Pockthorpe ' and ' St. James's,' which have had, for many years, good schools, both church and dissenting, whilst certain active religious-political gentlemen here have carried on addresses on Sundays and week days, till now our most fashionable street, St. Giles's, and St. Stephen's our great thoroughfare, give the police far more trouble than those once-styled ' worst ' parts of the city.

" *Without doubt great improvement has taken place,* although still fluctuating employment, causing many hundreds to vibrate between the workhouse and the bench or loom, low wages, and the lingering effects of corruption in Parliamentary and municipal elections, render the population here the lowest and least educated that I have ever seen. Any charlatan gets their ear for awhile ; nobody, either good or bad, for long. . . . As to corruption, I do not think either side would venture to claim more than 1000 to 1200 thoroughly pure votes. If the Liberals gain more than 500 majority, it is all bribery; if the Tories get more than 2000 on the whole, they must not only pay their own men, but must be bribing the other side immensely. All inquiry into election matters here was lately swamped by arrangement of the leaders on all three sides, Whig, Tory, and Radical, or our revelations would have equalled those of Yarmouth. . . .

" All this is, no doubt, the result of generations of mistreatment of men, of corruption and bad education, with latterly declining trade. The city is becoming more and more a county town which has seen better days. Meanwhile the old evils are dying out slowly by inanition, and *there is certainly far more reading and thinking, a far better spirit between classes, and a sounder feeling of trust in the men*, both as between themselves and as regards employers and the richer orders. As elsewhere, there has been far greater personal intercourse between the labouring and higher classes of late years than formerly, which has tended to a more human feeling on both sides. The one specialty of Norwich, music, has greatly helped this result. That gift has no respect of persons, and nothing can hinder an oratorio or church-choir or chapel singing-pew from becoming a glorious meeting-point for persons of different ranks and degrees of education. The 'tonic-sol-fa' was the invention of a lady here, while visiting one of the schools, whence it extended itself; but there are now several classes, public and private, for singing, and several bands also are at work on various instruments.

"Strikes have been very mischievous, and when they have lately recurred have manifested the old spiteful spirit. In one case they precipitated the almost total withdrawal of one firm, a large one, to Bradford. The weavers of Norwich are as yet irreclaimable on that point; but they are dying out.

" As to sobriety, *without doubt the working men are much improved;* and though we have a terrible number of public-houses, they depend mostly on the market-days and country custom."

We subjoin another statement by a gentleman also familiar with the working classes of Norwich, comparing those of thirty years ago with those of to-day. Although more favourable than the one above, it yet tallies with it in the main, and brings out a few new aspects of the question:

" I think," the writer says,—

" 1. That they" (*i. e.* the working men) "are, generally speaking, very much improved; and particularly

" 2. That they are less hostile to religion, less disloyal, less brutal, more susceptible to kind efforts and wise counsels;

" 3. That the leaders of the people in working class agitation, for instance in the Reform movement, are different men from the old Chartist leaders; more moderate, more reasonable, more moral, less violent in temper and language. I observed that all the working-class speakers at the largest Reform meeting we have had here for years, were religious men; local preachers, or Sunday-school teachers. The president of the 'Norwich Political Union' is superintendent of the 'Sunday-school Union' for the district. I was struck, the other night, with the proposal made at a meeting almost entirely composed of working men, that a hall recently used by the Mormons should be hired as a 'Working-Men's Hall and Mission-room,' for preaching on Sundays, and for politics, or a reading room, or co-operative meetings, etc., on week-days. The men who will manage this room will be all (or nearly so) religious men and radicals. And these are the men who just now have the ear of the masses.

"4. I find a much better feeling amongst the lowest class in regard to religion than was observable twenty or even ten years ago. The Revival movement, the Temper-ance movement, and above all Sunday-schools, have done very much towards this. The public-house is now *the* enemy."

Surely the above picture, unflattering and painful as it is, suffices yet to show positive moral improvement springing up in the working class, even from amongst the depths of political corruption, and developing itself side by side with economic decay.

PART VII.

CONCLUSION.

WE have attempted to describe in these pages the advance made by the artisans of England, chiefly towards the accomplishment of certain self-imposed tasks to which they had devoted themselves as matters of duty. In doing this, we have sought to notice every movement in which working people have engaged as organized bodies. We have not deemed it necessary to recount what sections of them have attempted, and failed to accomplish, still less to canvass opinions and dogmas. Chartism for instance, as a political programme, needs no argument to controvert or justify it, now that Radicalism and Conservatism are terms scarcely differing in their application; whilst Chartism, as a form of violence, was a miserable failure. Of the Owenite Socialists, whose influence during the period we have been reviewing was far from inconsiderable, especially in the manufacturing districts, it may be said that they were a sect rather than a great popular party; and entertained opinions and sought to carry out principles not shared in, nor indeed understood by the great majority of the working people, even in those districts where they were most successful. Their doctrine of the " formation of character," whatever objection may be held to it as a dogma, was, considered in its application, but a peculiar form of the great question of national education ; whilst their views as to " community of property " were regarded by themselves as matters for private experiment rather than general acceptance. After some few years of peaceable agitation, such experiments as lay within their means were tried, and failed. From that moment the adherents to Mr. Owen's views fell back amongst their less speculative fellow-countrymen, and lent their aid in forwarding the less ambitious but more practical schemes of social amelioration which have since then engaged public attention.

But we must now conclude this sketch. Lengthy as it may seem, we are ourselves chiefly conscious of the gaps which are left in it, of its shortcomings and deficiencies. Such as it is, however, we venture to think it abundantly proves that the progress of the working class in our country since 1832 has been general and continuous. Even the agricultural class, we believe, has participated in that progress—partly through the spread of education, partly through economic causes—such as the general development of wealth, the depletion of the agricultural labour-market by means of public works, emigration, the growth of manufactures, etc.*

* Among the most cheering signs of such progress, to our minds, are the movements which have taken place within the last year or two among the farm-servants of Kent, and the Scotch ploughmen, for raising their wages and bettering their condition. But, in the Southern counties perhaps especially, there is very much yet to do. Dr. Drew, in a

Exceptions to such progress there are, no doubt; those, namely, of certain quarters of the Metropolis and of our larger towns, where, through the gradual withdrawal of the wealthy, then of the comfortable classes, either to other quarters, or to country residences, the poor have been left alone, to become poorer, more ignorant, and more degraded;*—of certain other towns and quarters of towns, where, through some sudden influx of prosperity, or again, through the demolitions caused by railways or other public works, the population has become accumulated under bad sanitary conditions, often in dwellings hastily run up by speculators, and has fallen a prey to similar evils;—or, lastly, of particular trades which have either remained exceptionally depressed through peculiar circumstances, or in which, conversely, through exceptional prosperity, the rise in the price of labour has outstripped the development of the legitimate wants of the worker. Nor do we, we repeat it, pretend to say that the progress which we affirm to have taken place has been as rapid—that it has been

paper on " The Moral Effects of the Poor Laws," read before the Social Science Association in 1865 (Transactions, p. 556), tells of a Sussex labourer's wife, who said that her husband had joined a sick-club, but she " persuaded him to leave it. Why should a poor man pay 1s. or 6d. a week just to screen the parish ? . . . We know very well why the gentry and farmers try to get up such clubs ; but poor people here know better than to spend their money just to save the rates." So alien is still all idea of associative forethought to these Sussex hinds.

* It is well known that large districts, even parishes in London might be quoted, where there is not a single resident left who keeps a servant. A quarter in Liverpool has also been cited to us, where twenty or thirty teachers resident in the neighbourhood could formerly be found for a Sunday-school, and to which scarcely six or seven can now be brought, all from a distance. Here there has been positive retrogression.

carried as far—as it might have been; that the working man has made the fullest use of the opportunities which have been offered to him. But we believe, nevertheless, that the history of no people under the sun will show a period of the same duration in which, without any great political or social revolution, so great an advance has been achieved by the working class, and that chiefly through influences which God has been pleased to evolve from the bosom of the class itself.*

Without, therefore, in anywise subordinating political reform—the means—to social reform—the end—we wish to express our conviction (now fully shared, we are glad to see, by nearly the whole Conservative party) that the time has come for the working classes of England to exercise, as of right, a far larger share of political power than has been till now doled out to them. They are not perfect; but their faults and their vices, if not always the same as those of the governing classes, have at least their equivalents among those classes. They are not perfect,

---

* We fear the middle classes have not made similar progress. A return, quoted in the 'Times,' of February 16, 1867, shows that in the nine years ending April, 1865, while population had scarcely increased 10 per cent., the number of taxed men-servants had increased over 17 per cent. (from 140,092 to 163,697), and of taxed male servants under 18 (including under-gardeners and under-gamekeepers), 39 per cent. (from 69,420 to 96,535). Allowing for a proportion of gardeners and under-gardeners, who, as productive labourers, ought to be deducted, the above figures show a growth of flunkeyism which is appalling, and which obviously belongs chiefly to a middle class aping one above (witness the extraordinary multiplication of boys under eighteen). It is really too bad that the productive workers of this country, agricultural and industrial, should have to maintain such a swelling host of " Jeameses " and " Buttonses."

but the vice with which they are most taunted is, by the most ardent opponents of that very vice, made a ground, not for withholding the suffrage from them, but for extending the suffrage to them. The most advanced section of the Temperance party declares that they are the victims of the publican, not his friends, and that "any Reform Bill" is "an Alliance gain." We go further, and we say that, with such a history as the working classes of England furnish for the last thirty-five years, the question of to-day should have reference to the advantages, rather than to the danger of their admission to political power. Fear lest the "pot" should "boil over"—to use Mr. Henley's words—is hardly a sufficient reason for a great political reform. It is not with fear, but with hope, that a nation like England should face the future.

Class exclusiveness has surely hitherto furnished no guarantee for Ministerial honour or Parliamentary purity. The Walpoles, Pelhams, Butes, and Norths, were the subjects of charges which nobody would now dare to make against the integrity of any public man ; whilst the House of Commons was little better than a market, in which the minister of the day paid in money and emoluments for such voices and votes as he deemed necessary for the maintenance of his power. Wraxall's account of the Parliament of England in those days is borne out by nearly every writer who makes any allusion to the same times and circumstances. "A friend of mine," says Wraxall, "knew Roberts, who was Secretary of the Treasury under Pelham, and who assured him that there were a number of members who regularly received from him their payment at the end of every session in bank-notes."* " The sums, which varied according to merits, abilities, and attendance of the respective individuals, amounted usually from five hundred pounds to eight hundred pounds per annum." " I took my stand," said Roberts, "in the Court of Requests on the day of the prorogation of Parliament, and as the gentlemen passed me in going in or returning from the House I conveyed the money in a squeeze of the hand." How Mr. Pitt regarded the interests of the owners of rotten boroughs may be inferred from the fact that, in the draft of his Reform Bill, he made provision for a large sum of money as compensation; whilst at the time of the Union the Irish owners of such boroughs as were extinguished by that Act drove very hard bargains with Lord Cornwallis for the money price of their Parliamentary influence, which was about to be taken from them. That there was policy in Pitt's proposal, as well as validity in the claims of Irish

* 'Historical Memoirs of my own Time.' Wraxall, vol. ii. p. 515. Compare also the following passage in a letter from Lord North to George III. :—" The expenses of the Westminster election amounted to more than £8000; Surrey, to £4000; the City, to £4000; the amount of all three to more than £16,000. These three contests were unhappily not successful, and therefore the expense is the greater grievance; but Lord North must, in justice to the members who were assisted to come into Parliament, say that they all behaved with very steady attachment to the end. The elections in 1779, 1780, and 1781, will cost £53,000, but there had been no additional pensions promised. Lord North begs leave to submit to his Majesty that at the time of the election it was thought of the highest importance to secure a number of friends in the House of Commons, the opposition was eager, numerous, and powerful, and the times were distressing upon gentlemen." (Correspondence of George III. with Lord North, from 1768 to 1783.) See also Mr. Heneage Jesse's recently published work.

noblemen and gentlemen, may be seen by the fact that im mediately before the passing of the Reform Bill of 1832, Lord Camelford sold Old Sarum—then a two-member borough—to the Earl of Caledon for £60,000, though its land and manorial rights were not worth more than £700 a year.*

The demand for a Reform Bill, which had its accomplishment in 1832, did not originate solely in a desire for political privileges on the part of those who had them not. Unbearable as it might be to see Bramber, with its population of 97 all told, returning two Members of Parliament; and Old Sarum, without a house of any kind within its bounds, also returning two members, whilst Manchester and Birmingham, with their teeming thousands, were unrepresented; still the change then brought about was much hastened by a prevailing sense of the political immorality and corruption which such a state of things generated and fostered. Nor were the hopes entertained of the effects of political reform altogether falsified. The widening of the basis of the Constitution, by the admission of the middle class to a share in the political power of the country, to a certain extent purified the political atmosphere. New men with new interests came upon the stage, and—partly perhaps because they were not in a position to share the spoil—they demanded a more disinterested and honourable administration of the nation's affairs; less nepotism, and consequently more justice in public appointments; more economy also, seeing that family aggrandisement could not be made so directly a reward for ministerial support.

* Smith's 'Parliaments of England,' vol. iii. p. 100.

But the class, above all others, that can profit least by a sinister administration of public affairs, is the working class. Whatever is wise as a policy, foreign or domestic, must be of benefit to working men. Religious or political disabilities are painfully felt by them. Restrictions on commerce affect them most injuriously. A defective or ill-administered system of national education can only produce evil to them. There are no monopolies in land that can bring them wealth. Their sons cannot be lifted over the heads of competitors by undue influence. And as any attempt to serve their interests by an improper exercise of their Parliamentary power would be certain to unite all other classes, as well as the honest and conscientious of their own class, against them, their prime duty must always be to give their aid in the promotion of measures likely to serve the general welfare. What is more, they have still that keen sense of political justice which our middle class possessed in country and town 200 years ago, which seems to have well-nigh died out in it now. Throughout the country, for instance, the instincts of the working men may be said to have anticipated that late magnificent charge of the Lord Chief Justice's on the illegality of martial law, and the atrocity of its exercise in Jamaica, which a Middlesex grand jury proved actually incapable of understanding. They are always ready to sympathize with every noble cause. Of the best men amongst them, it is the firm conviction of both the writers of this volume that, for strong sense, keen insight into the substantial merits of questions and policies, cautious resolve, but sturdy determination, steadfast honesty of purpose, faithfulness to a once trusted leader,—nay, for a genuine courteousness of mind worth far more than all outward gloss of manner, they have no superiors in any other class of our countrymen.

Power placed in the hands of the working men exclusively would no doubt be abused, as it always has been when so possessed. But as the political enfranchisement of the operative classes in England will be the completion of the national fabric, and not the usurpation of dominion by a class, these people can bring no danger with them which the good sense, patriotism, and power of the nation cannot overcome. The cries of alarm uttered on this subject are simply such as have always been heard when important changes in the constitution or laws of the country have been proposed. We have seen how absurd and irrational they have been in regard to the changes which have taken place during the present century. Let us trust that the " flood-gates of revolution," with the throwing open of which we have always been threatened, are as little likely to be burst at this moment as ever they were; that the " foundations of society," which, according to politicians in a minority, have always been on the point of being uprooted, are at least as firmly fixed, as broadly and deeply laid in the affections of the people, as at any previous period of the nation's history; and that the same God who has watched over our country till this day will never leave her nor forsake her.

THE END.